THE BIBLICAL MOSAIC

THE SOCIETY OF BIBLICAL LITERATURE
SEMEIA STUDIES
Dan O. Via, Jr., Editor
William A. Beardslee, Associate Editor

THE SWORD OF HIS MOUTH: FORCEFUL AND
IMAGINATIVE LANGUAGE IN SYNOPTIC SAYINGS
by Robert C. Tannehill

JESUS AS PRECURSOR
by Robert W. Funk

STUDIES IN THE STRUCTURE OF HEBREW NARRATIVE
by Robert C. Culley

STRUCTURAL ANALYSIS OF NARRATIVE
by Jean Calloud, translated by Daniel Patte

BIBLICAL STRUCTURALISM: METHOD AND
SUBJECTIVITY IN THE STUDY OF ANCIENT TEXTS
by Robert M. Polzin

STORY, SIGN, AND SELF: PHENOMENOLOGY AND
STRUCTURALISM AS LITERARY CRITICAL METHODS
by Robert Detweiler

CHRISTOLOGY BEYOND DOGMA: MATTHEW'S CHRIST
IN PROCESS HERMENEUTIC
by Russell Pregeant

ENCOUNTER WITH THE TEXT: FORM AND HISTORY IN
THE HEBREW BIBLE
edited by Martin J. Buss

FINDING IS THE FIRST ACT: TROVE FOLK TALES
AND JESUS' TREASURE PARABLE
by John Dominic Crossan

THE BIBLICAL MOSAIC
Changing Perspectives

edited by
Robert Polzin
and
Eugene Rothman

FORTRESS PRESS
Philadelphia, Pennsylvania

SCHOLARS PRESS
Chico, California

Library of Congress Cataloging in Publication Data

Main entry under title:

The Biblical mosaic.

(Semeia studies)
Papers from a colloquium held in Oct. 1977
at Carleton University, Ottawa, and sponsored
by the Jewish Community Council of Ottawa et al.
Bibliography: p. 225
1. Bible. O.T.—Criticism, interpretation,
etc.—Congresses. I. Polzin, Robert.
II. Rothman, Eugene. III. Carleton University.
IV. Jewish Community Council of Ottawa.
V. Series.
BS1192.B44   222'.06   81-67307
ISBN 0-8006-1510-7   AACR2

9030I81   Printed in the United States of America   1-1510

Contents

Foreword: On Joseph Heinemann (Judah Goldin)   vii

Preface: Robert Polzin and Eugene Rothman   xi

INTRODUCTION

Chapter 1:   The Mosaic (Robert Polzin and
             Eugene Rothman)   3

PART I   Rabbinic Perspectives

Chapter 2:   Toward a Rhetoric of Midrash: A Preliminary
             Account (Lou H. Silberman)   15

Chapter 3:   A Homily on Jeremiah and the Fall of
             Jerusalem (Joseph Heinemann)   27

PART II   Philosophical Perspectives

Chapter 4:   Deuteronomy and the Word: The Beginning
             and the End (Joseph Gold)   45

Chapter 5:   Word Reception as the Matrix of the Structure
             of the Genesis Narrative (Hugh C. White) . .   61

PART III   Three Divergent Traditions

Chapter 6:   The Problem of False Prophecy: Talmudic
             Interpretations of Jeremiah 28 and
             1 Kings 22 (Robert Goldenberg)   87

Chapter 7:   The Story of the Prophet Micaiah (1 Kings 22)
             in Historical-Critical Interpretation
             1876–1976 (Wolfgang Roth) 105

Chapter 8:   Micaiah ben Imlah: A Literary View
             (David Robertson) 139

PART IV   Dialogue Between Traditions

Chapter 9:   Interpretation of the *Akedah* in Rabbinic
             Literature and The *Akedah*: a Folklorist's
             Response (Anthony J. Saldarini and
             Dan Ben-Amos) 149

Chapter 10: "A Wretched Thing of Shame, A Mere Belly":
             An Interpretation of Jeremiah 20:7–12 and
             Jeremiah 20:7–12: A Literary Response
             (Michael Fishbane and Geoffrey Hartman) .. 169

CONCLUSION

Chapter 11: "Ruth Amid the Alien Corn": Perspectives and
             Methods in Contemporary Biblical Criticism
             (John Dominic Crossan) 199

Chapter 12: The Mosaic Revisited (Robert Polzin and
             Eugene Rothman) 211

Bibliography 225

Foreword:
On Joseph Heinemann (1915–1977)

Judah Goldin

Except for some notes or outlines which he may have left behind, or previously completed papers still awaiting publication, Professor Joseph Heinemann's essay in this volume may indeed be the last study he finished and sent to be published (he was already very sick by then). Let this study of his, therefore, represent something of Heinemann's constant interests and method. He called the study "A Homily on Jeremiah and the Fall of Jerusalem," and it is both detailed analysis and description of a *literary* unit in the *Pesiqta Rabbati*. Heinemann was emphatic about this.

I have still another reason for emphasizing the word "literary": although in whatever Heinemann wrote (in Hebrew and in English) there was always shining testimony to scholarly and critical discipline—the noting of variant readings and parallel passages, the attempted stratification of textual traditions, the close examination of language and vocabulary, and his wide-ranging consultation of sources including primary, secondary, and those at times overlooked by others—all this did not satisfy him. He was after more than that. He sought in the atomized texts he studied, their possible literary entirety. He wanted the organic whole in addition to the parts. He wanted to know not only what the words mean but what the design and purpose meant. We can see this instantly in the homily included in this volume: his fascination with the dark lady and the shock of her identity, and with the corresponding changing moods of Jeremiah, the prophet both of doom and of consolation. This concern with the literary as a whole is not confined to midrashic narratives and characters. He

vii

loves to follow a theme and its adaptations down through the centuries and varieties of environment. He will trace a version from the tannaite *Mekilta* and earlier, down through *Pirqe Rabbi Eliezer,* to reveal the applicability of the ancient teaching or reflection to the new pressures from the Islamic world. His writing is forthrightness itself.

Nor is this all. Because of his fine sense of primary literary structures, for example, he was able to call attention to the serious limitations of what had almost become a classic in the Palestine mandate at first, and later the Israeli school system, Bialik and Ravnitzky's *Sefer ha-Aggadah.* Of course Heinemann was not opposed to the teaching of aggadah and midrash in the schools; and of course he appreciated the esthetic and moral merits of the passages selected (and where need be, explained in Hebrew when the original was Aramaic). But Heinemann insisted that by adopting a modernization for pure and simple literary effect, Bialik and Ravnitzky drove out of sight the original liturgical literary framework of the haggadic material. The wrong kind of literary transposition, he felt, left no trace of the original literary form and role. Midrash is more than belles lettres; it had a base and cycle in synagogue instruction. It was not accommodation to the modern that he objected to. What he objected to was transformation which erased the original character of the literary composition, written or oral, or the original and relevant naturalness of a central Jewish institution. The aim of midrash is indoctrination, not merely to please.

When Professor Heinemann's volume on *Prayer in the Talmud* appeared (recently translated and published in English [1977] but first printed in 1964), it was as though fresh air had been admitted into an established field of investigation which had fixed ground rules. He argued and demonstrated, however, that precious as are literary finds in what was once upon a time oral literature, the place to begin is *before* the oldest texts, not just *along with* them. The oldest texts are already part of the finished process; but before crystallization or statutory prescription, there is flux, legitimate and approved variety, and spontaneity. This process can be observed in the mobility of recurring "formulae" from one prayer setting to the other. One is tempted to say that his knowledge of forms of written literature (he read extensively in literary criticism) led Heinemann to recognize the features of the oral. From this view he could move forward to the categories of prayers modeled after the idiom of court pleadings, prayer in the idiom of the academy, obligatory and communal prayer, private devotion, and so on.

Then again, there was his refreshing suggestion about the location of the *Petihtas* (the proems of our midrashim), that such homilies were very likely introductory *to* the Torah reading in the synagogue, not sermons after the Torah reading. Make this assumption, and the literary brevity of the *Petihta* becomes appropriate and meaningful rather than a puzzling artificiality.

Heinemann never denied that philology was of fundamental importance, but he insisted, as in the case of the texts of prayer, that there were problems philology by itself could not solve. He was deeply impressed by the work (*Darke ha-Aggadah*, 1954) of his older namesake, Isaac Heinemann. In the essay in this volume Joseph Heinemann wrote, "In the manner of the aggadists [the author of the present homily] arrives at a solution by way of creative philology and historiography. To the extent that he has portrayed an integrated and persuasive picture of the prophet, he has done so by rewriting his story using scriptural material selectively, disregarding details that do not fit his plans, and inventing episodes that have no basis whatsoever in Scripture." The stance is recognizable by all students of the two Heinemanns. The two sentences quoted can stand as a governing statement of Joseph Heinemann's analyses in his *Aggadot we-Toledotehen* (see p. 309) (1974) as well.

A bibliographical compilation of Heinemann's publications by one of his Israeli students, critical reviews no less than independent essays and books, would be a service to contemporary scholarship. Such a compilation is, of course, no substitute for the man himself, who, even in his merciless last sickness still hoped to explore many liturgical, midrashic, and aggadic subjects that challenged his thinking. How much richer we might have been had he been able to do so, for he was, despite frequent assaults upon his health, astonishingly vigorous and creative intellectually. How much he had to offer! His works and the memory of him endure as a blessing.

Preface

In October 1977, more than forty scholars from across North America gathered at Carleton University in Ottawa, Ontario, to spend three days reflecting on the Bible from their various vantage points—whether historical, rabbinic or literary. Our hopes for this colloquium were modest: "a broadening of interests, an increase in knowledge, and a pleasant experience of fellowship."

If our expectations were exceeded during those autumn days three years ago, it was the result of the warmth and enthusiasm of all those involved who contributed their time and efforts with such generosity. We doubt that this volume, the outcome of that gathering, will provide either "the symmetrical vision of biblical literature" to which Kalman Bland of Duke University referred in his charge to the colloquium, or the "alternate vision" that Robert Alter of Berkeley proposed in his summation. We can only hope that the volume will convey some echo of those rare and magic moments when, for three days, scholars became friends and the pursuit of common understanding was a journey of shared curiosity, discovery and joy. To those who made such moments possible, our thanks.

Many contributed their advice and assistance both to the colloquium and the volume, and to all we are most grateful. We would particularly like to thank the Deans of Arts, James Downey and Naomi Griffiths, and the Dean of Graduate Studies and Research, Gilles Paquet, of Carleton University, for their moral and material support for the colloquium and the volume of essays. We would also like to express our appreciation to the following indi-

viduals and the institutions they represented: Earl Rooney and
Nancy Kenney, Office of Continuing Education, Carleton University; Jeremy Palin, the Carleton Library; Jane Forner, the
Canadian Broadcasting Corporation; and Mimi Taylor, the National Gallery of Canada. Of course, grateful thanks are due to
Christine Wirta for the otherwise thankless task of producing a
difficult manuscript with precision and to our wives for accepting
what we hope was excusable neglect with good cheer.

Finally, special mention must be made of the contribution by
the Jewish Community Council of Ottawa, its officers and its
Executive Vice-President, Hy Hochberg. The Council, a cosponsor
of the colloquium, not only generously supported the original
gathering but continued to encourage and assist us throughout the
preparation of the volume. Their continuing interest in and commitment to Jewish Studies has left its mark in many areas.

This volume is dedicated to Professor Joseph Heinemann of
blessed memory. Although his tragic illness deprived us of his
physical presence at the colloquium, his influence and impact were
with us throughout. We are very grateful to Moshe Greenberg and
Zwi Werblowsky of the Hebrew University for their efforts in this
respect. We cannot add to nor improve upon Judah Goldin's mov-
ing memoir of Professor Heinemann. We will, therefore, simply
express our personal thanks and appreciation to Dr. Judith Heinemann for permitting us to dedicate this volume of essays to the
memory of her husband whose insight and vision are still sign-
posts for us all.

Introduction

Robert Polzin and Eugene Rothman

Chapter 1

The Mosaic

Robert Polzin and Eugene Rothman

A previous volume in this series (*Encounter with the Text,*
Martin J. Buss, editor) shows conclusively that modern biblical
studies can benefit profoundly by approaches utilizing structural,
sociological, existential, linguistic, literary and other esthetic perspectives. The present volume in a sense continues this multi-
disciplinary encounter with the text, even though its scope is more
restricted and its dialogue on method differently structured.

Biblical studies have emphasized historical modes of interpretation for well over a century. One result of this emphasis has been
the neglect of the *literary* aspects of the biblical text. Thus present-
day biblical studies involve a hermeneutics that is still in its infancy with regard to literary criticism but well advanced in age
with reference to historical criticism.

What would happen if these two modern interpreters of the
Hebrew Bible—the elderly historian and the infant literary critic—
were to view their understanding of specific biblical texts in the
light of that traditional exegesis developed by the learned rabbis
of ancient times? This interesting question, and the unknown dimensions of an answer, provide the general perspective for the
present volume.

The essays by Lou H. Silberman and Joseph Heinemann are
superbly representative of the very best in modern rabbinic scholarship. How better to put into perspective the way we moderns interpret biblical material than to offer exquisitely detailed explanations of two ancient midrashic interpretations of particular biblical
texts? In elegance of style, depth of scholarship, and clarity of

3

presentation, Silberman and Heinemann brilliantly exploit key aspects of the biblical mosaic and in their own work recreate the midrashic genre.

In an impressive step-by-step analysis of a section of the midrashic collection, *Pesiqta Rab Kahana,* Silberman introduces us to ground-breaking considerations about the rhetoric of midrash. As he sketches for us the collage-like arrangement of biblical texts by which his rabbinic homilist constructed his *pesiqta,* Silberman traces a biblical path whose goal, Exod 19:1–2, is reached only after starting off with the concluding verses of the Book of Proverbs as a framework for significant reflections upon passages from Genesis, Exodus, Deuteronomy, and Jeremiah. The skillful inventiveness with which the homilist leads us from Proverbs to Exodus with exhortative stops all along the biblical route offers us much to think about concerning scholarly creativity in the interpretation of the Bible. More than this, one is led to reflect upon the contrast between the utter faithfulness with which Silberman explicates his homilist's text and the playful creativity with which the homilist rearranges the biblical text. We begin to see that questions of *peshat* (the simple or literal meaning of a text), and *derash* (the interpretative meaning of a text), and their mutual value are intimately connected with changing perspectives of biblical literature.

Joseph Heinemann's essay on a midrashic homily about Jeremiah and the fall of Jerusalem (*Pesiqta Rabbati, Pisqa* 26) exemplifies his own scholarly eminence as well as the genius of an ancient rabbinic homilist. Heinemann the rabbinic scholar reveals himself to be an excellent literary critic. He even points out how the homily he interprets is an example of a rare midrashic genre which treated the biblical text so freely that the rabbis, during certain historical periods, feared the public might mistake such accounts for authentic reflections on the biblical text itself. In other words, even among ancient midrashists, some midrashim were thought to suffer from an excess of creative interpretation. The modern problem of meaning versus significance (e.g., Hirsch), literal versus metaphoric sense, or authentic versus inauthentic word, has, as in so many other cases, ancient reverberations.

The section on rabbinic perspectives offers us an unusual opportunity to reflect upon the complicated relationships of *derash* and *peshat*. This is the case primarily because the essays of Silberman and Heinemann are splendid examples of modern *peshat* upon ancient *derash* and will have much to teach us about the important issues raised in this volume.

The immensely readable essay by Joseph Gold on Deuteronomy and the Word initiates philosophical, indeed semiological concerns, that continue on into the following essay by White. Gold finds in Deuteronomy the emergence of Mosaic monotheism that is coincident with a crucial stage in man's evolution: namely, man's emerging awareness of the centrality of language in his life. For Gold, Deuteronomy was written down in a literary form "which in spite of all cited parallels is utterly unlike any other document known to man." The book remains for him the earliest example of popular, universal and compulsory education. It is difficult to endow Deuteronomy and its central human figure, Moses, with more stature than Gold does in his essay of superlatives. How biblical scholars respond to the brash claims of this literary critic will be highly instructive for the changing perspectives of this volume, as it aspires to a shared vision.

Hugh White's analysis of the Genesis narrative is representative of the approach to the interpretation of biblical texts that characterizes younger scholars impressed with the insights of French structuralism. His interpretation embodies the hypothesis that the Genesis narrative develops as it does by a kind of semiological necessity: the nature of man's language and literary capacity dictates the very sequence of key events narrated in the Book of Genesis. The transition from prohibition to promise found between Genesis 1–11 and 12–50 and key moments within each of these two main sections enable White to map out the Genesis story on a grid which describes the process and progress of human awareness from a closed to an open semiology. White's thesis is provocative and his reading of the Genesis story will enable us below to pinpoint a number of key issues. In any event, in their essays, Gold and White offer us important examples of what happens when both a literary critic and a biblical scholar philosophize about a biblical text. Although neither essay's philosophizing tendencies are representative of the professional disciplines by which each author calls himself literary critic or biblical scholar, both essays illustrate the communal interests of the larger humanistic context in which these disciplines presently exist.

The three divergent traditions represented in chapters 6, 7, and 8 allow us to put in direct juxtaposition rabbinic, modern biblical, and literary critical perspectives on the question of false prophecy as it is represented primarily in 1 Kings 22, the story of the prophet Micaiah ben Imlah. For the first time in the volume we can see how each interpreter—the ancient rabbi, as well as the modern biblical and literary critic—approaches the same biblical text and deals with the problems which that text presents to him. Goldenberg, Roth, and Robertson, unlike the scholars of the next section, rarely speak directly to one another but rather to the text and to us. Nevertheless the variegated reading of 1 Kings 22 according to these three diverging views enlarges the biblical mosaic in a way that the various juxtapositions of the earlier sections could not do.

One of the important results of Goldenberg's survey of rabbinic teaching on the problem of false prophecy as it relates primarily to 1 Kings 22 and Jeremiah 28 is his claim that the rabbis, recognizing the implications of the Micaiah ben Imlah story, namely, "that the divine gift of prophecy can be more dangerous than anyone had ever imagined," were led to keep Micaiah's vision from standing. The rabbis were led to systematize their views on false prophecy through a fear of the consequence of having to believe in a deceptive true prophecy. To accomplish their purpose, Goldenberg infers from the talmudic evidence, the rabbis felt it necessary deliberately to invert the apparent meaning of specific biblical narratives. "When we moderns come upon a troubling biblical passage," Goldenberg writes, "we tend to discuss it to excess; the Talmud simply changes the meaning of the text without explicitly acknowledging the problem at all."

Goldenberg insists that, where the meaning of the Bible is concerned, the purpose of the rabbis differs from that of contemporary scholars. We moderns try to understand the text as well as we can on its own terms; talmudic exegesis could and did do this, but needed also to produce a religiously acceptable interpretation, so that when these two purposes came into conflict, it was acceptable to invert the apparent meaning of a troubling biblical passage. The rabbis were forced, therefore, "to sacrifice plausibility for mere defensibility as their criterion in accepting the interpretation which they did." Implicit in these remarks, as Robertson will be quick to point out in his own essay, is the belief that we know what a text is saying in its own terms, and that the rabbis could do this also but rejected such meanings when religiously dangerous.

In the end, Goldenberg believes that an investigation of the manner in which talmudic sages dealt with troubling passages about false prophecy such as 1 Kings 22 teaches us very little about what we would today call plausible meanings of such texts. The most we can learn is their potential meaning. The crucial questions that Goldenberg raises about understanding a text in its own terms and about plausible and potential meanings will have to be faced later on when we attempt to assess the impact of all the essays of this volume on the biblical mosaic.

In Wolfgang Roth's contribution we have this volume's only representative of the historical-critical approach to a biblical text. Happily, this review of seven historical-critical interpretations of 1 Kings 22 is a masterful survey that highlights most of the important characteristics that distinguish historical-critical exegesis from the rabbinic approach described by Goldenberg and the literary approach to be proposed by Robertson. An important contribution of Roth's essay is his epilogue which deals with a number of methodological reflections about what the seven historical critics seem to have done in connection with the issues that directly concern this volume. As we shall soon see, Roth's contribution is pivotal for the conclusions we will draw from our multi-disciplinary experiment.

What Roth's survey brings out so well is that it is not always possible to put historical critics in the same methodological bag. In summarizing for us the exegetical positions of Wellhausen (1876–77), Kittel (1900), Gressmann (1921), Noth (1943), Montgomery (1951), Würthwein (1967), and Rofé (1976) on 1 Kings 22, Roth pinpoints their similarities and differences. Wellhausen comes across primarily as an historian: he selected and rearranged biblical texts to enable him to reconstruct the history of the religion of Israel. Rudolf Kittel also saw himself primarily as a historian, yet as Roth perceptively remarks, his commentary shows that the moral issue of Yahweh's allowing prophets to lie takes center stage in his treatment of 1 Kings 22. Roth's assessment of Kittel's interpretation turns out to be remarkably similar to the picture drawn by Goldenberg of the rabbinic midrashist striving to make troubling texts speak religiously acceptable truths. Roth writes, "Thus for Kittel exegesis serves to underscore his understanding of religious history as the never-ending movement from a lower order to a higher, purer view of the divine. He interprets the image of Yahweh as liar in 1 Kings 22 as an episode in that movement." Roth finds Gressmann's interpretation of 1 Kings 22 impressive and gives a number of reasons for this. In addition, the utter reverence and faithfulness of Gressmann's procedure, as Roth describes it, in treating the text in all its smallest details stand out clearly. Noth, on the other hand, subjects 1 Kings 22 to an extensive redactional analysis and represents a much greater hermeneutical distancing than do Kittel and Gressmann. For example, the moral questions in 1 Kings 22 about divine deception that so taxed Kittel and Gressmann and the rabbis before them are not confronted by Noth. When Roth introduces us to Würthwein's position, we see the fragmenting nature of historical-critical analysis at its highest level as Würthwein finds literary layers within layers within layers in 1 Kgs 22:1–38.

Roth concludes his survey with a valuable epilogue which sets up key issues arising out of his impressive review. What immediately strikes one who has just finished the Goldenberg article is Roth's description of his seven historical critics in terms that recall the rabbinic midrashist struggling with troubling texts. Roth writes, "In all cases their reading of the text is not an end in itself; it is a means to an end. . . . All these exegeses move into a positive but critical distance from the text, for the sake of literary deconstruction and literary and/or historical reconstruction." When we add to this the fact that the historical reconstruction was often in terms of a grand scheme of religious evolution, the external religious purposes of the rabbis whereby they rearranged their biblical texts do not seem so far from the external purposes of the historical critics surveyed by Roth. The distancing from the text involved in both cases turns out to be remarkably similar, even if the directions in which they move differ.

The literary view of 1 Kings 22 that David Robertson presents begins with a parable meant to lead us to reflect upon the absolutely central concept of hermeneutic frame of reference when we bring together traditional interpretations and modern interpretations in an interdisciplinary dialogue (as we are doing in this volume). Robertson reminds us that we discuss these issues not to engage in rational argument but to *testify* about those frames of reference which express our deepest convictions and to *understand* and appreciate the frames of reference cherished by our colleagues. In this regard Robertson points out how helpful Roth's essay is in describing the basic frames of reference of the historical critics he has surveyed for us in the previous essay. Robertson also shows that the concept of frame of reference helps us to rephrase the problems Goldenberg's paper raises about apparent and distorted meanings, or plausible and potential meanings, of the text.

Robertson then puts himself in a literary frame of reference and gives us a reading of 1 Kings 22 that is at once both imaginative and plausible. Utilizing the idea that a narrator communicates his meaning by ringing changes in the genre in which he chooses to tell his story, Robertson details for us how 1 Kings 22 sets up expectations in us that are not fulfilled in any straightforward way, so that the narrator may effectively distance himself from the characters of his story and from some of the conclusions we may want to draw from reading it. Robertson suggests that in the case of 1 Kings 22 ambiguity may be the direct result of looking at this text from a literary point of view. Although Robertson ends his rewarding essay by suspecting that literary criticism may involve a drastic alteration in the way we view the Bible, it remains entirely possible that the juxtaposition of Goldenberg's, Roth's, and Robertson's essays on the "divergent" rabbinic, historical and literary approaches to 1 Kings 22 has uncovered important similarities among them that are as striking as their differences.

To cite only one similarity which we will explore in more detail shortly: Goldenberg has shown how the rabbinic midrashists distanced themselves from troublesome biblical texts for a religious or theological purpose; Roth describes in great detail how each of his historical critics had distanced himself from the biblical text for the purpose of historical or literary re/deconstruction; and

Robertson uses a literary frame of reference to argue for a narrator of 1 Kings 22 who deliberately distances himself from the characters of his story for purposes of his own. The important concepts of frame of reference and of distancing that are respectively the starting point and conclusion of Robertson's essay are heuristic devices that will allow us to raise some important questions not only about how a biblical text "writes itself" but also about how ancient and modern commentators on the Bible have interpreted both their object and each other.

To summarize, this journey through the concrete mass of biblical texts has so far comprised the following stages. Silberman and Heinemann stand out as parade examples of modern interpretative scholarship; the rabbis they write about come across almost as paradigms of ancient imaginative interpretation. *Peshat* illumines *derash*. With these first two essays we see that precise faithfulness to the details of their rabbinic text yields striking illustrations of the creative playfulness whereby the rabbis altered or rearranged the biblical texts. White's and Gold's philosophic interpretations of Deuteronomy and Genesis have put in bold relief a number of humanistic assumptions shared by modern commentators on the Bible, the most obvious of which is the absolute centrality of language. These two papers almost tell us more about ourselves than about the biblical texts they explore.

With the juxtaposition of Goldenberg's, Roth's, and Robertson's essays, the reader strangely experiences a feeling of déjà-vu as he progresses through the three articles. When confronted with the story of Micaiah ben Imlah in 1 Kings 22, what Goldenberg says the rabbis did, Roth says his historical critics did, and Robertson says the biblical narrator did. Each, we are told, distanced himself from the text he narrates or interprets for purposes external to the text itself. Up to now, the insights we have gained have resulted primarily from the *juxtaposition* of differing traditions or perspectives (only Robertson made any reference at all to another essay in the collection); the dialogue, such as it is, is only implicit, if at all.

The next group of interpretative essays extends the discussion to an explicit *dialogue* between divergent traditions. In the interchange between Anthony Saldarini, the rabbinist, and Dan Ben-

Amos, the folklorist, on the binding of Isaac (the *Akedah*) in Genesis 22, we are first given a review of the main approaches and perspectives of rabbinic literature to this popular biblical story, a review that brings to light the diversity of both positive and negative responses of the rabbis to the reading of Genesis 22. On the positive side, the ancient commentators express admiration for the obedience of Abraham and Isaac, and on the negative side, a muted, even defensive, attitude toward God's command and Abraham's intentions toward his son. Although Saldarini is in full control of the historical contexts of the rabbinic texts he surveys, Ben Amos is quick to point out that Saldarini has given us only a literary, thematic, almost synchronic survey of important rabbinic texts concerning the *Akedah,* and that we now need "to examine texts in their relationship to the culture, ideas and events of distinct historical periods."

The conversation between Michael Fishbane and Geoffrey Hartman on the meaning of Jer 20:7–12 brings our multi-disciplinary dialogue on specific biblical texts to a fitting climax. Fishbane's essay is a detailed literary analysis of Jeremiah's heart-wrenching prayer that uncovers for us how its dynamic structure and Jeremiah's renewed hope and confidence are intimately connected. Although Fishbane, like virtually all biblical scholars today, is well trained in matters of historical criticism, he has recently been engaged in new and exciting research on the hermeneutics of the biblical text. His essay is an apt starting point for the literary-critical gifts of Geoffrey Hartman. His essay brilliantly inserts a helpful critique of Fishbane's essay between a prescient outline of critical issues confronting biblical scholarship in general (and this volume in particular) and a valuable justification of Jeremiah's prayer in 20:7–12 as belonging to the genre of "crying or shouting rather than speaking or the modalities of speech which we usually associate with literature."

It is clear from both Fishbane's and Hartman's contributions that we already have in this volume an answer to the questions of David Robertson about how different the literary frame of reference is and how drastic an alteration it promises in the way the Bible is seen. Fishbane's and Hartman's essays demonstrate, as Robertson's did earlier, that a literary frame of reference prom-

ises new and exciting interpretations of the Bible which have
much to commend themselves in terms of adequacy, imagination,
and completeness.

Finally, John Dominic Crossan concludes these essays with his
own assessment of and prognosis for the present state of biblical
studies. He sees biblical studies changing from a single discipline
to a field discipline, established by an influx of a host of new
methods in studying the Bible, methods whose twin axes are historical (genetic) and structural (synchronic). In the exercise of
this new field discipline, Crossan plausibly argues for the operational (in his terms, "logical") priority of structural analysis to
historical analysis. Sharing the optimism of Robertson, Crossan
concludes with a metaphoric prediction for the future of biblical
studies: "We are going to find ourselves like Ruths gleaning in
strange and alien fields, in places we have not seen before, among
companions we have not met before, but with gains we have not
known before."

Part I
Rabbinic Perspectives

Lou H. Silberman
Joseph Heinemann

Chapter 2

Toward a Rhetoric of Midrash: A Preliminary Account

Lou H. Silberman

A critical examination of the structures of a midrashic collection necessarily includes the attempt to understand the form and function of the collection at hand—attending, of course, to text-critical questions because this is, in a broad sense, redaction criticism. The question is quite simply, what is the intention of the redactors? The answers to this question vary with each collection, for different collections have different intentions. Thus one may not begin with a generalization concerning midrash as a genre but only with a particular collection. If one is successful in grasping the intention of the particular redactor, then one can move back through and behind the redactional undertaking to an examination and analysis of the materials which the redactor had at hand and used to fulfill his intention. It may then become evident that those materials vary in their formal structures and in their previous functions and intentions. Careful consideration of these blocks of material may disclose again their composite nature—their construction from yet smaller pieces of several forms, each having a particular function in a yet earlier situation. The obligation of the critical scholar is to discover the form and the function of the materials on the several levels he or she may uncover, holding in mind that earlier forms and their functions may be lost or distorted within the larger whole in which they are subsumed.

An analogy to this, indeed a model for it, may be a collage. In this art form fragments of materials are brought together to compose a new something that is more or less indifferent to the previous form and function of its parts. One must say "more or

15

less," for these previous forms and functions may or may not play a role in the intentionality of the artist. Thus, a torn piece of newspaper may be present in a collage because of its colors and texture. Its immediately previous function may have been to stop a hole in a broken windowpane. Before that, it may have been used to wrap some hot chestnuts, and somewhere back along the line, to convey news about the outbreak of a war, the execution of a criminal, the awarding of the Nobel peace prize, or the birth of an infant. Any, all, or none of these previous functions and of the early form or forms of the material may be involved in the intentionality of the artist. It is not wise, however, to push the analogy beyond this point, for one must recognize the difference between a collage and a literary work.

If one turns to contemporary literary works for help, one finds that some poets have quoted or referred to the writings of other authors within the body of their own work to set up a resonance of ideas in the reader's mind. If the reader is unacquainted with this material, however, then the ideas do not resonate. In fact, they are lost, although other parts of the poem may be grasped and may illuminate the uncomprehended lines.

The critic, on the other hand, is sent to the sources. Part of his or her task is to observe the form and the function of the materials in those sources without insisting that they remain the same in their new environment. It may be that the later author has misunderstood or distorted, consciously or unconsciously, the earlier form and function. The critic may argue the intentionality of the author on the basis of the tension between the original form and function and their present state in the work at hand. This is suggested, not because one follows blindly the methods of contemporary critics but because if one is aware of them, one looks at the material of interest differently. It is examined with some concern, first for the poetic sensibility and the intellectual sense of the redactor and then for the sense and sensibility of the author or authors of the material he or she has redacted, at whatever levels of form and function are disclosed.

This essay will examine a limited but representative block of material in a particular midrashic collection, *Pesiqta de Rab Kahana*. This is a collection of *haggadic* midrash, i.e., interpretation or exposition of Scripture not for legal (*halakhic*) conclusions (what may be called the structure of life), but for the sense of life therein contained. It is organized around the extraordinary liturgical cycle of the synagogal year—the *mahzor*—as contrasted to the ordinary cycle, the *siddur*. The latter is the regular structure of Sabbath worship in which a consecutive lection of the Pentateuch (*Humash*) with its conjoined but not consecutive prophetic lection (*Haftarah*) is read. The *mahzor*, on the other hand, represents the cycle that complements the regular Sabbath cycle with lections for holy days, festivals, fasts, and also provides additional pentateuchal and prophetic lessons to supplement the regular readings on extraordinary Sabbaths. These lections are not consecutive but are dependent, as the Sabbath cycle is not, on the particular and special nature of the occasion on which they are read.

Our interest will be focused upon the material related to *Shabuot*, Pentecost. The first item in this section presents us with a formal structure: the *petiha*, the proem. As Leo Baeck, following the lead of Bloch, suggested and as Joseph Heinemann has demonstrated, it is a particular liturgical device that introduces the reading of the Scriptural lesson of the day and is not—as was once thought—the introduction to a homily on that lesson /1/. It begins with the statement that R. Judah b. R. Simon began his introductory discourse by quoting the concluding verses of the Book of Proverbs /2/:

> *rabbot banot 'asu hayil ve'at 'aleet 'al kullana sheqer hahen*
> *vehevel hayyofee 'ishah yir'at Adonai hee' tithallal*
> *tenu lah mippree yadeha vihaleluha bashe 'arim ma 'aseha.*

"Many women have done excellently,
    but you surpass them all."
Charm is deceitful, and beauty fleeting,
    but a woman who fears the Lord
    is to be praised.
Give her of the fruit of her hands,
    and let her works praise her in
    the gates.

The reason for choosing this verse to introduce a homily that will conclude by quoting the first verses of the Pentateuchal lesson

of the day (Exod 19:1–2: "In the third month of the going forth
of the children of Israel from Egypt. . . .") is certainly not immediately evident. Indeed, considerable debate has revolved around
the question of the so-called "extraneous" verse. I am, however,
prepared to argue that whatever internal reason (i.e., some con-
gruence of ideas) there may be, there must always be an external
connection between the opening verse or verses and the opening
verse or verses of the pentateuchal lection. That external connection is invariably the assonance of some word or words in the two
passages /3/. In the *petiḥa* at hand this assonance is far from
obvious but it is present. In Prov 31:30 the word *ha-ḥen,* "charm/
grace," is used. In Exod 19:2 two words occur that are assonant
with it: *vayaḥanu,* "where they encamped," and *vayiḥan,* "Israel
pitched tent." There is no lexical connection whatsoever between
the two roots *ḥnh* and *ḥnn.* All we have, to begin with, is assonance. The internal connection between the extraneous verses and
the text is more subtle, as we shall see. The preacher begins with
the assumption that the verses have, in addition to their commonplace meaning, a second level, i.e., an internal connection that he
is to bring to the surface. It is to how he did it that we now turn.
The "many" of "many women" who have done excellently is understood to refer to a series of persons who, within the pentateuchal narrative beginning with Adam, have displayed their valor
by subjecting themselves to divine commandments. The first of
these, Adam, said the preacher, was commanded to observe six
commandments concerning idolatry, blasphemy, judges (i.e., law
courts), bloodshed (i.e., murder), sexual misconduct, and theft.
All of these are derived from one verse: *vayetzav Adonai 'elohim
'al ha'adam le'mor mikkol 'aytz hagan 'akhol to'khayl*; "The Lord
God had commanded the man, saying, 'From every tree of the
garden you may indeed eat' " (Gen 2:16). The derivation is accomplished by breaking the verse into single words or word clusters and then quoting another verse from elsewhere in Scriptures
that permits for one reason or another the word in question to be
understood as a reference to the commandment specified. These
proofs are, of course, not direct. They depend entirely upon some
resonance with the text word—and that resonance is, in most instances, tenuous indeed.

In the case of the first word of the Hebrew text, *vayetzav*, "and he commanded," it is verbal assonance that suggests a resonance of content and allows the text word to be understood as referring to idolatry. The assonance is between *vayetzav* and the word *tzav* in Hos 5:11, (*ho'il halakh 'ahare tzav*) "doggedly pursuing that which is worthless." The two words are actually unrelated in meaning; indeed, *tzav* in Hosea is an *hapax* /4/ and its meaning, "worthless," may well depend upon its own assonance with *shav* in Exod 20:7, *lo' tissa' 'et shem Adonai 'elohekha lashav*. However that may be, assonance gives rise to resonance of meaning: *vayetzav* refers to idolatry.

The second instance, the prohibition against blasphemy, is based on the occurrence of the Tetragrammaton in the verse, which is tallied with Lev 24:16, "whoever utters the Tetragrammaton shall be put to death." Since, however, the Tetragrammaton occurs frequently, the connecting of its occurrence in these verses is completely arbitrary but is apparently allowable as a conventional rhetorical gesture.

In the third instance, the command to establish courts, the word *'elohim* is understood as a reference not to God but to judges, an interpretation that is by no means novel here but occurs elsewhere in other settings.

The words *'al ha'adam*, "unto man" or more specifically "man," are connected with *'adam* in Gen 9:6 (*shofekh dam ha'adam ba'adam dammo yishafekh*, "he who sheds man's blood, by man shall his blood be shed,") in order to arrive at the prohibition against murder. Again, the application of the word from Gen 9:6 to Gen 2:16 is completely arbitrary but, according to the convention here at work, it too is entirely acceptable.

Even more arbitrary is the connection of the infinitive *le'mor*, "saying," with the prohibition against sexual misconduct. It is tallied with its counterpart in Jer 3:1, *le'mor*, the introductory word to that verse. Its presence there is obscure, but since the verse refers to the pentateuchal prohibition against the remarriage by a man of his divorced wife after she has been married to another man (Deut 24:1–4), that is quite sufficient to permit the inference.

The derivation of the commandment against theft from the

words "from all the trees of the garden you may eat" comes from the continuation in the next verse "but from the tree of the knowledge of good and evil you must not eat," a straightforward derivation /5/.

The block of material is not the preacher's own /6/. It belongs to an exegetical tradition available in a variety of circumstances to support or to illustrate diverse positions. It is effective in the case at hand because it enables the preacher to begin his chain of excellent or valiant persons at the very beginning and thus to build, as we shall see, to a climax.

The chain continues and in most instances there is no need to engage in the kind of proof we have seen in Adam's case. The command to Noah not to eat flesh cut from a living animal is found in Gen 9:4: "But you must not eat the flesh with the life, which is the blood, still in it."

Abraham receives the commandment concerning circumcision in Gen 17:9-11. The next figure, Isaac, seems, however, attached to the chain by the sheer necessity of completeness. Indeed, the preacher is careful not to say that Isaac was commanded to be circumcised on the eighth day; the audience knows that it was Abraham who had been so ordered, in the continuation of the commandment just referred to (Gen 17:12). Hence the preacher chose another term, *hinnekh*, "he inaugurated." Isaac *inaugurated* the eighth day, i.e., he was the first one circumcised in response to the commandment. Here again, as in the case of Adam, an inference rather than reference to a direct proof-text is called for.

The preacher treats the restriction against eating "the sinew of the hip" (Gen 32:32) as though it were a commandment given to Jacob although the biblical text does not make an explicit statement. However, the legal discussions of the subject in the Babylonian Talmud (*Hullin* VI) make it evident that its scriptural basis was located here.

Judah, we are told by the preacher, received the commandment concerning levirate marriage. Now R. Judah surely knew that the specific statement concerning such a marriage is found in Deut 25:5ff., but since Gen 38:8—his proof-text—clearly states that Judah instructed his son Onan "to do his duty as the husband's brother," he was free to conclude that Judah had indeed been commanded concerning this requirement. It may well be that this position was part of a body of commonly accepted ideas with which the preacher was working.

At this point one may at last comment on the internal connection between the extraneous verse and the Torah lesson to be read. That lesson, beginning with Exod 19:1 and continuing through Exodus 20 describes the giving of Torah and contains the Ten Commandments. If we omit, in our enumeration of the worthies commanded, Isaac who was not commanded but rather who inaugurated the observance of a commandment, we find a list of ten commands corresponding to the Ten Commandments of Exodus 20. Thus an internal connection is established by the preacher between the introductory verses from Proverbs and the lesson. The *peshat,* the simple meaning of the latter, and the *derash,* the interpretive meaning of the former, refer to ten commandments. Hence an internal connection is established.

This whole chain from Adam to Judah has emerged from the four words: *rabbot banot 'asu ḥayil,* "many women have done excellently." Now R. Judah turns to the second half, "But you excel them all," adding another link to the chain: *zeh doro shel Moshe shenitztavu 'al taryag mitzvot,* "this [the half verse] refers to the generation of Moses that was commanded concerning 613 commandments" /7/. R. Judah continues. The 613 commandments were divided into two parts: "248 are positive commandments, corresponding to the 248 members of the human body, each member saying to a person: please perform thus and such a commandment through me! 365 are negative, corresponding to the 365 days of the solar year. Each day calls to a person: do not do thus and such a transgression on me!" This statement of the number and division of the commandments is found in the Babylonian Talmud (Makkot 23b–24a) in the name of R. Simlai, an amora of the second generation, i.e., two generations earlier than our preacher R. Judah. What is not present in that passage are the phrases: "each member saying," "each day calling," with their continuation. Thus one may assume that the homilist has taken up a commonplace (he does not quote it in the name of R. Simlai, who said that 613 commandments were communicated to Moses, but our homilist has shifted the center of attention to the genera-

tion of Moses, saving Moses for a later verse) and has given it
immediacy by adding the phrases noted.

The interpreter, continuing his examination of the passage from
Proverbs, quotes a part of v 30: *sheqer ha-ḥen vᵉhevel ha-yofee,*
"grace is a delusion and beauty fleeting." This is understood to
refer to two of the worthies already mentioned, Noah and Adam.
The word *ha-ḥen,* echoing its occurrence in Gen 6:8, *vᵉNoah
matza' ḥen bᵉayne Adonai* permits the preacher to interpret the
half verse as referring to Noah and thus to draw the conclusion,
sheqer haya ḥinno shel Noah, "Noah's favor was or became a delusion." This conclusion, it seems to me, is not arbitrary but is
derived from the assonance with *vayyishkar,* "and he became
drunk," in Gen 9:21. Although this latter verse is not quoted, it
seems to have provided the interpreter with his clue, whether
recognized by the audience or not. Noah's grace, *ḥen,* became a
delusion because of Noah's *shikkaron,* drunkenness. To reverse
the Latin tag *"in vino veritas," bᵉshikkaron sheqer,* "in drunkenness, delusion."

Some such relationship seems to be present in the interpretation
of the next phrase: *vᵉhevel ha-yofee,* "beauty is fleeting." The
preacher understands it to refer to Adam: *hevel haya yofyo shel
Adam ha-rishon,* but how Adam was chosen as the referent of
the verse is obscure for the expected connecting verse is absent.
In its place there is a block of material dealing with the beauty
of Adam that has all of the earmarks of a redactional insertion.
I suggest this first because of textual variations at this point. One
text has an introduction, "said Rabbi" with the name missing;
another begins, "said Levi," while a third has no attributive introduction. The second reason for the surmise is that the block
occurs earlier in the *Pesiqta* (chap. 4, sect. 4) in a passage in
which R. Levi quotes it in the name of Rabbi Simeon b. Menasya
and where it is an integral part of the interpretation of a biblical
verse. The passage reads:

> The heel of Adam's foot outshone the sun. Do not be aston-
> ished at this assertion! Is it not customary that when a man
> makes two salvers, one for himself and the other for a close
> friend, he makes his own lovelier? So too when Adam was cre-
> ated, was it not that he might serve the Holy One, blessed be

he, Whilst the sun was created to serve creation. Should not then Adam's heel outshine the sun and if that is the case, how much more the beauty of his countenance.

This in no way assists us in understanding why *hevel ha-yofee,* "beauty is fleeting" refers to Adam. The only possible tally I can conjure up is that between *hevel,* "fleeting" and *hevel,* Abel, the son of Adam, with the supposition that with the murder of Abel, the beauty of Adam was turned into something ephemeral.

In terms of the introductory analogies with collage and with the use of quoted material in the writings of contemporary authors, this passage is instructive. It is an item that was not part of the original exposition of the verses in Proverbs. Its addition by the redactor shifts the center of interest—at least momentarily—away from the interpreter's movement toward a climactic disclosure. The redacted text gives us something more or something other to ponder than did the interpreter's text. In a scholarly work the insertion would be relegated to a footnote from which position it could but peripherally affect the text. In a literary work such as we are reading, its presence distorts for a moment the intention of R. Judah b. R. Simeon, the preacher.

R. Judah, however, continued his interpretation of the text of Proverbs, *'isha yirat Adonai hi' tithallal,* "a God-fearing woman is to be praised," with yet another reference to a figure from the past: Moses. We have already been told on the basis of "you surpass them all" that the generation of Moses excelled all those previously mentioned; is Moses to be set on a level with that generation or is he to be raised above? There is no comparative available in the biblical text, so the preacher prefaces his quotation with the word *mikkullam* ("more than all of these"): "more than all of these is a woman who fears the Lord, Moses, to be praised." Thus is Moses' superiority indicated. The preacher then quotes the concluding verse: *tnu lah mippree yadeha vihalleluha ba-she'arim ma 'aseha,* "Give her of the fruit of her labors and let her deeds praise her in the gates." At this point the redactor found it necessary to insert a statement from a much later teacher, R. Jose bar Jeremiah, explaining this odd circumstance that feminine figures in Proverbs are understood to refer to men, in this case Moses. "Why does he [Lemuel to whom the chapter is attributed] compare the prophets to women? Just as this woman [in Proverbs] is not bashful about presenting the needs of her household to her husband, so the prophets were not bashful about presenting the need of Israel to the Holy One, blessed be he." Again this is a learned note that belongs in the classroom, not in the pulpit /8/.

R. Judah continues: "Said the Holy One, blessed be he to Israel, 'My children, read this lesson every year and I will account it to you as though you are standing before Mt. Sinai and are receiving the Torah!' " *Aymatai,* "when" is this reading to take place? The answer comes in the form of the first verse of the pericope itself: *bahodesh ha-shelishi la-tzet bene Yisrael me-eretz Mitzrayim,* "In the third month of the going forth of the children of Israel from Egypt."

What, we ask, is the point of this emphatic statement; is this lesson to be read in the third month? In the normal Palestinian lectionary in which the Pentateuch was read through in three or more probably three and a half years, it would not be read every year. Thus the preacher insists it has a special function outside of that cycle. How is this special function to be determined? By the occasion on which it is read. When does that occasion fall? In the third month. What occasion outside of the regular cycle falls within the third month? *Shabuot,* Pentecost, the Feast of Weeks. Thus, the preacher is saying, the proper lesson for the festival is Exodus 19 that introduces the Sinaitic theophany and, presumably, Exodus 20 containing the Decalogue. He is, indeed, rejecting the explicit statement in the Mishna that Deut 16:9ff. is the lesson for the feast day. That pericope refers specifically to *Shabuot* but it contains no reference whatsoever to the giving of Torah which according to rabbinic tradition took place on that day. On the other hand, Exodus 19 and 20 make no reference to *Shabuot* so there seems to be no justification for reading them on that occasion. But, of course, there is the opening verse just quoted: "In the third month . . . ." Thus R. Judah's *petiha* that leads up to the reading of Scripture builds up support for this position. It emphasizes the giving of Torah at Sinai and the superiority of the generation who received it there over all preceding generations and then promises to join the present community to the past community in worth, if it asserts by the liturgical act of reading the lesson dealing with the giving of Torah on *Shabuot* that *Shabuot* is, indeed, the Feast of the Giving of Torah.

I have suggested along the way how the preacher built his argument. Let me go back, in conclusion, and attempt briefly to put it all together. The text as we have it from the hand of the redactor contains two learned footnotes: one deals with the beauty of Adam; the second justifies obliquely the use of feminine terms in Scripture to refer to masculine persons. Remove the footnotes, after recognizing the role they play in the redacted text, and what remains is the preacher's homily. But it too is a composed piece, although in a different sense. R. Judah has offered as the framework for his development three verses from the Book of Proverbs. He and his audience know, of course, where the exposition is to end—with the opening verse of Exodus 19. Tension thus arises in the audience's mind—how is he going to get there? And how does he intend the text to be understood? When we examine the exposition, we discover that some, at least, of the material is not of his own invention but is drawn from a common stock of ideas used elsewhere by other expositors for other purposes. But this ought not astonish us. The love of novelty was a late arrival in many cultures. Indeed, it is entirely possible that the presence of the already-existing in a new context, as I have suggested in the opening remarks about collage and some poetry, may have been more highly regarded than the new material. That, indeed, is what I understand the preacher's art to have been: the choice of the framework verse or verses and the building upon that framework, using pieces of received and recognized materials, in such a fashion as to arrive at an expected goal in an unanticipated fashion. He has, of course, not merely quoted from the common stock; he has fitted it in with skill, occasionally adding his own qualifying phrase to give the item the particular significance he has in mind, so that at the end, out of the old he has composed the new. And in doing so, he has made his argument and has, he hopes, thus convinced his hearers that the overriding meaning of *Shabuot* is not *hag habikkurim,* the festival of first fruits, but *mattan Torah,* the giving of Torah at Sinai.

And these, persuasion and conviction, are the goals of the rhetor's undertaking.

NOTES

/1/   See J. Heinemann (1971:104ff.). The references to Baeck and Bloch are found in the bibliography of that essay. Professor Heinemann's untimely death is a great loss and I wish to dedicate this essay to his enduring memory.

/2/   The transliteration of Hebrew in this paper does not pretend to be "scientific" but is more or less phonetic, although not technically so. It is intended to make it possible for one who does not read Hebrew to follow the argument of this paper by reading the words aloud—a most necessary part of the argument.

/3/   This against Heinemann (1971:101) who states that the opening verse is selected "because of some inner link or association with the theme of the pericope."

/4/   Its occurrence in Isa 28:10, 13—a difficult text—is incommensurate with its use here.

/5/   This, according to Ms. Oxford. See B. Mandelbaum (1:202–4).

/6/   This conclusion is drawn from the fact that the passage occurs in a number of other places in quite other contexts. It is the basis of the concept of the Noachide commandments incumbent on all mankind.

/7/   This, indeed, is what Ms. Carmoly does. See Mandelbaum's variant readings op cit. His own text, however, and the reading in *Yalkut Shemoni* do not have the words, "the generation of Moses" but, given the structure of the exposition, it is clear they belong here. The variants, however, are interesting for they seem to turn directly to the audience: "but you were commanded at Sinai concerning 613 commandments." The direct address, it seems to me, would have brought the homily to its conclusion.

/8/   What is particularly strange about this insertion is its place, for the concluding verse of Proverbs to which it is attached is not interpreted as referring to any of the aforementioned but to the congregation present at the moment.

Chapter 3

A Homily on Jeremiah and the
Fall of Jerusalem
(*Pesiqta Rabbati, Pisqa* 26)

Joseph Heinemann /1/

This wide-ranging and well-constructed homily on Jeremiah and the fall of Jerusalem is unique in many ways. While all other sections of *Pesiqta Rabbati* (henceforth *PR*) use as a heading the first verse of the day's Torah lection on which the homily is based, this section opens with a few lines of an ancient *piyyut,* which it then expounds: (*And it came to pass/ When the sheep rebelled/ And would not obey their masters' words/ For they hated their shepherds/ Who were their good leaders/ And withdrew far from them.*) There is no example of this anywhere else in midrashic literature. Then, too, throughout the other homilies, the first verse of the day's lection may be repeated over and over again in any one of its various sections—such as at the conclusion of the proem and elsewhere. Here, no quotation of verses from the day's lections in Torah or Prophets appears at all /2/.

It is impossible to even know for sure the occasion for which the homily was composed in the first instance. Its subject, the fall, points to the fact that it was intended for the period between the 17 of Tammuz and Tish'a (the ninth of) B'Av; however, there is no clear indication as to which of the three "Sabbaths of Doom" it belongs (the Sabbaths between the above-mentioned days on which prophetic pronouncements of Israel's doom are read) or whether it was composed for Tish'a B'Av itself. Its position in *PR* shows that the editor of the *Pesiqta* meant it to serve as the *pisqa* for the first sabbath after 17 of Tammuz, on which the prophetic lection is Jeremiah 1 /3/.

Unlike other *pisqas* or chapters in the midrashim, this *pisqa*

27

pisqa; chapter

continuous narrative about Jeremiah

shows no evidence of having been compiled of several independent units /4/; it seems to have been originally composed by the author as one integral piece. If, nonetheless, he made use of existing midrashic materials, he reworked and stylized them in such a way that it is almost impossible to isolate the components. In the entire *pisqa,* long as it is, not one homily or saying is cited in the name of its author. The section is not constructed according to any traditional plan or familiar pattern. It is an unusual attempt to create a continuous narrative about Jeremiah from his birth to after the fall, consisting of a medley of verses and verse fragments from the Book of Jeremiah (but not in the order of their appearance), of paraphrases of biblical stories, of freely invented legends that are not anchored in the text at all, and of midrashim that explain and enlarge upon the story in different ways. Its subject is the destiny and personality of Jeremiah, but subsumed under them is the story of the city and the people, their destinies being inextricably intertwined.

How this piece was originally composed, whether orally or in writing, is difficult to determine. Its length, the comparative scarcity of wordplays and other rhetorical devices, and perhaps also the fact that it has been preserved only in this fairly late work, point to the second possibility. If we have here written literature, its author did not follow the practice of other compilers of homiletic midrashim, because this is not a compilation of various independent units, but has been fashioned into a literary, stylistic, and structural whole. Clearly, this well-integrated piece cannot be attributed to the compiler of *PR,* since he is no more than a collector who does not leave such a mark on the materials of the work as would obscure the style and form that characterize each of his sources. Moreover, there is nothing like this section in the whole book.

Here is an outline of the contents /5/:

1. "When the sheep rebelled," Jeremiah was prophesying to them by the holy spirit.
2. He was one of four humans called "creatures."
3. The moment he came forth into the world he shouted loudly, "My bowels, my bowels, I writhe in pain . . ." (Jer 4:19).

4. He immediately opened his mouth to rebuke his mother saying that her behaviour was that of a *śoṭah,* a woman suspected of adultery. (To clarify such a woman's status, Numbers 5 ordains an ordeal by drinking a special potion, administered by a priest.) When she expressed surprise at this, he said to her, "Not to you, mother, am I prophesying, but to Zion."

5. The Holy One, blessed be he, said, "Before I formed you in your mother's belly, I appointed you to prophesy to my people." When Jeremiah refused and said, "I cannot speak for I am a child" (Jer 1:16), he answered him: "I love children, as it is said, 'When Israel was a child, I loved him' (Hos 11:1) . . .; take this cup of wrath and make the nations drink" (after Jer 25:15). He said, "Whom shall I make drink first?" He said, "Make Jerusalem and the cities of Judah drink first." When he heard this he cursed the day he was born (Jer 20:14).

6. He was one of two (Job was the other) who cursed the day of their birth. He said, "Whom do I resemble? A priest, whose duty it is to subject a *śoṭah* to the ordeal by drinking." They brought the woman to him; he uncovered her head, dishevelled her hair, /6/ looked at her and saw that she was his mother. . . . He said, "Woe to me because of you, Mother Zion! I thought I was to prophesy good things and consolations to you, and behold, I am prophesying words of doom."

7. He was one of three prophets who prophesied in that generation. He would say to the people, "If you turn back from your evil deeds and listen to my words, the Holy One will exalt you, but if not, he will hand you over to the enemy. . . ."

8. When Nebuchadnezzar came intending to exile them, the Holy One turned compassionate toward them and he made Mattaniah king over them, renaming him Zedekiah. He made him swear not to rebel against him, but even before Nebuchadnezzar returned to his country, Zedekiah rebelled against him.

9. When the Chaldeans came a second time to besiege Jeru-

salem, the Egyptian army marched against them and they
fled to Chaldea. Jeremiah said to King Zedekiah and his
princes, "The Egyptian army will depart, and the Chaldeans
will capture the city and burn it" (after Jer 37:9ff.).

10. Jeremiah set out for Anathoth to partake of the priestly
portion with his fellows (Jer 37:12ff.). Shelemiah, the
son of Hananiah (a false prophet whose death Jeremiah
prophesied [Jer 28:1ff.]) who was stationed at the gate
of Jerusalem, seized Jeremiah and said to him, "You are
defecting to the Chaldeans to make peace with them." The
princes became enraged with him and put him in prison, in
the house of Jonathan the scribe (Jer 37:9ff.).

11. Zedekiah sent for him and asked, "Is there any word from
the Lord?" He said, "There is. The king of Babylon will
exile you." Jeremiah begged not to be sent back to the
house of Jonathan the scribe. The king acceded, and al-
lotted him a loaf of bread a day; so Jeremiah stayed in the
court of the guard (Jer 37:17ff.).

12. The princes heard that he had prophesied, "He who stays
in the city shall die by sword, famine, and plague." They
took Jeremiah, threw him into the pit, and he sank in the
mire (Jer 38:1ff.).

13. Ebed-Melech the Cushite came to the king and said, "If
Jeremiah dies in the pit, the city will fall to the enemy."
So the king ordered that Jeremiah be brought up out of the
pit, and it was done (Jer 38:8ff.).

14. Nebuchadnezzar appointed Nebuzaradan commander of
the army and ordered him to conquer Jerusalem, but he
could not do it, since the decree against it had not yet been
sealed.

15. The famine was severe in the city and the daughters of
Zion scoured the marketplaces for food but could find
none.

16. At that time, the Holy One said to Jeremiah, "Get up, go
to Anathoth and buy the field from Hanamel your uncle"
(after Jer 32:10ff.). As soon as Jeremiah left the city,
an angel came down and breached its wall. The enemies
then seized the high priest and slaughtered him. . . .

17. Zedekiah and his sons sought to escape, but Nebuzaradan captured them. Nebuchadnezzar put out his eyes and led him to Babylon, and thus the prophecy of Jeremiah came true, "You shall go to Babylon, but Babylon your eyes will not see" /7/ (after Jer 39:4ff.).
18. At his return, Jeremiah found Jerusalem going up in flames and he cried, "You have enticed me and I was enticed!" (Jer 20:7). He followed the exiles to comfort them. Then he thought, If I go to Babylon with these, who will comfort those that remain? So he left them.
19. Jeremiah said, "When I returned to Jerusalem, I saw a woman dressed in black, with dishevelled hair, calling out, 'Who will comfort me?' She said to me, 'I had seven sons; my husband died and my sons too.' I said to her 'You are no better off than Mother Zion.' She replied, 'I am Mother Zion.' I said, 'Your affliction is like Job's, and just as in due time he comforted Job, so the time will come when he will comfort you.' "

This homily paints a broad canvas of dramatic events, though it does not include all the events that befell the prophet as related in the various parts of the Book of Jeremiah. Almost every scene is a dialogue, with the participants constantly changing. First, there is a controversy between Jeremiah and his mother in paragraph 4, then a confrontation between him and the Holy One, blessed be he, at his commissioning (par. 5). Following these are a variety of conversations between Jeremiah and Mother Zion. Characteristic of most of these scenes is an unexpected turn or a surprise ending that heightens tension. Here are just a few: Jeremiah harshly reproaches his mother—and it turns out that he is really accusing Zion (par. 4). When Jeremiah tries to avoid his mission with the excuse "I am just a child," God replies, "But I love children, as it is written 'For when Israel was a child, I loved him.' " In spite of God's declaration of love for Israel, he nevertheless commands the prophet to give Jerusalem the cup of wrath to drink (par. 5). Jeremiah is like a priest who officiates at the ordeal of a *soṭah* and discovers that she is his mother (par. 6). Just as Jeremiah leaves the city, an angel comes down to breach its walls (par. 16). While the enemies are busy conferring about

changing dialogues

Surprise endings

their next move, angels descend to set fire to the Temple (par.
16). At his return, Jeremiah sees a mourning woman, who turns
out to be Mother Zion herself (par. 19). In almost every scene,
there is a turn, and expectations are not fulfilled. Not only are
ironic tensions thus formed, lending the homily a certain depth,
but these minor reversals prepare the reader for the major one—
the fall of Jerusalem, which is the subject of the homily. As for
the prophet, individual instances of unfulfilled expectations deepen
his disappointment at the realization that he did not succeed in
saving the city.

The homilist manages, by and large, to unify the components
of the homily through various literary devices, as L. Prijs has
shown at length (39, n. 56). Here are just a few: in paragraph 2,
four "creatures" are mentioned; in paragraph 6, two men who
cursed the day they were born; and in paragraph 7, three prophets.
Both at the beginning and the end of the homily (pars. 6, 19),
Job is mentioned as an example and an analogue. Before his death,
Hananiah commands his sons to find some pretext for doing Jeremiah in (par. 10), and in the course of pleading before the king,
Jeremiah says, "We ought to learn from the wicked, who never
do anyone in before finding some pretext for it" (par. 11). Twice
the *pisqa* has Jonathan the scribe deride Jeremiah (end of par.
10, par. 12); a third time it portrays Jeremiah expecting further
derision and on that account not responding to the call of Ebed-
Melech the Cushite (par. 13) (Prijs: 58, 59). And finally, the
subject "parents and children" in many variations appears in almost all parts of the homily: Jeremiah and his mother, the priest
and his mother, the *śoṭah,* Hananiah the false prophet and his
sons, the daughters of Jerusalem and their offspring, Zedekiah
and his sons, Job and his sons, Jeremiah and Mother Zion, Zion
as a bereaved mother, and more.

Especially noteworthy are two motifs that provide highly significant connecting threads for the elements of the homily and
serve to give it form. At the beginning, the figure of the *śoṭah* is
central: Jeremiah accuses his mother (Zion) of behaving like a
śoṭah (par. 4). When he is commanded to give Jerusalem the cup
of wrath to drink, an echo of the draught given the *śoṭah* is audi-

ble (par. 5). Prijs rightly notes (36ff. and n. 49) that in order to conjure up that echo, the homilist omitted the word "wine" from the verse that reads "Take this cup of the wine of fury at my hand" (Jer 25:15). Immediately afterward, Jeremiah compares himself to the priest who officiates at the ordeal of the *śoṭah* and finds that she is his mother (par. 6). An echo of this motif recurs in the closing paragraph (par. 19): Jeremiah meets a woman after the fall, who is "dressed in black and her hair dishevelled," and of the *śoṭah* it is said that the priest "clothes her in black" (Mishna *Śoṭa,* 1.6) and that he also "lays hold of her clothes . . . and dishevels her hair" (ibid. 1.5). But in our case there is a difference: these are not signs of a *śoṭah* but signs of mourning, and this change in the meaning of the symbols reflects the radical change in Jeremiah's attitude to Mother Zion. At first he took her for a *śoṭah* and was filled with rage; now he sees her as a bereaved woman stricken by fate. He is filled with pity, and seeks to comfort her. Another expression of his equivocal attitude toward Zion is this: at the beginning of his mission, the prophet compares himself to Job and curses the day he was born, because he was obliged "to humiliate" his mother (par. 6). In the concluding passage, the analogy to Job recurs, but this time Jeremiah realizes that it is Zion's fate that is comparable to Job's (and indeed, the description of the death of her sons is drawn from Job 1:19) and that it is his duty to comfort her (par. 19) (Prijs: 75).

A device that pervades this homily, and of which it can be said that style amounts to substance, is the interpretation of names. Jeremiah's admonition, "If you repent of your wicked ways and listen to my words, the Holy One will exalt (*yeromem*) you above all the kingdoms" (par. 7), is a play on the name Jeremiah, as Prijs has correctly noted (43). And as the name of the prophet of doom heralds consolation, so too does the name of the last king. At least Zedekiah himself thinks so, for when Nebuchadnezzar gives him this name (*Sidqiyyahu*) (or when he himself takes this name /8/), he takes it as a sign that just men (*ṣaddiqim*) will descend from him. He did not realize that in his lifetime the Holy One would mete out strict justice (*masdiq 'et haddin*) to the Temple and condemn it to the flames (par. 8). The portentousness of names comes out again in Jeremiah's plea to Zedekiah that he not kill him, "What is more, you are called Zedekiah because you are a just man" (par. 11) (Prijs: 56).

These three clear allusions to the fateful significance of names make it likely that the homilist's use of the many theophoric names of that generation—names that herald redemption, as it were—is a deliberate stylistic device for creating an ironic gap and thus strengthening the feeling of unfulfilled expectations referred to above. He mentions such names frequently, sometimes even when there is no need for it /9/. We hear time and again about Jeconiah, Irijah, Shelemiah, Hananiah, Shephatiah, Gedaliah, Malchiah and others, so as to drive home how deceptive were all these heralds of good tidings—the names of the princes who persecuted Jeremiah and of the false prophets and their helpers who were really to blame for the fall of Jerusalem. In order to leave no room for doubt that he had a purpose in parading before us these resonant names so charged with vain hopes, the homilist offers an interpretation of a name apparently pejorative, but for once of a man deserving praise, Ebed-Melech the Cushite (Nubian): "Why was he called the Cushite? For, just as the Cushite is remarkable for his skin, so was he remarkable for his good deeds" (par. 13).

The inner quality of the homily is seen in the correspondence between the opening and closing sections. We have already noted, for example, the double treatment of the suffering of Job in the beginning (par. 6) and at the end (par. 19). More important is the personification of Zion (symbolizing, as in Lamentations, both the city and the people) which is clearly expressed in paragraphs 4, 6, and again in the concluding paragraph. This personification is a means of representing the personal involvement of the prophet with the fate of the city and people. The confrontation between Jeremiah and the people takes place in the conversations between him and Mother Zion. His attitude toward Zion is revealed, in all its complexity, in the changing uses of the figure of the *soṭah* and in the analogy with the sufferings of Job. These passages play a decisive role in the structure of the homily which is emphasized by a unique stylistic device. In only two passages does Jeremiah speak in the first person (preceded by the words "Jeremiah said"):

Main concern: Jeremiah's personality

in paragraph 6, in the parable of the priest who officiates at the ordeal of the *soṭah* and finds that she is his mother, and in the concluding paragraph, when he meets the mourning woman (Zion). Moreover, in both passages, and in these alone, what Jeremiah says is the invention of the homilist and not quotations from Scripture. On the other hand, even though they are formally monologues—and herein lies their stylistic peculiarity—Jeremiah quotes an exchange between him and Mother Zion, a dialogue full of dramatic tension.

The main concern of the author of this *pisqa* is undoubtedly Jeremiah's many-faceted personality. He comes to grips with the essential contradictions in the prophet's personality which emerge from Scripture itself. The prophet who before birth was charged with a mission, refuses to accept it; however, after the charge of being the prophet of doom was thrust upon him, he fulfills it in an exemplary way and with dedication. In spite of this, we find in his book (especially in chap. 20) complaints about his bitter fate in which he reproaches God and curses the day of his birth—words of unmatched harshness in the prophets. Even so, he continues to fulfill faithfully his role as "the prophet of wrath" to the end, to the very fall; then, he straightway becomes the prophet of comfort! It goes without saying that our homilist does not raise these issues in an analytic or abstract manner; he is not concerned with criticism of the scriptural story or with adjusting the discrepancies in it. In the manner of the aggadists he arrives at a solution by way of creative philology and historiography. To the extent that he has portrayed an integrated and persuasive picture of the prophet, he has done so by rewriting his story using scriptural material selectively, disregarding details that do not fit his plan, and inventing episodes that have no basis whatsoever in Scripture. According to the homilist, Jeremiah was meant from birth to be the prophet of divine wrath; this is expressed concretely by having him reproach Mother Zion immediately after being born /10/. Nevertheless, at his commissioning, he tries to evade the tragic role of one who is called upon to "humiliate" his mother, to prophesy doom to her instead of the "good things and consolations" that he would have liked. Yet he accepts the mission of prophet of doom and carries it out faithfully in spite of all the

refuses mission

curses his birth

"creative philology and historiography"

suffering and personal hardships that it entails. Only after the fall
does his poignant protest burst forth ("You have enticed me and
I was enticed"); from then on he laments over the fate of Zion
and comforts her.

The homilist presents Jeremiah, then, as torn by conflicting emotions from the very beginning. At times anger prevails; at times,
love and pity. For the homilist, the key to understanding this
complicated figure is a supposition he clearly implies though nowhere states in so many words: Jeremiah agrees in spite of everything to play the role of prophet of doom, only because he is convinced that in this way he will succeed in saving Zion from
destruction! He prophesies unceasingly of the coming disasters, but
he perceives his prophecy as a last-gasp measure of averting
them. The most trenchant expression of this singular conception
of the homilist is an invented episode, not merely without basis in
Scripture, but even in contradiction to it. On the very eve of the
fall, God sends Jeremiah to Anathoth to purchase a field from
his uncle Hanamel. In the scriptural version, a purchase takes
place, but in Jerusalem, when Hanamel comes to the court of the
guard (Jer 32:6ff.). It is impossible to mistake the meaning of
the biblical text, for it says repeatedly that Jeremiah was imprisoned in the court of the guard and did not leave it until the
fall (ibid. 38:13, 28; 39:11–14) /11/. This striking deviation
from Scripture is highly significant; in the homily's sequence of
events, immediately upon Jeremiah's leaving Jerusalem, the angel
descends to breach the wall and the city falls. The implication is
that the fall could not occur so long as Jeremiah was in the city;
the prophet's very presence protected it. The homilist, indeed, does
not say this outright, but he hints at it when he has the angel say,
"Let the enemies come and enter the house, whose master is no
longer within . . . let them enter the vineyard, whose watchman
has gone away and left it, and cut down its vines!" The image of
the watchman who has forsaken the vineyard must refer to Jeremiah—though, to be sure, it is formulated ambiguously (it would
seem on purpose), and can be interpreted (albeit with strain) as a
reference to God, paralleling the image of the house "whose master is no longer within" (which signifies that the fall could not
occur until the Divine Presence left Zion). The matter is settled

NB

in contra, to scripture

↓ deviation

Conflicting emotions —
anger, love, pity

by the cry (the occasion for which cannot be fixed by scriptural data) "You have enticed me and I was enticed" that the homilist puts in Jeremiah's mouth precisely when, after his return from Anathoth, he finds Jerusalem in flames. Retrospectively, Jeremiah interprets the command to go to Anathoth as a deception on the part of God; God tricked him by sending him out of the city, so that he could destroy it—just as God tricked him at his commissioning by giving him the false impression that his prophecy would be one of consolation, since God indeed loves Israel! Thus did the Holy One, blessed be he, set at naught all of Jeremiah's unflagging efforts of many years, in which "he prophesied words of doom"—only in order to save Jerusalem from destruction.

That indeed the author ascribed protective virtue to Jeremiah's presence in the city is corroborated elsewhere in the homily. We recall once again Jeremiah's words at the start of his mission; "If you repent of your evil deeds and obey my words, the Holy One will exalt you above the kingdom . . ." (par. 7). While this is not ground enough to assert that the mere presence of Jeremiah in the city could save it from punishment, Ebed-Melech's statement to Zedekiah (which has no basis in Scripture) is: "Know that if Jeremiah dies in the pit, the city will be handed over to the enemy" (par. 13).

This is how the homilist resolves all the discrepancies in Jeremiah's behavior. In spite of the pain and suffering attaching to his duty to prophesy doom, he undertakes it, for he is sure that his actions can save Zion. The prophet clings to this hope until the very last. When he is commanded to go to Anathoth, "Jeremiah thought in his heart and said, 'Perhaps he is giving the place to its owners' " /12/ (following the Parma ms.) (par. 16). At his return, when he sees smoke rising from the Temple, "he said to himself, 'Perhaps Israel is offering sacrifices in repentance, for there is the smoke of incense ascending' " /13/. Hence his bitter disappointment and burning anger—toward God!—when he realizes that the city has been destroyed while he, the "watchman," "had gone away and left it," trustingly obedient to the divine command to purchase the field in Anathoth—an act in which he saw an indication of salvation.

But there is another side to the coin. With the fall, the prophet

is freed from the cruel task of being a prophet of doom. After the
failure of his long and persistent effort to defend Zion against destruction, he can now do what he longed to do from the first—to
honor "his mother" instead of "humiliating" her and to prophesy to
her "good things and consolations." That this is his purpose after
the fall we must make out by reading between the lines, inasmuch
as it is difficult to make sense out of the statement of the prophet
at the end of paragraph 18: "Jeremiah said to himself, 'If I accompany the exiles to Babylon, who will comfort the exiles that
remain?' " Why should he prefer "the exiles that remain" to the
exiles that were deported to Babylon; and why should those be
more in need of comfort? It is no explanation to say that the
Babylonian exiles do not need him since they already have a
prophet of their own, Ezekiel. Ezekiel is not mentioned at all in
the homily, whereas, in Erez Israel (according to our homilist),
two other prophets were active alongside Jeremiah—Zephaniah
and Hulda (par. 7).

The real meaning emerges from the concluding paragraph which
describes the poignant meeting between Jeremiah and Mother Zion,
in which he does indeed begin to speak words of comfort to her.
It is not the "exiles that remain" then, whom the prophet has in
mind, and not them that he wishes to comfort, but Mother Zion.
A complete shift of perspective occurs. The fictional character of
Mother Zion takes the place of the Temple and the city which
she was supposed to symbolize; she becomes a reality, as it were.
The reality of the symbol is so strong in the concluding paragraph,
that a certain opposition between it and what it is supposed to
represent develops. The quasi-poetic passage concentrates in the
figure of Mother Zion what the city and the people are to Jeremiah
and thus forms an impressive conclusion.

In this homily, Jeremiah is conceived of as an eminently patriotic figure, something not necessarily equivalent to what Scripture
itself tells about him /14/. It is an image fitting for the homilist
to conceive because he seeks to give encouragement and comfort
to his audience, who have suffered yet another fall and upon whom
lies the cruel yoke of a hated foreign power. The scorn shown the
enemy throughout the homily serves the same purpose. It is not
the might of the enemy that brought about the destruction of

Jerusalem: "Do not say in praise of yourselves that you conquered it—a conquered city you have conquered, a dead people you have killed" (par. 16). This appears again in the picture of angels who descend and set fire to the Temple, while the enemies are conferring on how to do it! They manage to overcome the high priest and his unfortunate daughter and slaughter them, but we do not hear that they attack the soldiers with equal heroism. On the contrary—Nebuchadnezzar "is afraid" that his may be the fate of Sennacherib and so turns over command of the army to Nebuzaradan (par. 14). Indeed, "they could not conquer Jerusalem because its fate had not yet been sealed" (par. 14). When the Egyptians approached, the Chaldeans "fled"—a term that is not found in Scripture in this context and is inconsistent with it (par. 9) /15/. The patriotic interpretation of the homilist finds its most manifest expression in what he omits. When he quotes the scriptural warning of Jeremiah to the people, "He who stays in this city will die by sword, famine and plague" (par. 12), he does not quote its continuation, which sounds like a call to treason, "and he who goes forth to the Chaldeans shall live; he shall have his life as booty and live" (Jer 38:2). Much less does he mention the prophet's explicit statement to Zedekiah, "If you will go forth to the king of Babylon's princes, then your soul shall live and this city shall not be burned with fire; and you shall live, you and your house" (Jer 38:17).

The figure of Jeremiah as depicted by the homilist is surely complex and many-sided. The prophet is caught in a difficult conflict which induces his troubled and inconsistent behavior. But under the hand of the homilist, he becomes more understandable. His motives, apparently in conflict with one another in the biblical story, are now harmonious. The figure is no longer an enigma but credible and convincing. It is, paradoxically, the fall of Jerusalem that resolves his conflict, freeing him from his role of prophet of doom, which he hated. The concluding scene, in which he meets the mourning Mother Zion, marks the end of his struggle, for from then on he has a new mission, suggested by the depiction of its first moments: he must now do what he has always yearned to do— prophesy to Mother Zion "good things and consolations" /16/.

midrash is

see Holtz 179 "a way of resolving crisis"

NOTES

/1/   This article was written by Joseph Heinemann shortly before
his untimely death. The editors would like to thank Professor Moshe Greenberg, Hebrew University, for his generous and invaluable assistance in
overseeing the completion of the English version.
/2/   Compare H. L. Strack (213).
/3/   But see the commentary of M. Friedman there, par. 1, and also
L. Prijs (21f.).
/4/   See J. Heinemann (1971a:145ff.).
/5/   For convenience I have adopted the division into paragraphs
suggested by Prijs in his above-mentioned book. In his commentary, Prijs
has hit the mark in many matters, among them matters of style and
composition of the homily. However, he does not comprehend the whole
pisqa as an integral literary creation, having a unified design and single
purpose. The text we have is corrupt. The critical edition in Prijs' book
does not improve matters much, since we have at our disposal only one
manuscript, Parma, which contains many corruptions. The same applies
to the edition of our pisqa, also based on ms Parma, published by William
G. Braude. Unless stated otherwise, I have followed Prijs. Since in most
cases the variant readings are not of decisive importance for our purposes,
I have chosen the reading in each case that makes the most sense to me.
/6/   See Prijs (40) and variant readings (84).
/7/   There is no verse in the Book of Jeremiah which says, "But
Babylon your eyes will not see"; see Prijs (70).
/8/   The readings we have are ambiguous on this point.
/9/   It is surely not necessary to identify Irijah, the gatekeeper, as
the grandson of Hananiah the false prophet. Moreover, Hananiah dies
only in Zedekiah's fourth year (Jer 28:1, 17). In any case, there was no
reason here to tell at length about the confrontation between Jeremiah and
Hananiah, about the death of the latter, about the will he made out to his
son and his son's will to his son after him, etc.
/10/   This is the import of the expression in the Pesiqta "Jeremiah's
coming forth into the world." Compare Prijs (29) with M. Friedman.
/11/   Compare Prijs (65ff.). But we cannot be satisfied with his explanation of this striking deviation from the plain sense of Scripture—
namely, that the homilist wanted to describe three imaginary journeys of
Jeremiah and that his departure from the city symbolizes God's departure,
which was the necessary condition of Jerusalem's fall. Compare Targum
Sheni of Esther, 1:3 (A. Sperber: 178ff.) where similar if not identical
motifs are found, such as that it is impossible to destroy the city as long as
Jeremiah is in it, because he prays for it, and only when he leaves for the
land of Benjamin can Nebuchadnezzar overcome and destroy Jerusalem and
the Temple.
/12/   Neither the reading nor the meaning are completely clear. Compare Prijs (64) and the variant readings; in his opinion, the meaning is
that God will give—or will leave—Anathoth in the hands of its inhabitants;
similarly, M. Friedman. But Braude, in his English rendition of PR, (534),

thinks that the reference is to Jerusalem. In any case, it is clear that Jeremiah sees in this command to go to Anathoth a hint of some kind of salvation.

/13/   The following formula, "Jeremiah thought to himself and said," which recurs many times, is meaningful; its role, apparently, is to emphasize the prophet's thoughts and desires which serve as a key to understanding his behavior.

/14/   Although in Scripture, too, Jeremiah prays on behalf of the people; compare on this the article by Yochanan Muffs. So too, the sages see in Jeremiah a prophet who was concerned for the honor of both the father and the son (= the people of Israel) (*Aboth de-Rabbi Nathan*, beginning of chap. 47). But according to the singular conception of the author of our homily, the prophet acts to save the city not by means of prayers—these are not mentioned at all by the homilist—but by means of his rebukes and warnings.

/15/   For the Chaldeans evidently lifted the siege in order to fight Pharaoh's army.

/16/   Attention should be paid to the literary genre of *pishah* 26, which belongs unmistakably to what G. Vermes has called the "re-written Bible"—in itself a clear indication that we are dealing with a rather late literary creation. For while this genre was popular and widespread in late second Temple times, not only in sectarian circles (Jubilees) and in those close to hellenist influence but also even among authors who belong to the pharisaic stream or are close to it (e.g., the author of *Liber Antiquitates Biblicarum*), it disappears utterly from talmudic-midrashic literature (except for occasional brief paraphrases of short biblical passages, e.g., *Tanh, Lekh Lekha* 5)—certainly not just by coincidence. Apparently, the rabbis conceived a danger that the public might take such freely treated accounts of the Bible for authentic reflections of the text itself. Only in the early Middle Ages does the genre reappear (*Pirqe Rabbi Eliezer* in the eighth century)—according to L. Ginzberg (72)—through the influence of the Moslem "stories of the Prophets" until its full development in works such as the *Chronicles of Moses* and the late *Sefer Ha-Yashar*. I have not referred to the surprisingly strong links between this *pisqa* and the pseudoepigraphic Syrian *Book of Baruk* (which neither Prijs nor Braude note). The matter has been discussed already by L. Ginzberg (19:2, 1556); cf. also L. Gry; but it would have taken us too long in the framework of this paper. Let it be noted, though, that in using material, almost quotations from the *Book of Baruk,* he still uses it freely and reworks it for his own literary purposes.

Part II

Philosophical Perspectives

Joseph Gold
Hugh White

Chapter 4

Deuteronomy and the Word: The Beginning and the End

Joseph Gold

As human beings are created into a world formed by the word of God, so they end their pentateuchal evolution armed with the word made human. Moses is the figure to whom the past has led and from whom the future grows.

The literary critic must feel some misgiving at venturing into fields that have long been thoroughly hedged about by the landed gentry, so to speak, of biblical studies. It ought to be obvious that this promised land is best cared for and will flourish most luxuriantly under many hands and different talents. The gates cannot forever be locked by the documentary hypothesis (J, E, D, P). It is time to admit some fresh air into the garden.

I am not, however, altogether clear as to what a literary critic theoretically does when approaching a work of language art. So many different things are done in practice that one professional category hardly seems to cover all the activity. For the moment, I cannot but agree with Eliade (4–5), who says:

> It is regrettable that historians of religions have not yet sufficiently profited from the experience of their colleagues who are historians of literature or literary critics. The progress made in these disciplines would have enabled them to avoid unfortunate misunderstandings. It is agreed today that there is continuity and solidarity between the work of the literary historian, the literary sociologist, the critic, and the aesthetician. To give but one example: if the work of Balzac can hardly be understood without a knowledge of nineteenth-century French society and history (in the broadest meaning of the term—political, economic, social, cultural, and religious history), it is

nonetheless true that the *Comédie humaine* cannot be reduced to a historical document pure and simple. It is the work of an exceptional individual, and it is for this reason that the life and psychology of Balzac must be known. But the working-out of this gigantic *oeuvre* must be studied in itself, as the artist's struggle with his raw material, as the creative spirit's victory over the immediate data of experience. A whole labor of exegesis remains to be performed after the historian of literature has finished his task, and here lies the role of the literary critic. It is he who deals with the work as an autonomous universe with its own laws and structure.

The last sentence is worth bearing in mind and points to the properly self-contained quality of a language construct. When the literary critic turns his attention to the Bible, he has several immediate problems and tasks. Biblical scholars would necessarily, or at least commonly, know Hebrew, Greek, perhaps Latin, possibly Aramaic, and numerous other languages. Certainly they would know German. Literary critics may or may not know these languages. If they are English scholars their profession has not of itself dictated Hebrew and German, for example, as prerequisites. There are three possible options, it seems to me, for literary critics. They can become biblical scholars and learn the appropriate tools. This is difficult and time-consuming. While a few may have done so, it seems unlikely that even the best of critics who have spent long lives in English studies, like Cleanth Brooks, Lionel Trilling, or F. R. Leavis, would undertake such a course. What most have done is elect for option two, the use of the King James translation of the Bible as a work of original merit and beauty and the high point of the English Renaissance, perhaps indeed the magnum opus of the Reformation. This path has been chosen by such men and women as C. S. Lewis, Helen Gardner, T. R. Henn, Margaret Chase, Quiller-Couch, and numerous others.

It should be noted in this regard that no modern Jewish translators of the Bible have failed to pay profound respect to the 1611 version. Whatever the biases and inaccuracies of this version, it reflects the immense learning and piety of its creators. What they sought was a language not merely fitted to a rendering of Hebrew sense, but a style and elegance that would reflect the grandeur and sublimity of their subject. Their awe and their responsibility called into play all the language resources of a time of linguistic explosion, the culmination of centuries of vernacular experiment.

But there is a third option for the serious critic of the Bible and it lies somewhere between these two. It is what I would call the comparativist method. It demands some knowledge of Hebrew, a large dependence on the work of other biblical scholars, and the patient comparison of appropriate translations: for instance, the Authorized Version, the Revised Standard Version, the Jewish Publications Society Edition, the rabbinic commentaries which often are a particular translation, and the New English Bible. With a text of great antiquity, even the most detailed knowledge of classical Hebrew will not free us from dispute. The work of Hans Walter Wolff on Hosea is an elegant example of a linguistic arena which one enters only at the risk of never coming out alive. The search for the original text produces similar dilemmas in English studies. The struggle to achieve a pure text, even of quite recent origin, can be so all-consuming an obsession as to create a blindness to the work of art, or to hold up publication indefinitely. The perfect work never gets printed.

Deuteronomy is an instructive example. The controversy is enormous. I have read the views of Albright, Buber, Craigie, Driver, Goldin, Gordon, Harrison, John Miles, Rashi, and Ryle /1/. Opinion ranges from a date at the end of the pre-Canaanite period to one of a number of postexilic choices; from an authorship by Moses or by Moses and Joshua jointly to Hilkiah or some monarchic prophet or to a fraudulent, but presumably pious and literary Josiah himself. Three sources and one source have been argued, and different dates for different parts. How does all this leave the reader who, in some way and over thousands of years has believed in this and other texts, believed that it mattered and spoke to him? The critic of the Bible cannot evade this question and the educational responsibilities it implies. We must not, like a new school of obscurants, found another church with our own self-generated "Latin," the jargon of our journals.

There is no doubt in my mind that the entire Graf-Wellhausen tradition has, along with other nineteenth-century positions, contributed to a decline in popular Bible study and learning and an increase in skepticism. The Bible has been the victim of religious malaise as well as of antisemitism. The greatest loss in all this has been the loss of literature. Nothing short of a literary response can restore these texts to popular enthusiasm. As we can see from Elinor Shaffer's brilliant book *"Kubla Khan" and the Fall of Jerusalem,* what we are now doing as critics is joining hands with the eighteenth-century pioneers, Eichorn, Lessing, Herder, and Coleridge. It is true that literary critics must examine the provenance and setting of the work in order to avoid blatant misreading. External data, where available, must condition our thinking. The history, culture, language, and archaeology are the lighting and framing for our picture. To be guilty of anachronistic or socially impossible readings is to be wasting our time and energy. The external data should become part of our perception and ideally our imagination should be enriched by our learning.

Rather than avoid these questions in so far as they affect Deuteronomy, let me state my own views about date and authorship. Honorific ascription is so widely accepted a device in literature, ancient and modern, that the literary critic will naturally be somewhat puzzled by the nagging controversy about author identity in this and other cases. Who wrote any of the Bible? It is customary in Japan for master potters not to sign their work, for the Zen view of artistic perfection, the "truth" of the work, is that of a mystery emerging through the artist and not of a mere product extension of the person himself. Ownership ends at completion. In forming his art, he has partaken of so much which is not him, that clearly a signature would distort, misrepresent and take away from the object itself. Once it is made, ownership is extraneous. In the same way the holy truths of scriptural writing were so sacred as to preclude human claims of authorship. Ascriptions to Moses and Solomon and David are appropriate as legendary honor, for these figures are of such stature that no harm is done by such gifts. But it is possible to argue that this ascription is proper in a religious framework only because it is honorific. Moses and the law are one, but the compositions in writing about these matters are another thing. This model of self-effacement is followed by the translators of 1611. We know who some of them were and that is all we know. Obviously, so much ignorance as we have about such matters can only be the result of the most careful planning of secrecy on the part of those who wish it to be so. They are right, of course, and our response to the text is not mediated by any human psychology or other biographical sleuthing.

The fact that God is continually named as creator, that indeed his own name may mean creator, is further evidence that writing about his works must not be attributable. This anonymity of text would also help to preclude the danger of writing as idolatry, the danger of the text becoming itself a god, for if God is the divine inspiration that becomes written language, then this is a process in which human authors should not claim credit. When we are told that Moses is being quoted, we have no right to ignore the omniscient author model here employed. Practices which we accept in all authorship from Jerome to modern journalism are at once subject to suspicion and distortion in biblical criticism.

As to the dating we are equally and designedly in the dark. Clearly the events synthesized in Deuteronomy are over and the work is retrospective *and* prophetic. The only question is how soon after Moses died was the book written, only to come to light later. It has been argued that the actual writing of what we have is pre-Canaanite /2/. But to argue that this is possible is not to say it is true. For some this argument depends on or is reinforced by a tradition of Mosaic authorship, which I have shown above is at least a suspect literary proposition. The internal evidence seems to me to point to a postmonarchic period. In the light of Samuel's reluctance to embrace monarchy, this book, especially chap. 17, suggests considerable experience of monarchy. This experience can hardly be derived from non-Hebraic kingship, since the injunctions about the king's responsibilities in writing and reading the law seem so intimate and clear. Josiah's response also suggests a regeneration of purpose rather than a discovery of completely new ideas. Ryle has presented a much neglected but elegant case for Deuteronomy as the first book of the canon. Here we must distinguish between a long, widely known oral tradition and the writing down of this tradition in a literary form, a form which in spite of all cited parallels is utterly unlike any other document known to man. Why should this material have been written at all? When is idolatrous practice most likely to flourish? Why does prophecy appear when it seems most alien to its social setting, to its subject?

I would like to speculate that the written record becomes a compelling necessity during a time of peace and ease, when moral fiber and purpose is weakened, when signs of decadence abound, when idolatry and assimilation flourish, and when poets and priests foresee social breakdown and dispersion as a real possibility. It is reasonable to suppose that the jars of Qumran were hidden by those who feared the destruction of their contents. The written record would broadcast and keep alive a threatened tradition, and this objective has been astonishingly fulfilled. The success of the writing is no mean argument for speculating thus about its origins. The history of publication, printing, censorship, and reading can illuminate our understanding of Bible and Talmud.

After all this is said and done, the critic and his perception are alone with the text. It is then that the reader's mind engages with the mind or minds that made the literature. As Norman Perrin (1974:5) puts it,

> The relationship between historical criticism and hermeneutics is, then, in my view, that of a first and a second stage of the total process of coming to understand a text and of entering into meaningful dialogue with it. In the case of texts from the past or from a different culture the task of historical criticism can be both difficult and quite inordinately complex, but in the case of any text it is essential. I would never accept a view of hermeneutics which did not see historical criticism as the essential first step in coming to understand any text, whether it be from the ancient past or today's newspaper. At the same time historical criticism is only the beginning of the process of coming to understand a text, not its end.

Literary criticism, as I have said, means different things to different people. Certainly Norman Habel, in his little book *Literary Criticism of the Old Testament,* means something quite different from what I want to say here. I have come to think that the act of criticism is an artistic act or it is nothing. Criticism is literature whose stimulus is other literature. It is rapidly becoming clear that literary criticism will increasingly embrace questions of perception and ontology. Language will be encountered as a kind of action, rather than a pointing to action. Word and event may be inseparable, but in any case the critic will henceforth have to explore the implication of such a problem. The old Platonic assumptions underlying traditional literary approaches all at once seem irrelevant. We cannot yet be more than tentative about what some call cognitive criticism; I feel sure, however, that it will be tied to discoveries in neuropsychology and will develop along with increased understanding of the cortical functions, particularly the processing of language. What we must remember is that the Bible passages we are considering are symbol systems constructed by a brain like ours and intending to render the world as metaphor— that is, in language—in the only thoroughly decodable way in which human brains communicate. This metaphoric world is the only systematic reality that we have, that is, in words and numbers. By this means we construct our perception, our own and others'.

Literary criticism of the Bible will have the shape that we call midrashic and will accrete to the original material, if it is good enough in itself—if it makes sense to others *of* itself. An interesting book *about* the Bible is really about itself. That is, if the Bible prompts me to write this essay, then that is because the Bible has become part of my perception, a shaping force. For anyone interested in making this essay part of their perception, a knowledge of the Bible would be part of their process, as it is part of the essay writer's.

How can I read Deuteronomy? Can the Deuteronomist's mind speak to me across the two-and-one-half-thousand years of intervening history? Is the world it creates apprehensible to me after the holocaust? That the answer to these questions is yes, results in part from the fact that my mind has already been shaped by the Deuteronomist—that in reading him I am necessarily also reading myself. Moses has become part of us, part of the evolution of our brain-processed language; Moses *is,* like my parents and their parents, me. We are always the last of a series of magic mirrors that have a cumulative record of imagery, forever modified, forever enduring and multiplying. Adaptation and selection, survival and evolution itself, became in human beings linguistic, the development of metaphor being as profound a shift and of the same

order as bipedal posture. All human development became linguistic in the broadest sense and, as we see now, extrasomatic.
The way we will be in the future depends largely on what we say
and write in the present—on how we process and create our per-
ceptions. The functioning of the neocortex, especially in language,
will henceforth evolve ourselves. Could the Deuteronomist, in any
sense, have known any of this? I think so, and I will try to show
so. It is essential to keep before us the Hebrew title of the book's
beginning, *These are the words*. This is a book about words and
the covenant form is a form of words.

The literary approach to a work cannot really isolate one chapter. Whoever wrote chap. 34 inextricably wove it into the fabric
of the whole, and its vision is an isomorph of the psychic tenor of
what precedes it. What are some of the primary impressions
gleaned from the text? It is a narrative, in the dramatic form of
implied dialogue. Moses, with God in the wings, addresses a
gathering of all the people of Israel. We read a narrative about
making history, about how history is made, or at least about
ethnography, and we are also forced to be part of the audience.
Why some places are destroyed, some left intact, why victories are
won and defeats suffered, some places settled and some avoided—
all these are mysterious dispositions of the Hebrew God who
shaped the world as the Deuteronomist knew it. Without this God,
nothing has happened and through this God everything that is has
its special shape.

The two outstanding features of this God in Deuteronomy are
first his omnipresence (4:7) and then again his statutes and ordi-
nances which are the source of human wisdom and understanding.
It is this latter—in a word, the Word—which, over time, evidences
the former. The highest moral and civilizing characteristic of the
Hebrews is this placing of wisdom and understanding as the goal
of human aspiration. This is what Julian Jaynes calls consciousness (as opposed to bicameralism)/3/. This wisdom is the Hebrew
link with God. Loss of wisdom separates from God. Wisdom and
understanding *are* somehow God and the human realization of
both is language. Those who do not cultivate this triune wisdom-
God-language must do something else. What they do is worship
idols and false gods. The Hebrew mind, or the writing mind,

writes about itself. The act of writing is to create an extrasomatic, transmittable, preserved, and decodable reality. This is quite different from conversation. Even the remembered and orally told tale depends on the life of the teller. The written narrative gives a conquest of space and time and is coincident with the full flowering of monotheism. It fixes the record like a lifeline to the minds of the past /4/. Idols are the signs of people who cannot write about their own minds. The wooden passivity of the idol is a perfect image of the mind that created it. The very existence of the Bible on the other hand is evidence that "He is your God—there is none else." Neurologically speaking, there can be no other God than the god capable of being realized through language, realizable by the human power of poetic formulation.

The form of raising consciousness embodied in Deuteronomy is the exhortation composed of threat and reward, a psychological model based on the assumption that the listener is capable of decision and choice. "I have set before thee this day life and good, death and evil . . . the blessing and the curse; therefore choose life, that thou mayest live, thou and thy seed." There is a death in life. For human beings to live lives of bestial instinct only is a living death. The power to choose, to reflect, to internalize, to create a moral system and a linguistic order: this is the demonstration of Moses' discourse. Perhaps here is the key to the uniqueness of Hebrew culture.

There are two kinds of threat and reward in Deuteronomy. One is organic and personal, psychologically based and realized internally: e.g., if you do certain things you will lose your power, your understanding; you will be undifferentiated from idolatrous peoples and therefore overwhelmed, wiped out by superior numbers, for population size will be your only distinction. The other kind of exhortation is from an older time, is anthropomorphic, externally power-structured and nature-based: e.g., the rains will cease, pestilence will follow, etc.

In conveying this wealth of intellectual history Moses is the consumate, the paradigm teacher, the moral instructor of all people, as opposed, for instance, to the exclusive Socrates of the esoteric dialogue. I suppose that a teacher might be excused for reading Deuteronomy as a lecture, a brilliant cross between a

sermon and a tutorial, but bias aside, I have read of no parallel to
this, the earliest example of popular, universal and compulsory
education. Moses coaxes and threatens, pleads and warns, enter-
tains and drills, and his speech is the model for what he advo-
cates. In a sense this is Torah as Talmud. It is hardly surprising
that the whole of midrashic, rabbinic tradition should be teaching
and learning centered. Commentary is at the heart of Torah itself
and the Hebrew models are all education paradigms. The Bible
persistently explains itself through the complexities of metaphor,
which is not to say that it is easy to represent in terms other than
its own. Quite the contrary, in fact; it means that one must return
continually to the text. Moses enjoins the people to two things. He
tells them to "take heed of themselves," i.e., to exercise a watch-
ful and practiced consciousness, a continual self-awareness so that
action and judgment may be united and not divorced as they are in
all automistic cults and magic, where judgment is deliberately suppressed by orgy, drugs, hypnosis, etc. The second lesson Moses
inculcates is the instruction imperative: the necessity to teach the
children and the childrens' children to know the statutes and the
history (in effect, to read), so that the truths about humanity and
wisdom, the metaphors of experience may be transmitted and also
kept alive in the teller, for in the telling the metaphor is revital-
ized. It is difficult to improve on Driver's (lviii–lix) general description of Deuteronomy:

> The imaginative revivification of the past, by means of dis-
> courses, conversations, and even of actions, attributed dra-
> matically to characters who have figured upon the stage of
> history, has been abundantly exemplified in literature: the edu-
> cational influence, and moral value, of such creations of human
> art have been universally allowed: the dialogues of Plato, the
> epic of Dante, the tragedies of Shakespeare, the *Paradise Lost*,
> and even the poem of Job, to name but a few of the great
> imaginative creations of genius, have never been condemned as
> immoral frauds, because the characters introduced in them did
> not always—or ever—use the actual words attributed to them.
> But the author, in each case, having a message to deliver, or a
> lesson to teach, placed it in the mouth of the person to whose
> character it was appropriate, or whose personality would give it
> force, and so presented it to the world. *Mutatis mutandis*, the
> procedure of the Deuteronomist was similar. No elaborate lit-

erary machinery was needed by him: a single character would suffice. He places Moses on the stage, and exhibits him pleading his case with the degenerate Israel of Josiah's day. In doing this, he assumes no unjustifiable liberty, and makes no unfair use of Moses' name: he does not invest him with a fictitious character; he does not claim his authority for ends which he would have disavowed; he merely develops, with great moral energy and rhetorical power, and in a form adapted to the age in which he lived himself, principles which (as will appear immediately) Moses had beyond all question advocated, and arguments which he would have cordially accepted as his own.

This is not how I would now put it, but it is a sensible, traditional literary justification.

Deuteronomy reads like the end of an epic, the closing scene of a vision. Moses is its hero, appropriately enough not one of the hereditary patriarchs, but the chosen one who came out of Egyptian chaos, where not only are rebellion and assassination inevitable, but where Hebrew strikes Hebrew in a sign that union of suffering has not led to communion of belief. From Egypt Moses is called to receive the eternal fire of the truth and return with it to the underworld of Egypt, to the fleshpots where the spirit languishes, to release the imprisoned souls. It is Moses who brings the people from the darkness of Egyptian paganism and error into the light of Sinai; and it is Moses who writes the law, thus giving human shape to a divine power.

What is this law? The law is to the story of Israel what language is to the metaphor of evolution. Moses functions like the inventor of writing. He is the hero of a story about the nature and hope of mankind, a divine messenger, the prototype of less human figures like Prometheus, and to my mind, Jesus. Moses, in addressing the people, analyzes their morality and instructs them in the central metaphor of Israel, namely, the occupation and enjoyment of the promised land. To achieve this they must so arrange their minds as to shed all illusions (i.e., other gods), and adhere to the law, the emblem of order, the touchstone of which law is that they shall love their one God "with all thy heart and with all thy soul and with all thy might!" This requires a lifetime effort but it is the only formula by which the promised land is to be occupied. If Israel is in a sense modern man, and the promised land is Earth,

then the key to human survival and meaning will be an understanding of the link between Yahweh and language. This God of
the Hebrews, of mind, soul, and heart, of *Nefesh,* is inside man,
known by the language that we make and read and teach. "The
secret things belong unto the Lord our God, but the things that are
revealed belong unto us and to our children forever, that we may
do all the words of this law" (Deut 29:29 RSV). What things are
revealed, what revelation never departs? Those who worship idols
will perish as the dinosaurs perished. Israel will house the word
in its ark because it can be internalized, known and transmitted.
The worship of the Torah is a response to its being in language.
It is not a thing but a process. The worship of Torah is an ascription to the Divine of the power to formulate the perceivable.

We are told that "the word is very nigh unto thee, in thy mouth
and in thy heart, that thou mayest do it." God enters the story at
various points to talk to Moses, his language intermediary, and in
chap. 31 he tells Moses to write chap. 32. Chap. 32 is a song;
this and chap. 33, the poetic blessing of the people, are clear indications that the lawgiver is really a language giver, a visionary, a
poetic seer, and that the God of the Bible is a God whose sign
among human beings is the gift of human language.

What of chap. 34? "Moses went to the top of Pisgah . . . and
the Lord showed him all the land . . . ." What could be more
poetically right than Moses' destiny? The "problem" of Moses'
death arises from reading this text as though it were unedited history. As he looks over the future of Israel, Moses acquires a
stature hardly attained by any other figure in literary history. He
is the human embodiment of the divine command, the symbol of
the transmittable, humanly-ordered, language-centered history on
which all future human events will be based. Moses takes humanity
to the brink of human fulfillment. Having given all that is necessary he gazes into the future and attains a vision not given to any
other person. The future must actually and always be fulfilled by
the children, by the untainted next generation, but that generation
must be steeped and learned in the wisdom and tradition of the
past, schooled in its laws and shaped by its hopes. The future
which Moses surveys is magnificently captured here as a spatial

metaphor, an image startlingly appropriate to Israel's history. Time is seen as apprehensible only by events played out in a spatial dimension. Events are metaphors of time, and language is the synthesis. There is little to say about the marvels of a metaphor in which the leader of people, the servant of God, looks and points to a future which he has helped make possible but which he cannot live himself because of the very humanity that marks him at every point. We are at one moment shown his immense strength and his human frailty. The future always belongs to others.

Moses is the paradigm of the striving-to-be-realized in human beings, from argument with God at their first encounter to their immersion in the Divine. To make a promised land fulfill its promise will require a humanity based upon the Mosaic foundation. The laws of Moses and the humanity of Moses are inseparable. This last chapter is a miraculously poised time and space barrier, with Moses as the guide pointing to an eternal promise. There is no trace of melancholy here. Moses is alive then and now and so "no man knoweth of his sepulchre unto this day." His power and truth live forever, because they live in the most powerful of human media; so it is that "his eye was not dim, nor his natural force abated" (RSV), for both are the signs of language, the law which he understands better than other men. His eye is the sign of understanding, truth and honesty, and the vehicle of perception. His natural force is his intellectual vigor, the human clarity of his knowing and making. Has he not just finished making a great song for God? It is his life that is celebrated at this point and after the formal period of mourning, Moses' spirit is seen anew in Joshua. Who was this man, Moses? He was a prophet and there has not arisen a prophet since in Israel like unto Moses, one who saw the Lord face to face, that is, one who knew God by his word and who reflected God in his mind and heart. Yet—and this is crucially important—with all the mighty works that Moses wrought, he was human and his destiny had a human determination. He was not free from God's judgment; he was not God and he was not perfect. He was not carried off by angels, but he shared the fate of his human followers and could do no more than lay the foundation for the future, nay, not even that, for he could only (how dare I say, only?) show how foundations can be laid. He was created so that we can recognize and relate to him.

Poised on the birth of civilized history, Moses brings the law down to the people, humanizes it and embeds it in a brilliant exhortation of threat and promise. His is a present, live and apprehensive audience, filled with its sense of divinely ordained destiny and fraught with the weight of a racial responsibility nowhere else (that I know of) recorded with such conscious precision. And in all this Moses speaks as one of the people. What we find here is a myth conveying the end of myth and the beginning of metaphor; once language comes to be seen as a vehicle of reality-shaping perception, then the mythic passivity of man is over and active metaphor-making is all. Deuteronomy's blend of law and anecdote, of rigor and gentleness, of curse and blessing is in itself an astonishing literary feat. As such, it is the commencement of a national literature, the natural conclusion to the creation phase of human evolution, a myth about metaphor—metaphor being the form of the Hebrew God.

It is instructive to note that the precise difference between Christian and Hebrew thinking is conveyed by the endings of two great books, Deuteronomy and *Paradise Lost*. For Milton, man's history commences with a loss of paradise, with two human creatures taking their solitary way (an interesting word, solitary, each of them hand in hand, alone while together), exiled from the promised land until God, in human form, can rescue them from despair. Deuteronomy ends in promise, not with man and woman entering the wilderness but with the people leaving it, about to enter the promised land of history, armed with the word and guided by the prophet. This is the informing Hebrew image. The people are not solitary but a company bonded by common knowledge of the word. Their God is present always, housed in the tabernacle, ready and waiting to be understood. There is no whining here at the human lot and no surprise that Moses must die, now rather than later. There is only awe that a person can do so much. Milton pines for a lost perfection, a harmony of mind, body, geography, and nature, free from struggle. The deuteronomic poet rejoices in the struggle which defines human experience, the struggle to understand and to express the word of God. The promised land of chap. 34, seen from the top of Pisgah, is inseparable from the word of God embodied in the preceding chapters—the word always available and regenerated in all prophets since Moses, who is their founding father. The word, not secreted by the oracles—the sybils and the priestesses—of hallucinating pagans, but fulfilled and restored to all who will read and hear, is the godlike faculty of man. The promised land, says the Deuteronomist, is for all who will read and hear what he has written about Moses and his people and their book. If those who carry the Torah, who have been given the sacred truth of the Word, who know the import of their exemplary mission, if they cannot create a land of promise in the promised land, then who can? This Hebrew metaphor is the pattern woven into the very fabric of Western culture. Moses uttered the seminal truth when he cried out, "Would that all God's children were prophets!"

NOTES

/1/   The reference here is to papers presented by John Miles and Judah Goldin to the Ottawa Symposium, November 1977.

/2/   R. K. Harrison and K. A. Kitchen among others.

/3/   Here and elsewhere in this paper my debt to Prof. Jaynes should be obvious. While I admire his book and am grateful for his metaphors, I am applying them in my own ways here.

/4/   Because writing evinces the minds of its past makers more precisely than anything else (though artifacts and architecture are important statements) we depend heavily on it where we have it. The picture of the ancient mind becomes obscure, however, in prewriting times. For this reason the work of Alexander Marshak on very early notation seems to me to have profoundly important implications.

Chapter 5

Word Reception as the Matrix of the Structure of the Genesis Narrative

Hugh C. White

Developments in the discipline of linguistics beginning with Ferdinand de Saussure in the early years of this century have stimulated the development in France of new modes of narrative analysis. The purpose of this essay will be to draw together some insights from these new developments and apply them experimentally to certain central passages in the Genesis narrative: the story of the fall in Gen 2:4b–3; the promise to Abraham in Gen 12:1–3; and the attempted sacrifice of Isaac in chap. 22.

This mode of analysis will not deal with historical or textual criticism, but will rather aim at uncovering the linguistic and semantic structure of the nodal word events in each of these passages, and the underlying connections between these events which may provide the generative matrix for the meaning of the narrative as a whole. The sources for this method of analysis are the French literary critic Roland Barthes and, to a lesser extent, those French psychoanalytic writings which have influenced Barthes. The method used here, however, will in no sense be strictly imitative of Barthes's approach.

This article will thus give the outlines of a new approach to the Genesis narrative. It is still very experimental, however, and no definitive conclusions can be expected within the brief format of this article. It is designed only to serve as a new starting point for the discussion of many of the longstanding problems of the Genesis narrative which were not resolvable within the limits of traditional historical and literary criticism.

The point of departure for many new approaches to narrative analysis in France today is the understanding of the structure of the linguistic sign in the thought of the Genevan linguist, Ferdinand de Saussure. For Saussure, the oral word is termed a "signifier" or "sound image." It stands in close relationship to its semantic content, or "signified," which he also terms a "concept." (66, 67, 102). The primary signifying relation is thus the relation between a word and one's mental image of the external object to which the word refers, and not the relation between the word and its external referent. It is this signifier-signified relationship which makes it possible for the word to perform the function of signifying. But an uncertain factor is built into this relationship. Even though the signifier and signified are as inseparable as the two sides of a coin, the relationship of the sound image as a material form to the concept is semantically arbitrary. Any sound could, in principle, refer to any concept. This uncertainty is overcome by the implicit agreement by which society has connected, for example, the word "cow" with the mental image of a cow.

But, as Anthony Wilden has pointed out, it would perhaps have been clearer if Saussure had said instead, that the signifier stands in an arbitrary relation to the object of reference (216). This brings into clearer focus the distinctive Saussurian insight that language functions as a signifying system not by virtue of its relation to real objects, but by means of its own internal system of relations between signs (union of signifier and signified). As Wilden (217) says, language appears for Saussure as

> a system of signification arbitrarily related to "reality" and in fact only related to itself. "Wood," for instance, can only be finally defined by itself, because it is not any other signifier in the system.

The result of this understanding of the sign is to divide the study of language into two hierarchically ordered spheres: synchronic linguistics which takes as its object language seen as a closed system of mutually defining parts; and diachronic linguistics which focuses upon the linguistic effects of the acts of speech in the external temporal process. In the former, language exists as a state in the collective consciousness of society where it functions as a signifying system without regard for the historical circumstantial relativities connected with the individual speaker. As Saussure (18) said, "Language is comparable to a symphony in that what the symphony actually is stands completely apart from how it is performed." As performance, language is a sequential process which unfolds through individual utterances. The intelligibility of the performance, however, depends upon its observance of the rules of the *system* of language which fixes the relations between signifier and signified.

But if the intelligibility of language depends upon its systematic character, this means that the individual in the *act* of speech adds nothing *essential* to the capacity of language to function as an intelligible system of communication. When it is recalled that the relation of the sign to its referent is also nonessential and arbitrary, then language appears as an autonomous system without meaning-producing relations either to the producing subject or the referent in the real world.

The possibility of understanding language as a closed system of mutually defining parts rests upon Saussure's view (103) of the indissoluble fusion (comparable to the fusion of hydrogen and oxygen in water) of the signifier and signified. This excludes the subject/speaker from the meaning-producing system.

Since formal logic also operates upon the basis of an understanding of meaning as a closed system of mutually defining parts, it is possible to move with the assistance of logic from Saussurian linguistics, which ends at the level of the sentence, to the analysis of narratives. Narratives can be reduced to propositional statements which can be analyzed in terms of the logical relations. This leads to a purely logical matrix as the generative source of narrative meaning and even narrative structure. Such has been the general path followed in different ways by Claude Lévi-Strauss in his study of chiefly Amero-Indian mythology (10) and by A. J. Greimas in his study of folktales, and other more contemporary narratives (141–171).

Roland Barthes, however, has taken a different route from Saussure to narrative analysis. Barthes, while making use of the basic terms of the Saussurian understanding of the sign, does not accept the absolute separation of signifier-signified (sign) from the subject/speaker, but argues for a larger role for the act of speech and writing in the signifying process (1964:18–23). This causes him to attribute a greater role to the act of writing in generating the signifying structures in the narrative (1974a:3, 4):

> The primary evaluation of all texts can come neither from science, for science does not evaluate, nor from ideology, for the ideological value of a text (moral, aesthetic, political, alethiological) is a value of representation, not of production (ideology "reflects," it does not work). Our evaluation can be linked only to a practice, and this practice is that of writing.

For Barthes, in "writing" (he means primarily imaginative, literary writing) a signifying act occurs which creates a second language between the excluded, heterogeneous self and the closed system of natural language. Whereas a person has no choice regarding the use of his or her native tongue, the person does have a choice with respect to the creation (or one could add as well, the transmission) of literature. In this free action (though always constricted by circumstances of history, society, economics, language, etc.) the heterogeneous subject enters a formal linguistic structure explicitly. This heterogeneity is expressed in language in the mode of desire.

This results in the creation of a new grammar and even a new language beyond the restrictions of the natural language. Barthes compares the structure of the narrative to the structure of the sentence, the protagonist being the nominal (or pronominal) subject, and the events that transpire, the predicate. Here the relation of the narrative subject and its predicate corresponds to the relation of the signifier and its signified. The skill of the narrator is seen in his capacity to delay the conclusion of the predicate which would define or denote the initially open subject, thereby releasing the interest of the reader (1974a:76):

> To narrate (in the classic fashion) is to raise the question as if it were a subject which one delays predicating; and when the predicate (truth) arrives, the sentence, the narrative, are over, the world is adjectivized (after we had feared it would not be).

In the predication and thus definition of names in the narrative, a new second language is created: the narrator becomes a "logothete" (Barthes, 1974:35), a creator of the morphemes of a new language.

This means that the narrative offers the possibility for the portrayal of an open subject, a "subject in process," which permits
the heterogeneous dimension of the self to gain access to the common language (Kristeva, 1975:18). In narrative writing (and
reading) the closed self seeks to go beyond the logic of repetition
within which it operates (seen in the process of re-presentation,
re-cognition characteristic of the fixed system of signification) in
order to "found the logic of a renewal . . . in the interior of the
process of significance" (Kristeva, 1974a:156). Barthes sees the
essence of the narrative sequence as "a whole in the breast of
which nothing is repeated" (1966:26). This gives narrative logic,
"an emancipative value, and the whole narrative with it" (Barthes,
1966:26).

This liberating value of the narrative, which constitutes the
final horizon of its meaning, assumes a completely different understanding of the word from that which prevails in normal speech.
In place of the objective "signified" toward which natural language is oriented in the denotative mode, Barthes can describe
narrative (and poetic) language as being pervaded by the "profound, 'anormal' (removed from norms) energy of the word
(*parole*)" (1964:273). In *Writing Degree Zero and Elements of
Semiology* (1970:48) he had already described this strange sense
of the word, especially pervasive in modern poetic writing, which
stands beyond the limitations of normal language:

> The word is no longer guided in advance by the general inten-
> tion of a socialized discourse . . . The Word, here, is encyclo-
> paedic, it contains simultaneously all the acceptations from
> which a relational discourse might have required it to choose
> . . . The Word here has a generic form; it is a category. Each
> poetic word is thus an unexpected object, a Pandora's box
> from which fly out all the potentialities of language.

It is thus the word experienced apparently as something re-
sembling a pure metaphor generating meaning through connotation rather than denotation which constitutes the source of meaning in imaginative literature. Because metaphor is always dependent for its connotations upon fixed denotations, however, the
metaphorical language which does not become glossolalia ultimately reimposes closure upon the subject. But since it at least

momentarily presents the reader with a "subject in process," free and in subjective unity with his language, Barthes can say: "Literature becomes the utopia of language" (1970:88).

The question now is whether the perspective upon literature gained by Roland Barthes may shed helpful light on the structure of the biblical narrative. It should be emphasized again that this is a *preliminary, tentative* analysis that makes no claims to *formal* completeness. Further, it represents in many places an extension of Barthes's approach, and not a duplication of it.

Barthes explains that his approach to the narrative begins at the "narrational" level, rather than the level of "actions" (Greimas), or "functions" (Propp, Bremond) because "a function has meaning only inasmuch as it takes place in the general action of an actant, and this action receives its final meaning from the fact that it is narrated, included in a discourse which has its own code" (1966:6). This is consistent with his view that the act of writing generates a connotative dimension of meaning that pervades the whole of every narrative and transcends the closed meanings which may be established by the internal structure of the narrative.

This requires one then to begin narrative analysis with an assessment of the narrational code produced by the act of writing which connects the author/narrator with the reader.

This code is revealed in the posture which the author, as narrator, assumes with regard to the subject matter he or she is relating. On the basis of this analysis a typology of narratives can be established.

The two poles of this typology are represented, on the one hand, by the narrative from which all consideration of the act of narrating has been excluded (e.g., the scientific text, and most "realistic" novels), and on the other, by the narrative which relates the story of its own composition (e.g., the most purely represented by some of Mallarmé's poems, such as "un coup de des" [see Kristeva, 1974a:293], but also to some extent in a novel such as *Remembrance of Things Past* by M. Proust). In the first type the actual "I" of the narrator is totally displaced by the third person, and in the second type, the actual "I" of the narrator narrating is disclosed. In the former, the closed self is expressed as the object which receives the predication of the events he is recounting or living (as a personage in the story), while in the latter, the narrator recounts the story of the "arrival" of language through which he is constituted as a writer in the act of writing. These poles produce denotative or connotative meaning, respectively.

Before any segment of the pentateuchal narrative can be analyzed, it will thus be necessary to attempt to define the obscure relationship of the biblical narrator(s) to the narrative in terms of the inclusion or exclusion of the act of writing. This will then make possible the placement of the biblical narrative somewhere along the continuum between the poles representing the respective dominance of connotative or denotative meaning.

Narrators who exclude the act of narration from their discourse, assume the position of the closed, transcendent "I" who takes the persons and events of the story as objects for his or her act of recounting. Their language is denotative, i.e., is assumed to be a field of signifiers for which there are well-defined signifieds. The events which they recount exist entirely apart from their telling of them, and their act of recounting is insignificant; it adds nothing to the meaning.

Having covered over the possible significance of the relationship of the speaking subject to the words which they recount, i.e., the possible significance of the relation of humans to language, they must provide the events they recount with a translinguistic framework of signification. The signifiers of their narratives must refer to a signified structure of meaning outside of language such as the power of circumstance (fate), or psychological, economic, or political processes, etc. Through these signified referents outside of language, the signifying occurrences within the narrative are rendered intelligible in a denotative sense.

The code or system of signifieds that the narrators use must reflect not only their own private thoughts; it also must reflect the assumptions of their readers, and thus of the community to which they are addressing their narratives. As Barthes more broadly says, "Every time the narrator relates the facts that he knows, it is a sign of the reader, since the narrator does not speak to himself" (1966:19).

The relationship of the conventional narrator to his or her text can be illustrated, approximately, by diagram A which represents a modification of the signifier/signified schema used by Saussure in order to incorporate the position of the narrator with respect to both of these signifying systems.

DIAGRAM A:
ACT OF NARRATION EXTERNAL TO NARRATIVE

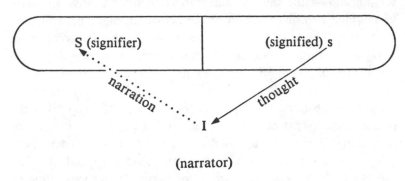

(narrator)

The narrating "I" uses signifiers which stand in a fixed relation to their corresponding signifieds. The narrator's self is not seen as implicated (e.g., through the phenomenon of desire) in the signifying process. Thus the narrator can view the *act* of narration itself as a neutral process which need not be mentioned *in* the narrative.

But the possibility exists for writers to make the organizing center of their narrative an "interrogation of the muse," as it were, where they place themselves as open, undefined subjects, before the word as signifiers with no fixed signifieds.

This might be done naturally, e.g., in the autobiographical writing of a professional writer. The logic of such a narrative would require, even if it began with a more or less realistic recounting of the events of childhood, that it include passage into the awareness of subjectivity over against the word, and end in the present with the author precisely in the act of writing, open to future meanings and events. Barthes' own recently published autobiography is an illustration of this. It lacks a continuous narrative thread (a signified) and ends with a brief, dated journal entry depicting a beautiful August morning and Barthes in a tranquil state of mind before his work: "Nothing is restless, neither desire, nor aggression; only the work is there, before myself, as a kind of universal being; all is full. This will then be Nature? An absence . . . of the rest? *Totality?"* (1975:182).

The signifying code which such a writer depends upon to convey meaning to the reader is now the model (see diagram B) which places the reader as an open subject before more or less undefined signifiers such as the questions, promises, and uncertainties which the writer faces. Author and reader are thus both cast into a model of becoming, oriented toward the word as an open signifier.

DIAGRAM B:

NARRATION AS SUBJECT OF NARRATIVE

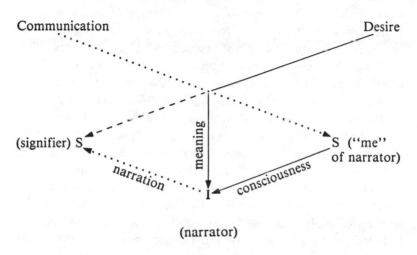

(narrator)

Here the signified has dropped out of consciousness, and has been replaced by the subjective self in the form of the signifier "me," representing the place where the word is received. The narrating "I" is describing the moment when the word "spoke" or "came to" him or her. The meaning of the event arises from the friction of the encounter between the narrator's own subjective self in the mode of desire and the word which "comes" to him or her. This friction imbues the word with material qualities of intonation, emphasis, etc., and may rebound against the self to produce other signifying effects /1/. The narration then incorporates both the signifier which has "come to" the narrator and his or her response to it. It is thus a narrative which takes the inner origin of the narrative in the moment of word reception as its subject matter. In so doing it brings into language the desiring self as an open subject in relation to language.

By making an adjustment within this perspective, it will be possible to understand the relation of the biblical narrator to the narrative. The pentateuchal narrator is characterized by his almost complete effacement. The narrator as narrator appears nowhere in the account. On the basis of the preceding considerations, this would seem to mean that the narrative is composed of a system of signifiers that refer to a process or reality beyond language which provides the explanation for the events of the narrative.

But in light of the absence of any concept of fate in the pentateuchal narrative, as well as the absence of any denotative philosophical or theological terminology, it is difficult to show that there is an objective translinguistic referent, a fixed narrative signified which can be relied upon to provide the meaning of the events recounted in the narrative (witness the long debate over whether there *can be* a "theology" of the Old Testament) /2/.

But if the narrative has taken the model of the open subject confronted with an open signifier as the generating source of its meaning, how can there be the total effacement of the narrator and the subjective process of word reception which one finds in the pentateuchal narrative? This question can be answered if one considers the possibility that the pentateuchal narrative might be an autobiography, but one whose subject is a nation and not an individual. The effacement of the narrator becomes understandable if one proceeds from the assumption that the narrator sees the nation itself as having been constituted by events in which its ancestors were constituted as open subjects over against signifying words which came to them (corresponding to a writer's experience of the word which comes to him or her). These words would not have given rise directly to a narrated or written story, however, but rather to a story written in the first instance in life and actions. The explanatory model the writer thus would use to provide significance to the events of the story and to connect him with his reader would be the portrayal of those events of word reception which constituted the ancestors as open subjects and set in motion the events which were to follow. Such events of word reception (prohibitions, promises, covenants) do, in fact, constitute the framework within which the events of the biblical narrative are made intelligible.

The narrative does not climax with the situation of the narrator narrating because the process of word reception, such as is normally the exclusive experience of the narrator or author of stories, is now a constitutive element of the social life of the nation whose actions he is recounting. Through the words which are brought to it chiefly by prophets, the nation is constituted as an open subject which then engages in writing the story of its own life in the actions which it takes collectively (or through representative persons) in response to these words. The narrator himself who recounts this process is forced to the outermost periphery in his act of narration since a model like that of the narrator vis-à-vis language has come to be the signifying model operative in the events he is recounting. You might say that the story writes itself in life and the narrator is formally (not actually) consigned to the position of the faceless recorder of the process.

The narrator is then in the strange position of not being able to conclude the story. It is beyond his control since the words come from a source outside of himself. The story can end only when the words cease to come to the nation.

Diagram C approximately illustrates the model at the center of the process of signification in the biblical narrative and the position of the narrator in relation to that structure.

The major change from diagram B is that the event of word reception now occurs outside of the narrator to a third party. This party is engaged in some action other than an act of writing and the word necessarily pertains to something other than the composition of a story per se. Since the author is writing about an event of word reception that someone else experienced, he must rely upon their account of it (or some intermediary). His third-person account thus presupposes an account structured similarly to diagram B. But this places him in a position of dependency upon tradition. Since the events of word reception in the Bible are sacred events, they generate a tradition that cannot be overtly altered by a traditionist not claiming an event of word reception

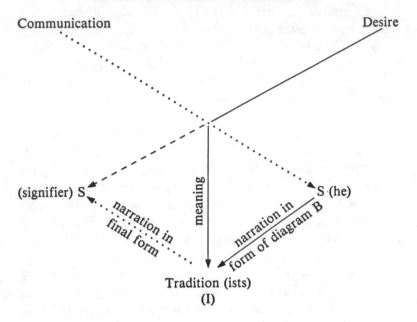

for himself (as the biblical narrator(s) of the Pentateuch does not!). Thus the "I" of the narrator is totally effaced.

The effect of this is to portray the word as a force shaping the lives of men and society rather than a force giving rise to narratives and poetry. The story becomes "history."

Thus the analysis of the relation of the narrator to his narrative has disclosed the possibility that the event of word reception constitutes a signifying model which served the writer both as a structure which united him with his reader and as a generative source for the meaning of his narrative. It now remains to begin the process of verification by analyzing these events to determine their inner structure. We move thus from the narrational level to the level of the analysis of particular sequences. Within the space of this essay, this analysis cannot be complete. The intention is only to lay out the basic perimeters and to suggest the conclusions that a more thorough analysis might establish.

If a narrative has incorporated the event of word reception as the generative matrix of its meaning so that the characters write their own stories with their lives as they respond to the words which come to them, then it is consistent with this premise to assume that the narrative could take as one of its major sequential divisions a juxtaposition of this open mode of existence with a closed mode of existence in which the identity of the characters is fixed from the beginning and their actions locked into a repetitive cycle. Through the juxtaposition of these two modes of existence the narrative would then generate meaning purely through connotation.

Further, the juxtaposing of these two modes of existence would indicate that the generative matrix of the narrative's meaning is the tension present in the relation of the human subject to language. One could thus expect to find in each of these major sequences the portrayal of word events in the lives of the personages which correspond to those occurrences of language through which humans are established in their respective modes of existence (i.e., closed or open, divided or integral).

But a problem can be foreseen regarding the establishment of the second mode of existence. Thus far we have seen the open mode of existence portrayed only in the moment of the writer (or narrator) before the empty page (or in the silence of receptivity) and in the course which the protagonist follows in the novel from initial indefiniteness to final definition. When a narrative attempts to portray the subject of the narrative's action as living permanently in the state of openness before the word that is characteristic of the narrator in his or her *moment* of receptivity, then the difficulty arises, first of all, of how to establish the personage in a mode of openness which is so detached from the closed systems of signification that prevail in language and life, and, secondly, how to prevent the events of the narrative which follow that initial opening of the subject from imposing closure once again.

The basic sequential divisions of the Book of Genesis correspond to the anticipated sequential content that is consistent with the needs of a narrative organized around the model of open subjectivity. The text of Genesis actually consists of three sequences: Gen 1:1–2:4a; 2:4b–11; 2:12–50. But Gen 1:1—2:4b contains a word event for which there is no human response. The word event which gives rise to the narrative does not occur until the second sequence, and so the second sequence of the text must be considered the first sequence of the narrative proper /3/.

The first major narrative sequence consists of a series of stories structured around repeated violations of prohibitions and the destructive consequences. The second major sequence beginning in chap. 12 consists of a series of stories that are initiated by the giving and receiving of promises and a move toward an open future, the content of which is foreshadowed by the objective referents of the promise. The fundamental meaning of the narrative arises in the form of connotations generated by the contrast between the two major sequences. The specific nature of this contrast can be illuminated by an analysis of the anticipated word events which are found in the initial segments of each of these sequences: the prohibition in Gen 2:16 and the promise in 12:1–3. Then a third segment, Genesis 22, will be analyzed which serves to resolve the anticipated problem of the establishment of the subject in a state of permanent openness.

It will be maintained that these three segments disclose the deepest signifying level of the narrative and constitute the proper starting point for understanding the structural relation of the other narratives to each other and to the whole. But this can be finally substantiated only by a more lengthy analysis of the entire narrative which extends beyond the scope of this article. The analysis of these segments must be confined to a brief examination of the structure of the word events themselves and cannot include here an exposition of the internal structure of the narrative segments in which they are found.

Gen 2:16, 17: The first word addressed to man by God in this narrative is a word of mandate and prohibition. In the same communication, God first gives man the entire garden for his enjoyment and needs. But by placing the objects of the world there only *for* man, God puts him in a potentially narcissistic relation to them. Then through the prohibition against eating of the tree of the knowledge of good and evil, man is introduced to the mode of difference which takes the implicit form of the contrasting options: obedience vs. disobedience.

To be made aware of ethical difference by the prohibition opens the possibility of entrance into the other primary differential, signifying systems in which humans live: language and sexuality. The need for a mate for man is thus expressed immediately following the prohibition. In the course of events leading to the acquisition of a mate, man is permitted also to make use of language in the *naming* of the animals. Naming the animals and woman are the only things done by man in the garden which are not transgressive. The practice of language itself is in conformity with the prohibition which establishes a differential system of signification based upon obedience.

But the reservoir of forbidden narcissistic desires blocked by the prohibition cannot be expressed except through a transgression. The prohibition imposes such absolute closure upon the subject that, aside from tending the garden, naming things, and harmoniously relating to woman, there is nothing for Adam to do. God, through the mandate and prohibition, is still finally the true subjective source of man's actions and not man himself. Since a transgression is also needed to set the classical narrative in motion (Greimas: 195) a violation is now to be expected. This is brought about by the deception of the serpent which consists of appealing to the latent narcissism of the human. The serpent tells the woman, who already is established in a mode of difference knowing good and evil in terms of obedience vs. disobedience, that there is a knowledge of good and evil possessed by God alone which can only be attained through disobedience, i.e., through the experience of eating the fruit of the forbidden tree. The assurance of the serpent is that she will be "*like God,* knowing good and evil," i.e., knowing in terms of oppositions which are beyond the ethical system ruled by the pair obedience vs. disobedience. Divine knowledge cannot be limited in this fashion. But the result of this narcissistic thrust toward ethically unlimited knowledge is personal inner and outer alienation represented by the donning of fig leaves, hiding, blaming of others, eventual exclusion from the garden, and death.

The narrative then goes forward in chap. 4 with human beings established in this negative mode of existence. Having forsaken the goodness that comes through obedience for the dubious wisdom which comes through disobedience, they are locked into cycles of repeated transgressions which now stem from, and lead to, alienation and death. The repetition of this cycle in Genesis 4—11 is broken only by the flood story which foreshadows the possibility of an end to these cycles through the promise. But the promise here affects only nature and not history.

Gen 12:1–3. In juxtaposition to the morbid cycles of human existence portrayed in the first eleven chapters of Genesis, the narrative now initiates a new sequence which begins with a new type of word event: the giving of a promise. This opens up the possibility of a new mode of subjectivity.

The narrator cannot explicitly denote it, but it is unmistakable that the deepest meaning of this narrative is that which is *connoted* by the juxtaposition of these contrasting modes of existence.

To understand this new mode initiated in Gen 12:1–3, it will be necessary to examine the structure of the promise.

From a strictly linguistic point of view, the "I" is only an instance of speech (Benveniste: 218). Since, however, this instance of speech gains its capacity to signify by virtue of its relation to a fixed closed system of signification which excludes the heterogeneous, subjective, desiring dimension of the subject, the "I" embodies an unconscious contradiction. One might express this contradiction by saying that the "I am" rests in the consciousness upon a forgotten contradiction with what "I am not," i.e., with what language cannot signify due to a combination of linguistic and social constraints. Psychologically this contradiction constitutes the place of the unconscious self which then serves as a reservoir for all sorts of negated desires that have no "place" in language (Lang: 255).

On the other hand, the "I" that occurs in the "I will" of the promise (in contrast to the "I am" of the statement) represents an instance of speech in which the unconscious desires of the speaking subject are provided a place of access to common language where they can be oriented to the positive values of society.

Likewise, the receiver who desires the promised objects must exist openly in the mode of desire until he receives the objects. The alienation of the desiring self and the "I" of discourse is overcome in principle. The formerly negated desires implicit in the "I" are now oriented toward a signifier which represents the promised action or object. The desiring subject is thus able to find a socially legitimate point of access to language.

But the price of this admission of desire into the realm of signifiers is that the entire system of signification is thrown into question. The promise is a word which has been explicitly separated from its referent. The promisor offers a word *in place of* a thing which will be supplied at a future time. This separation of the word from its referent injects an element of uncertainty into the relation of the signifier to the signified. When a man promises to bring me apples, I know what *I* think apples are (i.e., the signified of the signifier, apples), but I will not know what *he* thinks they are until he produces them. A word which is included in a promise is thus returned hypothetically to a zero state of significance and is restored to significance as an instrument of communication (between the two parties) only by the fulfillment of the promise.

Moreover, the emergence of desire in the signifying system makes the material form of the signifiers through which the heterogeneous aspects of the self are manifest also significant. In the original oral promise, the intonation, physical strength of the voice, etc., affected the capacity of the promise to be received as a signifying word.

When the biblical narrator initiates this sequence with a divine promise to Abraham, he thus makes possible the portrayal of a new mode of subjective existence for the promisee (also for the promisor, but this cannot be taken up at this time). Whereas the prohibition divided the subject in such a way that transgression was the only mode in which he could exist as a desiring subject, the divine promise opens the possibility of entrance into a positive mode of subjectivity and the consequent healing of the division in the center of his consciousness. The divine promise, which is given beyond the prohibition, does not negate the prohibition but opens up the possibility for the differentiated self to exist consciously as a place of desire and to act, subjectively, in some way *other* than as a transgressor. The promise to Abraham is thus coupled with a positive mandate, "Go."

The effect of the promise upon the subjectivity of the receiver, Abraham, would be to make possible his appearance in language as a desiring subject, his desire now, however, oriented toward the object values which are constitutive of society (land, nationhood [which implies children], fame, and the power to bless others).

But the fact that these desires appear in the form of a promise from another, rather than as a direct expression of the self, ultimately transforms the character of the desiring subject. First of all, these object values are given to Abraham in advance through the signifying word. When someone promises you an object, you become the possessor of that object upon receipt of the promise even though you do not materially have it. Your relation to the object thus is no longer one of pure desire. The flame of desire related to the object is partially quenched by the possession of the word which signifies it. This has the effect of bringing about a new and positive relationship between the desiring subject and a signifier. Initially the desiring subject stood in a relation of nonidentity with the signifier. Now, in receiving the promise, the subject gains a positive relationship of identity to a signifier expressed in the giving of a new name. By accepting the promise, he *becomes* the one who will be the father of a nation, etc. This eventually results in the substitution of a new name, Abraham (father of a multitude), for the original name, Abram (exalted father). The new name directly stems from the content of the promise and is given in Gen 17:5 before the beginning of the fulfillment in the birth of a son.

But this identification with the signifier has an internal ambiguity: it is a composite of desire and faith. The content of the promise represents objects which Abraham doubtless desires. But the possession of these objects is *mediated* by faith in the word of promise. He will gain these objects of desire only through faith in the word.

The possibility of faith is thus opened as a new mode of subjectivity. The object of *faith* is not the object of desire, but the signifier which represents (or more exactly, pre-sents) these objects. The material form of the signifier thus attains signifying capacity. The desiring subjectivity of the promisor is absolutely identified with the signifier of the promised object in a mode of giving, as the desiring subjectivity of the promisee is identified with the promissory signifier in a mode of receiving. It is the linguistic form of the promise that connotatively signifies these two internal states by means of the first person, "I," attached to the promise (and to the act of acceptance when there is one).

Since the referent of the form of the promise as an object of faith and commitment is only back to the promising subject (and forward to the receiving subject), it embodies the maximum degree of referential openness of which a signifier is capable if it is still to retain a signifying capacity. Its major reference is to the two subjects who are themselves identified only (in the primary sense) with the promise. It is the subjective mode of faith which takes as its object this open signifier. Faith thus constitutes the state of pure openness of the subject in language. In the narrative this serves as a contrast to the closed mode of subjectivity established by the prohibition.

But a subjective tension exists between faith and desire in relation to the promise. It not only is an object of faith; it also has an objective referent. If the promise is fulfilled, the word and its objective referent will again be united and the signified will be more firmly than ever attached to the signifier. The promise can no longer function as an object of faith. The desire of the subject will also now be satisfied by the object of desire, and the subject can thus slip back into its former negative state of closure until it is reopened by another promise. The relation of faith in which the subject existed prior to fulfillment will no longer be possible after fulfillment. The relationship between the two subjects united by the promise will become obsolete. The identity of the promisee will then be oriented toward the material object he received and not toward the word which signified it.

Although the promise to Abraham extended far beyond the gift of children (implied by the promise of nationhood and made explicit in Genesis 15), it is clear that the fulfillment of this promise represented the possible closure of Abraham's faith, since the son was the material instrumentality through which the remainder of the promise could be fulfilled. This problem of the closure of faith after the fulfillment is resolved by Genesis 22, Abraham's test of faith.

Genesis 22. This narrative begins with a specific summons from God by name to Abraham followed by a mandate unaccompanied by a promise. In an unusual prefatory comment, the narrator informs the reader that this which is to follow will be a test of Abraham. We are left to assume that it will be a test of his faith.

To see the meaning of this mandate, it will be necessary to refer back to the mandate in Gen 12:1. The mandate in 12:1 is implied by the promise. Faith in a promise implies an action which assumes the possession of the promised object or state. If a man is promised, e.g., a high salaried and powerful governmental post, then he begins to act as if he had at least some of the power of the position. The word is accepted in lieu of the real object. If Abraham accepted the divine promise as being as good as the reality, then he had to leave his present land and nation and go into an empty space (between the nations and lands) in which he might find his own land, the space where his progeny could become a nation. This implication of action is expressed in the form of a mandate from God accompanying the promise. Since this sequence begins a new phase of the story, the more dramatic arresting mandate actually precedes the promise in the text.

In Genesis 22, however, another mandate comes from the promissor, but this time not accompanied by a promise. This mandate is *not* implied by the fundamental promise given in Gen 12:1-3, however. More specifically, it is not implied by the *denotative content* of the earlier promise. In fact, it stands in striking contradiction to it. The son who was promised (implicitly) to Abraham in Gen 12:1-3 (and explicitly in chap. 15), now that the promise has been fulfilled, is to be sacrificed. But this mandate is not in contradiction to the unique form of the promise. The significance of the form of the promise arose from its capacity to bring the subjectivity of two parties into a relation of faith, of open subjectivity. The object orientation of the denotative content of the promise then stood in tension with the more fundamental connotative meaning of the form of the promise, since the material fulfillment of the denoted content would eliminate the need for faith directed toward the form. Thus the mandate to sacrifice the material object which has represented the fulfillment of the content of the promise, while contradicting the content, is an implicit necessity from the viewpoint of the form. The intrusion of this contradiction thus makes it possible for the promise to serve a mediating function between idolatrous materialism and the deepest form of faith in the word.

This discloses the underlying orientation of the signifying structures of the narrative. The mandate to sacrifice Isaac becomes understandable upon the assumption that the signifying structures of the narrative are finally oriented toward the establishment of a subject in a state of absolute openness toward the word. But the word now cannot be considered a promise, since a promise always has a denotative meaning included within it. When Abraham is commanded to sacrifice the denotative content of his fulfilled promise as a test of *faith*, then the ambiguity between faith and desire in the intermediate mode of subjectivity created by the promise is resolved by the elimination of desire. His faith, purged of desire for objects, finds itself oriented exclusively toward the word which is now divested of all objective reference. The rescue of Isaac *after* the test of faith is complete does not alter the meaning of the test for Abraham.

What kind of word is this that is beyond all denotation? Perhaps it is what Roland Barthes referred to as the "anormal energy of the word." Or perhaps it is what the biblical writers meant by the God whose name was, "I will be who I will be" (Exod 3:14).

In any case, the narrative near its beginning, through this surprising mandate to its first major protagonist, has found a way of posing the human subject in a state of final subjective openness (faith) toward the positive signifying power of the word. The continuation of the narrative toward the objective fulfillment of this promise through the rescue of Isaac allows the promise to continue its mediating role for succeeding generations.

Here, then, we reach what may well be the fundamental signifying matrix of the Genesis narrative which accounts for the sequential structuring of the narrative as a whole: Gen 2:4b—11:32 depicting the contrasting closed subjective structure; chaps. 12—21 depicting the emergence of open subjectivity under the mediation of the composite promise; chap. 22 representing the consummation of open subjectivity in the willingness of Abraham to sacrifice the fulfillment of the promise; and chaps. 23—50, the continuation of the promise as the mediator of faith to later generations. The inability of any fulfillment to end the narrative, however, suggests that the true end of faith can only be found by transcending even the fulfillment, as did Abraham at the beginning. But the end toward which the mediating process moves has appropriately been disclosed already in the faith of the narrative's first major protagonist. These are matters, however, that can only be clearly established by a much more detailed study of the biblical narrative than the scope of the present essay permits.

CONCLUSION

Although the generative power of the paradigmatic model of open subjectivity has not been tested with regard to most of the individual narratives of Genesis, it has shown itself capable of originating the fundamental sequential division of the narrative (Gen 2:4b—11:32, and chaps. 12—50), and has, as well, provided a basis for understanding why each major sequence begins as it does, and the necessity behind the otherwise shocking intrusion of Genesis 22. Further, the relations between these passages were shown to follow a logic which appears to presuppose the primacy of this paradigmatic model in the signifying system of the author(s) of the narrative.

Because the prohibition, the promise and the mandate to sacrifice the child of the promise constitute the pivotal signifying nodes in terms of which the other events of the narrative acquire meaning, the conclusion of this study is then that the paradigmatic model of open subjectivity which unites them merits serious consideration as a possible generative matrix for the Genesis narrative as a whole (and possibly for the entire tradition of biblical narrative writing). This can be determined, however, only through the separate examination of the structure of each narrative unit.

NOTES

/1/ See below in the discussion of the promise for examples of some such effects.

/2/ The critical thrust of this statement is toward the traditional pattern of speaking of the God of the Bible in Greek ontological categories. It is intended to leave open the possibility of speaking of deity in other terms more appropriate to a people whose understanding of reality was articulated in narratives rather than logic. A similar possibility was raised from a Heideggerian viewpoint by James M. Robinson (153): "Truth is more basically an 'unveiling' (a-lētheia) than a correlation of objects to a subject's patterns of thought." For a summary of the discussion of the viability of Old Testament theology see A. Jepsen (246–284).

/3/ The relation of Genesis 1 to this model must be taken up at a later date.

Part III

Three Divergent Traditions

Robert Goldenberg
Wolfgang Roth
David Robertson

Chapter 6

The Problem of False Prophecy:
Talmudic Interpretations of
Jeremiah 28 and 1 Kings 22

Robert Goldenberg

I

I wish here to discuss the problem of false prophecy as it is raised by a pair of scriptural narratives, and then to examine certain talmudic efforts to minimize the threat these stories pose. If left unresolved, this problem can destroy all confidence in revealed religion: there is little value in living one's life according to messages purportedly received from heaven if there is no way to judge their authenticity, or to know the intent lying behind them. These stories imply that there is indeed no way to know such things, and I propose to study the ways in which talmudic exegesis sought to negate this implication.

It will be helpful to begin by summarizing the stories in some detail. Nuances thus noted will turn out later to be important.

In Kings (2 Chronicles 18 differs only in minor details), a king of Israel identified in v 20 as the notorious Ahab and Jehoshaphat, king of Judah, have come together to discuss a joint campaign against the city of Ramoth-Gilead, now held by the Arameans. Jehoshaphat expresses a desire to "consult the word of the Lord" before they begin, so Ahab assembles no fewer than four hundred prophets, who duly assure the kings that they may proceed because the Lord will deliver the city into their hands. Jehoshaphat, perhaps rendered suspicious by their unanimity (b. Sanh. 89a, Josephus, *Ant.* 8.15.4 [402]) /1/, politely asks whether there might not be still another prophet to consult. Ahab answers that indeed there is, Micaiah ben Imlah by name, "but I hate him, because he never prophesies good concerning me, only evil" (v 8). Jehoshaphat quietly insists, and Ahab agrees to summon Micaiah.

The messenger sent to fetch Micaiah tells him what has been going on and pleads with him to agree with all the other prophets. Micaiah, however, in a reminiscence of the possibly better-known story of the heathen prophet Balaam, indignantly insists that he will speak only those words which the Lord instructs him to say. Meanwhile, one of the four hundred prophets, a man named Zedekiah ben Kanaanah, has made for himself a set of iron horns and announces in the Lord's name that with those horns the kings are destined to gore the Arameans and wipe them out. The confrontation has begun to build.

Micaiah arrives and, in response to the king's initial query, prophesies a glorious victory. His tone, however, must have been heavily ironic, because the king answers, "How many times must I adjure you that you speak to me only the truth in the Lord's name?" (v 16). Micaiah then predicts defeat and the king's own death in battle, whereupon the king, apparently a hard man to please, says to Jehoshaphat, "Didn't I tell you that he never says anything nice about me?"

This much of the story is only background to the really crucial section, however, and the religious problem to which the story now shifts its attention is urgent. Prophet has contradicted prophet; how does one know whom to believe? Micaiah knows by now that he represents a very small minority. He has presumably noticed as well the impressive antics of Zedekiah, and without doubt is aware that the king personally detests him and has tried to discredit his prophecy in advance. He must now try to authenticate his message and seeks to accomplish this by reporting the following astonishing vision (vv 19–23):

> Hear then the word of the Lord. I saw the Lord sitting on his throne, with the whole host of heaven standing before him at his right and at his left, and the Lord said, "Who will entice Ahab to mount a campaign, that he may fall at Ramoth-Gilead?" One said one thing, one said another, but a certain spirit (hā-rûaḥ) came forward and stood before the Lord and said, "I shall entice him." The Lord said to him, "How?" and he said, "I shall go forth and be a lying spirit in the mouth of all his prophets." The Lord said, "You shall indeed success-

fully entice him; go out and do so."
So now, behold, the Lord has put a lying spirit into the mouth
of all these your prophets; the Lord has pronounced evil over
you.

That, then, is Micaiah's vision—the profoundly disturbing vision
of a prophecy indeed sent from God, but sent to destroy and not
save. The prophet speaks in the name of the Lord, but what he
says is false, and woe to the hearer who follows him.

Zedekiah, the other prophet (it would be prejudicial to call him
"false"), naturally resents this oracle. He slaps Micaiah and asks,
"How is this that the spirit of the Lord has left me to speak with
you?" (v 24). Micaiah's only answer is to say, in effect, "Let's
just wait and see what happens." While expressing the prophet's
own confidence, this is not a response suited to convince others.
Sure enough, the king orders Micaiah's arrest, presumably on suspicion of false prophecy (a capital crime—Deut 18:20), and goes
off to resolve the issue on the field of battle. As predicted, Ahab
falls in battle, but Scripture never reports the fate of the two
prophets Micaiah and Zedekiah. Micaiah's arrest is the last we
hear of either of them and that is the end of my first tale.

The other story is in several respects much simpler. It involves
a similar confrontation, and is found in Jeremiah 28. In 594 B.C.E.
(Bright, 1970:195f.), the prophet Hananiah ben Azur accosted
Jeremiah in a public place and announced that within two years
the exiled king Jeconiah ben Jehoiakim would return to Judea,
together with all the nobles and sacred vessels which the Babylonians had seized four years previously, and that indeed the
power of Babylon would be broken forever. Jeremiah's response
is a patriotic Amen. He wishes it might be so, but it isn't. "The
prophets who came before you and me," he says, "in any age,
predicted war, and suffering, and pestilence over many lands and
many kingdoms. The prophet who predicts well-being—it will be
known that the Lord really sent that prophet when his word
comes about" (vv 8–9). Deuteronomy, more or less the contemporary of these people, offers (18:22) a simple criterion for
distinguishing authentic prophecy from false prophecy; if it comes
true, it was authentic. This seems to have been the criterion underlying the arrest of Micaiah a hundred-odd years before, but

now Jeremiah himself proposes a revision: only good prophecies must be confirmed in this way. Bad prophecies are prima facie genuine.

Hananiah, of course, is not convinced. Jeremiah had earlier (Jer 27:2) made himself a wooden yoke and had been walking around wearing it as a sign that the nation's subjection to Babylon had been ordained in heaven. Hananiah now takes that yoke off Jeremiah's neck and breaks it, as *his* sign that the subjection is about to be lifted. Jeremiah, apparently not knowing what to say, simply walks off. Once again prophet has confronted prophet, and at least for the moment even Jeremiah can think of nothing to say or to do.

Later, however, Jeremiah does think of a response (or, if one prefers, he receives a message from the Lord). Unlike Micaiah, who spoke in puzzling visions, Jeremiah characteristically reacts with direct violent denunciation. After first reiterating his political message advocating subjection to the Babylonians, he turns to the prophet Hananiah (vv 15–17):

> "Listen, Hananiah, the Lord has not sent you, and you have encouraged this people with lies. Therefore thus says the Lord: I shall indeed send you—right off the face of the earth /2/. You will die this year, because you advocated rebellion against the Lord!"
> And the prophet Hananiah died that year, in the seventh month.

Jeremiah's response, then, differs strongly from Micaiah's and entirely lacks its ambiguities. Hananiah's prophecy is not "genuinely heavenly but misleading nonetheless"; it is an out-and-out lie. Hananiah himself is not the victim of a heavenly deception. He is simply a fraud, and as such deserves and receives the penalty prescribed for all false prophets. On the other hand, Jeremiah fails to answer one question which Micaiah does resolve: Why does all this happen? The purpose and meaning of Zedekiah's false prophecy eventually become clear for us, but Hananiah is always described as "the prophet Hananiah" and Jeremiah's own initial silence suggests he had heard Hananiah prophesy before and had found no reason to doubt him. What leads an authentic prophet of the Lord suddenly to overthrow his mission and speak falsely in the name of heaven? Neither Jeremiah himself, nor the author of this chapter, seems to know.

II

The most extensive rabbinic treatment of the problem of false prophecy appears in each Talmud in a context not of theology but of law. Tractate *Sanhedrin* deals with the capital law of the rabbis; among the other capital crimes which it must regulate is the offense of false prophecy. Mishna (henceforth m.) *Sanh.* 1:5 mentions that one accused of false prophecy must be tried by a court of seventy-one judges, and m. *Sanh.* 11:1 mentions in summary fashion that a convicted false prophet is executed by strangulation. The real discussion appears just below that, in 11:5:

> A false prophet, one who prophesies what he has not heard, and what was not spoken to him—his death is entrusted to man. But one who suppresses his prophecy, and one who ignores the words of a prophet, and a prophet who violates his own words—his death is entrusted to Heaven, as it is said, "I shall require it of him" (Deut 18:19).

Now an example of each of these categories can be found in Scripture, and one could defend the claim that the criterion for assigning some cases to a human court and reserving others for direct heavenly intervention was simply that some biblical stories ended in one fashion, while others ended differently. Thus, the classic case of someone ignoring a prophet's injunction appears in 1 Kings 20:35–36, where a prophet orders another man to strike him. The second man refuses, presumably reluctant to commit an unwarranted act of violence, whereupon the prophet announces: "Since you have not heeded the Lord's voice, you will depart from me, and a lion will strike you down." That is indeed what happened; that is, this execution was carried out by heaven. The story of a prophet violating his own words can be found in 1 Kings 13; there too a lion carries out the heavenly punishment. The classic case of a prophet who tried to hold back his own prophecy is, of course, Jonah; his narrow escape from a watery death must simply be taken as an eleventh-hour reprieve from the heavenly executioner.

Deut 18:20, however, implies (especially by its initial particle *'ak*) that certain sorts of offenses may be punished by a court of flesh and blood, and the Mishna tells what these are: "A false prophet, one who prophesies what he has not heard, and what was not spoken to him." Are these three types of cases, or rather one, described first generally and then in detail? It is tempting to say "one," and indeed a well-attested variant of m. (Rabbinovicz: 241–2, n. 6, 7; Schachter:273) omits the words "his death is entrusted to man." In that case, it becomes necessary to punctuate the text as follows:

> A false prophet is one who prophesies what he has not heard or what was not spoken to him. But one who suppresses his prophecy . . . his death is entrusted to Heaven. . . .

and the purpose of the text becomes simply to limit the definition of culpable false prophecy.

Once that phrase is added to the text, however, the Mishna can be construed as containing two parallel lists of several items each. This is the understanding reflected in all talmudic discussions, and the relevant portion of m. now refers not to one sort of case, but to three. Tosepta *Sanh.* 14:14 has the following:

> "One who prophesies what he has not heard"—like Zedekiah ben Kanaanah. "And one who prophesies what was not said to him"—like Hananiah ben Azur, who would hear words from the mouth of the prophet Jeremiah. [Jeremiah] would prophesy in the upper marketplace, and he would go and prophesy in the lower marketplace.

An undatable, but ostensibly early tradition thus distinguishes between these two cases and furthermore explains to us exactly what each consisted of. Hananiah's prophecies had indeed come from the Lord—but not to him. Zedekiah's, by implication, were simple fabrications. A later talmudic *baraita* typically systematizes all this, and to eliminate all doubt begins by saying, "Three are put to death by man, and three are put to death by heaven" (b. *Sanh.* 89a; cf. *Sipre* Deut 177). The first triad consists of our two cases and also "he who prophesies in the name of an idol." The last case is brought in from m. 11:6. Apparently even the author of this *baraita* recognized that "a false prophet" in m. 11:5 is a general introduction, and not a separate category.

Thanks to the rabbinic penchant for clear legal thinking, we can therefore begin to clarify the talmudic idea of false prophecy and its several varieties. The distinction made by the Tosepta is not implausible on its own terms. It is one thing to invent messages from God, and another merely to take credit for such messages when they had in fact been revealed to another. Both are frauds, but the deception is not the same. If the rabbis wish to distinguish between them, while subsuming both under the biblical prohibition, that by itself would be perfectly all right.

The problem—our problem here—arises from the fact that in isolating and distinguishing the two cases of Zedekiah and Hananiah, and placing each within a general category, the rabbinic authorities have in fact inverted the apparent meaning of the biblical narratives themselves. Jeremiah tells Hananiah that he is a false prophet whom the Lord has not sent. Why then does the Talmud put him into the other category? Why did R. Joshua b. Levi, in the early third century, explicitly say that Hananiah was a true prophet (Jer *Sanh* 11:5, 30b)? According to Joshua b. Levi, Hananiah's ability to receive messages had for some reason lapsed, and he had adopted the expedient of stealing Jeremiah's prophecies, inferring from them some further "information," and publishing these conclusions as his own /3/. None of this comes from Scripture; why would anyone make it up? Similarly, why is Zedekiah called "one who prophesies what he has not heard"? Micaiah, the hero of that story, is perfectly willing to concede that Zedekiah's prophecy has the same heavenly inspiration as his own. He merely warns Ahab and the others against listening to it. (This, by the way, would put them all into the illegal category of "one who ignores the words of a prophet," but no ancient commentator raises this consideration.)

I think these transformations came into being as a response to Micaiah's vision and its implication that the divine gift of prophecy can be more dangerous than anyone had ever imagined. It had always seemed clear that the prophet was a divine messenger, carrying to his audience a communication which they would be wise to heed. On this assumption, the basic problem had been to distinguish the false prophet from the true: it was necessary to ignore and indeed to wipe out the former, and equally necessary to pay close attention to the latter and follow his or her message in all respects. The deuteronomic law therefore emphasizes the need to identify false prophets and gives the best advice it can as to how this might be achieved. The stories in the earlier parts of 1 Kings reinforce this message, as does the more famous episode of Elijah's confrontation with the prophets of Baal (1 Kings 18): just figure which prophet is the one whom the Lord has sent, follow that one, and no other.

Micaiah's vision overthrows all that. Zedekiah no less than Micaiah himself is a prophet whom the Lord has sent. The only difference is that Zedekiah will lead Ahab to his doom, while Micaiah is trying to save him from a conspiracy conceived in the very court of heaven. Put bluntly, Micaiah's message is that God himself cannot be trusted. Put more subtly, it runs something like this: It is not enough to identify the prophet sent by the Lord. You must also know *why* the Lord has sent that prophet and the result which the prophecy in question was designed to produce. Then you have to decide whether or not to follow it. All this, whether in the blunt or the subtle version, is crippling, because there is no way to answer such questions. The human audience of a prophecy is simply not privy to the secret thoughts of God. We know only the prophecy itself. If Micaiah's vision is allowed to stand, prophecy can no longer be trusted, and as noted here at the very beginning, the notion of revealed religion collapses.

The urgent need of talmudic exegesis, therefore, was to keep Micaiah's vision from standing. Its implication had to be denied, and the interpreters achieved this aim through a double tour de force. By reversing the apparent meaning of two stories, by causing each to exemplify a category which seems more directly suggested by the other, they entirely neutralized the otherwise devastating religious implications of one narrative in its original form. They did all this, moreover, *without ever indicating their purpose or aim.* It seems to me that only awareness of the danger implied in Micaiah's vision would have induced them to transform so thoroughly the apparent meaning of the biblical texts, but no talmudic comment ever directly addresses this central concern. When we moderns come upon a troubling biblical passage, we tend to discuss it to excess; the Talmud simply changes the meaning of the text, without explicitly acknowledging the problem at all.

This would not have been possible without certain details which the biblical text does contain. Hananiah, for one thing, is called "the prophet" in that chapter as frequently and as consistently as is Jeremiah. Even in reporting his death (in other words, after Jeremiah has declared him a fraud), the narrator calls him "Hananiah the prophet." Jeremiah, during the original confrontation, is forced to retreat precisely because he does know Hananiah to be a prophet /4/, and is not sure how to proceed in the face of Hananiah's conflicting prophecy. He even invents a new theological principle—only good prophecies need to be verified—to break the deadlock. (The Jerusalem Talmud, *Sanh.* 11:5, extends this particular dialogue, again with a characteristic inversion. Hananiah now defends his prophecy, and then challenges Jeremiah to do the same. After stalling a while, Jeremiah finally says, "Very well, my confirming sign is that *you* are going to die," which Hananiah does. And this is still another inversion: the death has been turned from punishment for false prophecy into confirmation of truth.) The basis on which Joshua b. Levi openly contradicted Jeremiah's own declaration can thus be detected right in the biblical narrative itself.

The Babylonian explanation of Hananiah's sin supports my contention that the rabbis knew they were transforming the sense of Scripture. It begins with the allusion to plagiarism already noted in Tosepta:

> Jeremiah stood in the upper market and said, "Thus says the Lord of Hosts, 'Behold, I shall break the bow of Elam' " (Jer 49:35).
> Hananiah reasoned *a minori*: If the Holy One, blessed be he, intends to break the bow of Elam, who only came to help Babylon, how much more must this be true of the Chaldeans themselves! So he went to the lower market and said, "Thus says the Lord . . . 'I have broken the yoke of the King of Babylon' " (Jer 28:2).

The discussion then continues:

> Rav Papa said to Abaya, "But [this isn't a case of one prophet stealing another's prophecy;] this wasn't spoken to another prophet either!"

He said to him, "Since the syllogism was inherent in the prophecy, it was as though spoken, but it was not spoken to him."

This contorted logic bespeaks a desperate need to find some legitimacy in Hananiah's seeming fraud. If Hananiah's and Zedekiah's acts were fundamentally different and if Hananiah's act did have some legitimacy, it becomes easier to believe that Zedekiah's had none.

The story of Zedekiah itself provides further support for this elaborate reinterpretation. The crucial verse is 1 Kings 22:21, translated earlier as follows: "A certain spirit (*hā-rûaḥ*) came forward and stood before the Lord and said, 'I shall entice him.' " Now the word translated "a certain spirit," *hā-rûaḥ*, literally means simply "the spirit," and rabbinic exegetes naturally wondered, "What spirit?" /5/. The definite article implies that everyone should know which spirit this was who volunteered to go and lead Ahab to his doom. Hebrew diction doesn't really require people to wonder this at all, but rabbinic interpreters raised this question at other places as well (e.g., Gen 14:13), and we can take it here as a standard query. The answer here, however, is remarkable—this must be the spirit of the recently executed Naboth the Jezreelite, whose judicial murder had been arranged by Ahab and Jezebel not long before (1 Kings 21).

The chain of reasoning which thus emerges, while not exactly compelling, does have a logic of its own. "The spirit" which entices Ahab is no longer a divine emissary, carrying out God's own command, but rather Ahab's previous victim, seeking on its own initiative a vengeance which God grudgingly lets it achieve. (This line of explanation receives its clearest statement in the early seventeenth century in *Hiddushei Aggadah* of R. Samuel Edels, but it is implicit in the talmudic sources.) How do we know God's consent was grudging? The spirit, while receiving the permission it sought, was also peremptorily ordered by God to "Go out!" (v 22). As we know (Ps 101:7), the speaker of lies is not permitted to stand in the sight of the Lord. The deception, then, has not come from God but from the aggrieved shade of the murdered Naboth. God has merely permitted an act of justice. Those of us who have abstained from acts like Ahab's have nothing further to fear.

Were it not for the context in which these legends appear, that is, the rabbinic effort to systematize the notion of false prophecy, and the fear of deceptive prophecy which 1 Kings 22 seems to raise, all these details might seem quite innocent—indeed, exotic. After all, midrashic efforts to identify anonymous minor characters are found elsewhere in rabbinic literature (b. *Nid.* 61a; b. *Sanh.* 89ab). So are unnecessary clarifications of grammatical particles, and moralizing elaborations of seemingly straightforward dialogue. Since both of these motifs, however—identifying the spirit as that of Naboth, and sermonizing on the verb "Go!"—are found in several places (b. *Sanh.* 89a, 102b, b. *Šhab.* 149b), it seems that rabbinic teachers found them important, and I think I have discovered why.

I mentioned above that the transformations I have tried to explain are not explicitly acknowledged anywhere in rabbinic literature (R. Papa's question is as close as one gets). In general, rabbinic teachers did not talk very much at all about the nature of false prophecy, or true prophecy either, for that matter. The talmudic discussions of the law in m. *Sanh.* 11:5–6 consist entirely of Scripture exegesis and the like; one gets no impression at all that these were also living issues for later generations. Yet it is known that the early Christian church was witness to a great revival of prophecy, so that the apostle Paul found it necessary to warn his followers to "not despise prophetic utterances, but bring them all to the test" (1 Thess 5:20–21) /6/, and the Montanist movement, which was extremely receptive to prophets, flourished precisely during the time of R. Joshua b. Levi, whom we have already had occasion to quote here. Rather than testing every spirit, however, these rabbis seem to have preferred that the spirit would just go away. I think that is why their treatment of this question remained so indirect; they really hoped that people would not think about it at all.

The problem of false prophecy is, after all, terribly troublesome for any community which still expects new revelations from heaven. Charismatic authority is often unsettling and sometimes quite destructive, and the opponents of charismatic figures never find it very difficult to convince themselves they are dealing with an emissary of Satan, if not the devil himself. The Hebrew Scriptures, while clearly affirming the value of the institution of prophecy as such, never developed a very good procedure for separating true prophecy from false. The deuteronomic law could suggest only that people wait and let events take their course. Even Jeremiah, who tried to make the theory more sophisticated, was vindicated in the end (as the Jerusalem Talmud saw) only because his rival died at a convenient time.

Rabbinic Judaism /7/ tried to deal with this problem by ending altogether the expectation of new prophets, and by eliminating all question of the validity and uniqueness of the canonical prophets, on whose authority they themselves in the end depended. The legends examined here represent one way in which they tried to achieve that goal.

III

The foregoing was designed to stand as a self-sufficient investigation into the talmudic treatment of a certain interesting question. Given the setting for which it was originally written, however, it might be useful now to discuss more explicitly my own assumptions and procedures.

Since I was trying to focus simultaneously on two different historical levels—the biblical and the talmudic—it seemed appropriate as a start to combine them by gathering all available rabbinic comments on the relevant biblical passages: Jeremiah 28, 1 Kings 22, and the parallel to the latter at 2 Chronicles 18 /8/.

Much of what I found was trivial or irrelevant /9/. In trying to organize what was left, I had the good fortune to notice something out of the ordinary: the rabbinic assignment of certain scriptural personalities to different legal categories did not seem to square with the biblical stories themselves. This was the key moment— the point at which an active, transforming intelligence could be seen to be at work. My task now resolved itself into the project of perceiving and describing this transformation as clearly as I could, and then of accounting for it. The line of questioning in a sense was simple: given that the ancient rabbis were no less intelligent than I, and no less capable of making sense of a text, why should they have distorted these in so striking a manner? Part II above represents my effort to frame and answer this basic question.

Other answers may, of course, be possible. I have not offered here a chain of deductions starting from purely empirical evidence and reasoning step-by-step to proven conclusions. The logic depends more on intuition and judgment: it seems to me that the alleged anomaly really is surprising, and no other explanation for it strikes me as equally plausible. Nor does it seem to me relevant to appeal to alleged differences between rabbinic styles of thinking and our own. We might consider it hairsplitting to distinguish in the first place among all those types of false prophecy, but no exegetical necessity or compulsive obscurantism forced these ancient exegetes to reverse the two characterizations in the manner I have described. The Talmuds offer abundant evidence of rabbis' ability to read a text and see what it says. When they read a text and find something else, we are entitled to wonder what has led them to do so.

While the ancient rabbis do not differ from us in clearheaded intelligence, however, they do differ from us in purpose. (By "us" I mean contemporary academic scholars.) Our purpose, once we have noticed a theologically perplexing biblical story, is to understand it as well as we can on its own terms—what does the text mean, what were the probable intentions of its author(s), etc. Any talmudic interpretation needed to fulfill one additional decisive need: it needed to be religiously acceptable. Scripture, understood to be a perfect divine revelation, had to be understood in such a way that later generations would be willing to base their lives on the religious implications they found in it, and certain really disturbing stories therefore provoked very complicated reinterpretations indeed. See the story of Elisha and the bears (2 Kings 2:23–24) and compare the comments at b. Śota 46a–b. For a similar reason, R. Simeon b. Laqish denied that the story of Job ever really took place at all (*Gen. Rab.* 57:4, and b. *B. Bat.* 15a). On these terms, any acceptable interpretation was at least potentially "correct," and any other was out of the question. I think it is this existential dependence on these texts that forced the rabbis in this case to sacrifice plausibility for mere defensibility as their criterion in accepting the interpretation which they did. In the absence of any such dependence, the modern academic scholar is under no such compulsion.

The comments examined here represent two different formats: the list of legal categories (with or without examples), and the free-floating exegetical legend. The first is relatively straightforward. The rabbis thought as lawyers most of the time. In the present case, they were listing types of capital crime, classified according to the method of execution. It was natural that examples from Scripture should be used to illustrate each category, especially in the case of a charge like false prophecy, which had generated few, if any, actual cases during the last centuries of Jewish sovereignty /10/. The use of legend is more interesting. These legends serve several purposes at once. They answer questions of all sorts, varying from matters of detail (What spirit stood up and volunteered? Why does it say "the spirit" as though we knew?) to matters of basic understanding (Why is Hananiah the fraud so often called "the prophet"? Was he a prophet, or wasn't he?). Hidden among all the more or less explanatory details which these legends offer is the answer to the biggest question of all: How could God do that to Ahab? Could there be a worse fraud than that?

The key to this format lies in a formal convention: it is never necessary for a legend designed to answer a question to formulate the question first. One must infer the question from the answer. One must remember all the time that rabbinic legends, expansions, interpolations, and the like are usually the answers to unstated questions, and not simply independent fragments of imagination. In the present case, where it was better not to acknowledge the question any more than necessary, this convention was very handy indeed. Just as the question is never stated, the answer is buried in a format which seems designed—which *was* designed—for another purpose altogether. It is possible to speculate further that this tendency of rabbinic interpreters to hide their own traces has influenced my own work here and resulted in the intuitive and hypothetical character of my reconstruction. The information needed for a tighter chain of deductions was systematically withheld from us by the ancient exegetes themselves.

I think this entire investigation has in the end taught us very little about the Bible. The talmudic sages were using the Bible to achieve purposes of their own, and all we can do is to note the hints they discovered in Scripture which enabled them to attain their ends. In the end, the only thing we can learn about the Bible is what they wish to teach us, namely, that the Bible *can* be interpreted to mean what they say it means, and that certain details, which we might have missed on our own, *can* be adduced in support of that interpretation. We can learn about the potential meaning of the Bible, but little or nothing about its historical origins or about meanings which we might plausibly attach to it today.

This outcome seems inevitable. Every text requires an interpretation because no text really has only one possible meaning /11/. In the present case, the opacity of the rabbinic comments is increased by the differences between their purposes and ours, and by the energetic manner in which the ancient rabbis generally left their own mark on earlier traditions. The problem, however, is a general one, and the question why a certain interpretation rather than another eventually prevailed always has more to do with the history of interpretation than with the basic text itself /12/.

NOTES

/1/ Josephus reports that Jehoshaphat "perceived from their words" that they were false prophets, but he does not indicate what led the king to that conclusion.

/2/ The phrase is Bright's.

/3/ The details can be relegated to a footnote:

Hananiah said, "Isn't the whole point this: 'When seventy years have been fulfilled for Babylon, I shall remember you'?" (Cf. Jer 29:10.)

"All of [King] Manasseh's years were fifty-five. Deduct the twenty years [of his youth] for which the Heavenly Court exacts no penalty, and add the two years of Amon and the thirty-one of Josiah." (N.B.: $55-20+2+31=68$.)

It is that which is written: "In that year, at the beginning of the reign of Zedekiah, King of Judah, in the fifth year, the fifth month, Hananiah ben Azur, the prophet from Gibeon, said to me . . . 'I have broken the yoke of the King of Babylon. In two more years I shall return to this place all the vessels of the house of the Lord which Nebuchadnezzar, King of Babylon, took . . .' " (Jer 28:2-3).

The arithmetic here omits the reign of Jehoiakim, and the logic is generally arbitrary and vague. The subcommentary *Mar'eh ha-Panim* trenchantly observes, "There are many more mistakes in Hananiah's calculation, but the Talmud took no care to be precise, since the whole prophecy was false."

/4/   L. Finkelstein's suggestion (150) that the talmudic exegesis masks a reference to the apostle Paul, is groundless. Hananiah is repeatedly called a "prophet," so Finkelstein's assertion that "Scripture contains no hint that Hananiah was ever a true prophet" cuts too fine a distinction to be useful. See above, end of Part I.

/5/   The inclination of some commentators to see here an early appearance of "the Spirit," with a capital "S" so to speak, strikes me as anachronistic, a case of theological wishful thinking. Cf. Gray: 403.

/6/   See also Acts 2:17-18, Matt 7:22, 1 John 4:1, 2 Pet 5:1. My colleague, David Suter, aided me in gathering these references.

/7/   I say "rabbinic Judaism," but I think it worth noting that all the significant statements considered above are attributed to people who flourished within a single century, ca. 225-ca. 325. Joshua b. Levi, the earliest, was a younger contemporary of the editor(s) of the Mishna, and Abaye, who defended the traditional understanding of Hananiah's offense against R. Papa's challenge, lived about a hundred years later. The identification of "the spirit" as Naboth's is uniformly attributed to R. Yohanan, younger colleague of Joshua b. Levi. Only the minihomily on "go out!" remains in doubt. B. Šhab. 149b and b. Sanh. 89a in all versions attribute the statement either to Rav Judah quoting Rav, or to one of these two people by himself; this again reflects the early or middle third century. B. Sanh. 102b attributes this statement to the much later Ravina, but even here manuscripts offer variants naming Rav Judah, or Rav, or both. See Rabbinovicz, Shab., 359, n. 2; Sanh. 132, n. 50, 242, n. 50. I have left this finding for a footnote because I am not yet able to say what it signifies. The matter requires further study.

/8/   Hyman makes this sort of task tedious but easy. Hyman lists, verse by verse for the whole Bible, the location of every scriptural reference in all talmudic and midrashic and in some medieval literature. Ginzberg was also very helpful at this point.

/9/   Irrelevant, that is, to the question of false prophecy. Triviality is always in the eye of the beholder. Some examples: (a) God consulted the angels before dooming Ahab. This proves no one should ever judge a case by himself (y. Sanh. 1:1-18a; cf. Abot 4:8). (b) Zedekiah's horns prove an ox usually does its damage with its horns (B. Qam 2b). (c) A proverb: "A man's feet take him where he is destined to go" (y. Ketub. 12:3 35b; cf. b. Sukk. 53a). (d) In the heavenly throne room, only God himself is allowed to sit (Tanhuma, Bereshit 5, Qedoshim 6).

/10/   By the time of the Maccabees there were no more prophets altogether (1 Macc 4:46; 14:41). The Christian prophets were not under rabbinic jurisdiction, and did not attract their attention.

/11/   These final comments have been greatly influenced by Scholem. See especially his essay "Revelation and Tradition as Religious Categories in Judaism," in *The Messianic Idea in Judaism* (New York: Schocken, 1971), pp. 282–303.

/12/   This paper has been revised since its presentation at the Ottawa Symposium. I wish to thank my colleagues in the Religion Department at Wichita State University, and Prof. Anthony Gythiel of the WSU Department of English, for their helpful observations and responses.

Chapter 7

The Story of the Prophet Micaiah (1 Kings 22) in Historical-Critical Interpretation 1876–1976

Wolfgang Roth

INTRODUCTION: THE TASK AND ITS SOURCES

I intend to review seven representative historical-critical exegeses published in the course of the period 1876–1976. The selection of these interpretations from the great number of those published does not imply a value judgment but is merely an attempt to offer typical examples of this method.

I begin with Julius Wellhausen's discussion of the passage in his book on the composition of the Hexateuch (1876–77) because he builds on the work of earlier scholars yet gives new directions to the exegetical enterprise of his time. This is followed by an analysis of the interpretation of Rudolf Kittel (1900) who is in some ways an opponent of Wellhausen. Hugo Gressmann's exegesis (1921) represents the "comparative study of religions" approach, while Martin Noth's contribution (1943) is oriented toward redaction criticism. James Montgomery's commentary (1951) reflects and synthesizes earlier interpretations. The recent, almost monographical exegeses of Ernst Würthwein (1967) and of Alexander Rofé (1976) conclude my review.

In the review of each scholar's exegesis I describe, as fully as the limits of this essay allow, its method, character, and results. In many cases I quote extensively, so as to let the exegetes speak at crucial turns of their argument. The thrusts of their interpretations are usually summarized and set into their contemporary context. The title of each section indicates the major interest of the exegete; for the deceased scholars I draw also on scholarly appraisals of their contribution to scholarship.

In the epilogue I sketch broadly the major features of the seven interpretations of 1 Kings 22:1–38, relate them to each other and to three recent brief exegeses of the text which are addressed to wider, more general audiences, and raise some questions in the light of views recently expressed.

JULIUS WELLHAUSEN AND LITERARY CRITICISM

Wellhausen discussed 1 Kings 22 briefly yet in some detail in 1876–77 in the third edition of *Die Composition des Hexateuch* (282–4) /1/. In chap. 7 ("Judges, Samuel, and Kings") of his equally well-known *Prolegomena to the History of Ancient Israel,* originally published in German in 1878, he also touched on 1 Kings 22 (1957:180–294). I base my appraisal of Wellhausen's interpretation of 1 Kings 22 on these two sources.

The first characteristic feature is Wellhausen's comprehensive literary approach. Biblical texts are not discussed as independent units but are seen in their literary interrelation and as part of larger compositions. To be sure, many chapters in Judges, 1 and 2 Samuel and 1 and 2 Kings contain cross-references of a theological nature, which the reader cannot miss, such as the promise-fulfillment pattern (cf. 1 Kings 22:38 with 21:19). But Wellhausen analyzed the web of literary connections; he came to the conclusion that 1 Kings 22 is part of a series of similar stories: "Ahab's war with Benhadad (1 Kings 20 and 22) begins another series of stories. Three campaigns are described: the siege of Samaria (20:1–21); the defeat of the Syrians in the Plain of Aphek (20:22–34); and Ahab's death in the battle at Ramoth-Gilead (20:35–43; 22:1–38). Perspective and mood of 1 Kings 20 and 22 differ noticeably from those prevailing in chapters 17–19 and 21 . . . From the same author as 1 Kings 20 and 22 comes also 2 Kings 3 . . ." (1876–77:283–4).

It is of little interest here how exactly Wellhausen assigns the biblical texts; suffice it to point out that he does so on the basis of literary criteria in a broad sense. The questions he asked were: What presupposes what? What follows what? What stands in tension or is contradictory? What viewpoints, what sentiments are evident and appear consistently in a given group of texts? In what way do the answers to these questions both suggest the existence of narrative strands and' bring to the surface their peculiar features?

As far as 1 Kings 22 is concerned, Wellhausen saw in it "an original story about the relation of the prophets to the king" (1876–77:284). The great number of four hundred Yahweh prophets before Ahab (1 Kings 22:5, 6) is a feature which argues for the historicity of this particular tradition. Generally, Ahab is pictured sympathetically; he is presented as a "human being (20: 31) and as a man of stature (22:34–35), feared by the enemy more than an army (22:32), what he has accomplished is told, not what his character was like" (1876–77:284). The names of his two sons Ahaziah and Joram are compounded with the name of the God of Israel—indication that he was and remained a Yahweh worshipper, the erection of a Baal temple in Samaria for his Tyrian wife notwithstanding.

The second characteristic feature of Wellhausen's approach is based on the first. Once coherent series of narratives have been litcrarily isolated in the Books of Kings, they are related to one another. Now questions such as these are asked: Which one presupposes which? Which one follows which? Is there evidence that they are secondarily intertwined and fitted together? What can be said of the perspectives of their respective compilers, especially in relation to each other?

Thus Wellhausen compared a second and later string of stories, to which 1 Kings 17–19, 21 and 2 Kings 1–2 belong, with the first, earlier one, of which 1 Kings 20, 22 and 2 Kings 3 are a part. To quote him (1878:290–1):

> With the help of these other accounts, among which there is a considerable group of uniform characters (1 Kgs 20, 22, 2 Kgs 3, 4:24—7:20, 9:1—10:27) favorably distinguished from the rest, we are placed in a position to criticize the history of Elijah, and to reach a result which is very instructive for the history of the tradition, namely that the influence of the mighty prophet on his age has after all been appraised much too highly. His reputation could not be what it is but for the wide diffusion of Baal worship in Israel, which is quite exaggerated. Anything

like a suppression of the national religion at the time of Elijah is out of the question, and there is no truth in the statement that the prophets of Jehovah were entirely extirpated at the time and Elijah alone left surviving. The prophetic guilds at Bethel, Jericho, and Gilgal continued without any interruption. In Syrian wars prophets of Jehovah stand by the side of Ahab; before his last campaign there are four hundred of them collected in his capital, one of them at least long known to the king as a prophet of evil, but left alive before and left alive now, though he persisted in his disagreeable practices . . . the kings are the prominent figures, and do well and according to their office in battle: Elijah stands in the background.

The second set of stories, however, turns the history of Israel into a history of prophecy—indication of a later perspective. Again to quote Wellhausen (1878:293):

It may be said of this class of narratives generally, that the prophets are brought too much into the foreground in them, as if they had been even in their lifetime the principal force of Israelite history, and as if the influence which moved them had ruled and pervaded their age as well. This was not the case; in the eyes of their contemporaries they were completely overshadowed by the kings; only to later generations did they become the principal personages. They were important ideally, and influenced the future rather than the present; but this was not enough, a real tangible importance is attributed to them. In the time of Ahab and Jehu the Nebiim were a widespread body and organized in orders of their own, but were not highly respected; the average of them were miserable fellows who ate out of the king's hand and were treated with disdain by members of the leading classes.

Both series of stories were combined and produced a *sacred* history marked by the theological thrust commonly connected with "The Former Prophets." Thus Wellhausen argued that, "what in the common view appears to be the specific character of the Israelite history, and has chiefly led to its being called *sacred* history, rests for the most part on a later re-painting of the original picture" (1878:293), and concluded: "The prophets did not form the tradition at first, but came after, shedding upon it their peculiar light. Their interest in history was not so great that they felt it necessary to write it down; they only infused their own spirit into it subsequently" (1878:294).

This leads to the third characteristic feature of Wellhausen's approach. Once coherent series of stories have been identified and placed in relation to each other, the task of reconstructing Israel's history can be undertaken. Now questions such as these must be asked: In what way do the series of stories elucidate the history of Israel during and after the events to which they relate? How do they fit into the total picture of the historical evolution of ancient Israel? For what period are they the proper historical sources— for the period of the events told or for the period of the story-tellers?

Wellhausen argued that older stories, closer in time to the events to which they refer, are in a large measure historical and portray the actual events. The further removed from the event in time a story's composition was, the more it became a source for the outlook of the storytellers themselves. Furthermore, the younger stories overlaid the older ones to the point of superseding them (1878:281-82):

> Only so much of the old tradition has been preserved as those of the later age held to be of religious value: it has lost its original kind of gravity, and assumed an attitude which it certainly had not at first. It may have been the case in Judah that the temple was of more importance than the kingdom, but there can be no doubt that the history of Israel was not entirely, not even principally, the history of prophecy.

Wellhausen noted that older stories were fitted into the later outlook through expansions of the older stories. Thus he suggested that all of 1 Kings 22:38 is a later addition; it was inserted to illustrate the literal fulfillment of the threat of 1 Kings 21:19—not successfully, though, because 21:19 predicts that dogs will lick Ahab's blood in Jezreel on the field of Naboth, while 22:38 has the dogs lick the blood in Samaria (1876-77:283).

Of the latest passages such as 1 Kings 13, Judges 19—21 or 1 Samuel 7—8, Wellhausen said that they are of "historical worthlessness" (1878:285). The theological outlook of Chronicles is similar (1878:285):

> In the Books of Kings . . . the tradition is not systematically translated into the mode or view of the law, as is the case in Chronicles. What reminds us most strongly of Chronicles, is

the introduction from time to time of a prophet who expresses himself in the spirit of Deuteronomy and in the language of Jeremiah and Ezekiel, and then disappears. . . .

We cannot characterize Wellhausen's outlook as one of thoroughgoing historical skepticism; he analyzed the stories or the series of stories and by comparing them with one another sought to determine their usefulness as historical sources for either the period of the events or the time of the story teller. Once he had arrived at his judgment, he confidently used the texts as sources for the reconstruction of literary and historical processes.

Wellhausen's reconstruction of the history of ancient Israel is well-known and need not be discussed here /2/. Suffice it to stress that Wellhausen's basic insight "lex post prophetas" (the law is later than the prophets) was reached and undergirded by his literary-critical interpretation of the biblical texts. This is the way in which he understood his work; he characterized it once in a scholarly review with reference to the study of the Pentateuch in this way: "The problem is a literary one, hence must be solved by a literary approach, that is, the layers are compared with each other, and then are related to the events of Israel's history which are reliably known" /3/.

As far as 1 Kings 22 is concerned Wellhausen's interpretation amounts to this: A prophetical insertion such as 22:38 notwithstanding, the unit 22:1–38 is relatively early and historical. The passage contrasts with the later units which precede and follow it. As source for the reconstruction of Israel's history it shows how kings, not prophets, made history.

RUDOLF KITTEL AND DIVINE DECEPTION

In comparison to Wellhausen we enter another world in Rudolf Kittel's commentary on Kings, *Die Bücher der Könige* (1900), and in his later use of the biblical text as historical source for his historiography *Geschichte des Volkes Israel* (1925:253–56). To be sure, Kittel based himself on Wellhausen's insights. Thus 1 Kings 20 and 22 belong together and are different from the Elijah stories in 1 Kings 17–19, 21 and 2 Kings 1–2; and 1 Kings 22:38 is a deuteronomistic addition. But he does not pursue Wellhausen's

approach further /4/; his commentary shows that the moral issue
of Yahweh allowing his prophets to lie takes center stage; and in
his historiography he uses the biblical text as historical source in
an undifferentiated fashion.

First, we note that Kittel's exegesis of 1 Kings 22 is part of a
full-scale commentary. Thus he offers many observations and
comments on difficult forms or concepts. For our purpose his discussion (1900:162–63) of 1 Kings 20 and 22 as belonging together and as different from 1 Kings 17–19, 21 and 2 Kings 1–2
is important. His arguments (1900:163) are similar to those of
Wellhausen:

> Chapters 20, 22:1–38 cannot come from the author of 1 Kings
> 17–19, 21 . . . Even though Ahab's death is decreed by Yahweh
> and he therefore is bound to die, his death is not motivated
> with his guilt, neither through his Baal worship nor through his
> murder of Naboth. This shows that another spirit is at work
> here. The story comes from other than prophetic circles. It be-
> longs to the secular sphere, close to Ahab . . . Most of all, the
> picture of Ahab is very different in comparison to chapters 17–
> 19 and 21 . . . The author is evidently sympathetic toward
> Ahab; his fall is a dark fate decreed by Yahweh, and his heroic
> death secures for him the reader's sympathy in spite of chap-
> ters 17–19 and 21.

This brings Kittel to the reliability of the text as source for the
reconstruction of history. He argues (1900:163):

> The date of composition is hard to determine . . . In its original
> sections the story must have been written by a well-informed
> man, hence it may be close to the events it relates . . . the time
> around 800 B.C. likely is the date of its composition . . . The
> place must be Ephraim; content, interests and attitude suggest
> this. . . .

Kittel's reconstruction of ancient Israel's history for "Ahab's
Wars with Damasq and Assur" in *Geschichte* (1925:253–56)
shows that he uses 1 Kings 20 and 22, along with Assyrian records, more or less as they stand as historical sources. Kittel saw
himself primarily as a historian; his work with the text (and as
those who owe to his initiative one of the standard scholarly edi-
tions of the Hebrew Scriptures, we are not in danger of minimizing
his textual achievements) was the basis for his historical work.

Hempel stresses this when he states in his eulogy of Kittel: "the text-critical work was only part of his life's work, a part especially close to his heart and full of importance for the future . . ." /5/.

This brings us to the second aspect of Kittel's exegesis: its historiographical goal. His commentary deals at length with the offer of "the spirit," made in the heavenly council before Yahweh, to become a spirit of deception in the mouth of Ahab's prophets. Yahweh's acceptance of the stratagem poses a serious moral problem: Is the God of Israel a liar?

In his discussion of that troubling question Kittel first points out that the spirit is here neither a human property or quality (as in 1 Kings 21:5) nor an aspect of the divine manifest, for instance, in prophetic activity (as in 1 Sam 10:10). Rather, "the spirit" is one of the heavenly beings who make up the heavenly council. It is personified, reminiscent of the personification of wisdom in Proverbs 8.

Kittel notes that it is strange that God wills this spirit to become a spirit of deception within human beings (1900:175):

> There is no doubt that the character of Yahweh was for the consciousness of the older Israelite period not free from features which do not fit a personality who acts according to moral principles only. On the other hand, it is not the opinion of ancient Israel that he never does anything which would not be acceptable among human beings. Wherever something like this is actually said (compare Num 23:19 or 1 Sam 15:29), one can always find by way of balance statements to the contrary, which show that one deals here only with *one* aspect of the matter, with *one* way of looking at it, but not with a comprehensive picture of the older Israelite religious consciousness.

Kittel points out that we would at best tolerate a divine acceptance of harmful human actions; in this biblical text, however, harmful human actions are the result of divine initiative and activity (1900:175–6):

> The God of Israel acts according to the principle of the ancient world, "Him whom God wishes to destroy, he first deceives." Thus he also hardens Pharaoh so that he does not allow Israel to leave Egypt (Exod 4:21, 10:1), thus he not only permits that there is a quarrel between Abimelech and Shechem (Judg 9:10) or that Rehoboam gives a foolish answer to Israel (1

Kgs 12:15) and that David commits the sin of the census (2
Sam 24), but he himself wishes and effects all these directly.
He is the one who instigates David to sin in order to be able to
punish Israel (2 Sam 24:1) or he is the one who instigates Saul
against David (1 Sam 26:19).

This is the case also here as far as the deception of Ahab is
concerned. It is not enough to say that this is only a nontruth
(so Dillmann, *A.T. Theologie,* 305) but not really a lie; if God
knows that the salvation prophecy of the four hundred prophets
is not true, then he lets them lie; one must of course not over-
look that such statements (even though not quite as frequently
and with quite the same emphasis) are also made by writers
whose spiritual and moral understanding of God is otherwise
not in doubt (compare Isa 6:10, 19:14, Job 12:24–25), and
that both ways of looking at the matter stand one against the
other.

This brings Kittel to the heart of the matter. For him, religion
generally and the religion of ancient Israel specifically moves up-
ward to ever more spiritual levels. It leaves behind "the lower
order" without ever being able to free itself from it completely
(1900:176):

> Just as anthropomorphisms mixed into the language and into
> the fabric of daily life are not the full expression of the under-
> standing of the divine, because they always accompany the lan-
> guage of deep religious feeling, so also statements about God
> hardening people or instigating them to do evil can always be
> used with reference to God, comp. 2 Sam 16:10, a word which
> could be spoken still today.

> It is not fair to deduct from such a passage the notion that
> Yahweh was in earliest Israel seen as a nonspiritual nature
> being, arbitrary and directed by blind passion. Such elements
> occasionally still occur in the texts, but features of a different,
> a higher kind struggle with them. And even if the higher aspects
> come rarely to expression in our naively popular stories, it is
> enough to know that they are present. That which is higher
> and religiously more important, weighs much more heavily; it
> shows that religion, even though it cannot free itself from
> statements of a lower order (no religion is really able to do
> that), is still seriously on the way to a purer view of the divine.

Thus for Kittel exegesis serves to underscore his understanding
of religious history as the never-ending movement from a lower

order to a higher, purer view of the divine. He interprets the image of Yahweh as liar in 1 Kings 22 as an episode in that movement /6/.

HUGO GRESSMANN AND ADVANCE IN THE HISTORY OF PROPHECY

In 1921 the second edition of Gressmann's commentary on Israel's early historiography "from Samuel to Amos and Hosea" was published: *Die älteste Geschichtsschreibung und Prophetie Israels.* It appeared in a nontechnical yet scholarly commentary series edited by such pioneers of the form critical and the comparative religion approach as Hermann Gunkel and Hugo Gressmann. The title of the series is instructive: The Writings of the Old Testament—Selected Portions Newly Translated and Explained for the Present.

Its format is appealing. The biblical texts were translated into a flowing German that sought to reflect broadly the Hebrew style; the results of textual criticism are incorporated and marked as such, the passages are given a heading and arranged in roughly chronological fashion, and each explanation has approximately the same length as the biblical passage it interprets /7/.

In the interpretation of 1 Kings 22 Gressmann begins by setting Ahab's battles with the Arameans (1 Kings 20 and 22) into the historical context of the rise of Assyria at the beginning of the ninth century B.C.E. He exploits the text as historical information: "Even though we here (i.e., in 1 Kings 20) deal with a saga, we gain from it an excellent idea of the historical circumstances of the period; the Assyrian records, on the other hand, are not as trustworthy" (278).

Gressmann follows earlier interpreters in isolating 1 Kings 20 and 22 from the preceding, intervening, and following Elijah stories; he argues that the portrait of Ahab in 1 Kings 20 and 22 is a positive one but "later storytellers have diminished the fame of Ahab by increasing that of Yahweh" (278). Chap. 22, however, he perceives to be literarily of one cast and to be a reliable basis for the reconstruction of the issue then at stake: the clash between the salvation prophets and the prophets of doom. Al-

ready Elijah stood in spiritual opposition to his colleagues; the
rift between the two groups widened until it led to outright separation in Amos' time (Amos 7:14).

Gressmann describes the two groups in this way (279):

> The *salvation prophets* are the great mass of the prophetic
> guilds and thus are out-of-date. Since they live off the king's
> table, they prophesy for him success and say what the king
> would like to hear (Mic 3:5). They have very shortsighted,
> patriotic viewpoints and pile salvation oracles onto Israel while
> keeping the threats for the enemies. They are not original at
> all; one proclaims what the other one says; in fact, they steal
> each others' words (Jer 23:30).

> The *doom prophets,* on the other hand are, as Micaiah, the
> exception. With them the history of prophecy advances. They
> are in Yahweh's pay but not in that of an earthly king; they
> proclaim what Yahweh is saying to them. Their criteria are the
> canons of morality, according to which they measure also
> Israel. If it acts not in keeping with the demands of Yahweh,
> these prophets are not afraid even to condemn their own people
> and to threaten it like the Gentiles with doom. The great
> prophets belong to this group, whose unique character has made
> them known beyond their time and place.

Gressmann goes on to explore how concretely Micaiah ben
Imlah makes the claim that his prophecy supersedes and explains
the opposing voice of the four hundred Yahweh prophets. It is
because he has witnessed the heavenly council meeting that he is
able to know what is to come over King Ahab. "What a mighty
feeling of exaltation must have gotten hold of . . . men who could
say this of themselves!" (280) The interpreter Gressmann continues (280):

> While Isaiah masterfully describes the majestic distance of
> the Holy God in the words of Isaiah 6, here the scene is pic-
> tured in precious naiveté, a naiveté we should not spoil by
> moral considerations. . . .

> How does "the spirit of deception" reach his aim? The fine
> point of the story is recognized only when v 15 is read in its
> original text. Micaiah, who knows of the whole plan and now
> tells it to the king, must of course say the truth since he has
> earlier promised it under oath to the messenger who fetched

him (v 14). It seems that the oracle is three times (vv 6, 12, 15) repeated in the same way, and yet there is a small change which is very important.

> The additional phrase "you will have success" is missing in v 6 and (probably originally) also in v 15. To the question, "Shall I go against Ramoth Gilead?" the salvation prophets answer immediately (and this is later repeated by Micaiah) with, "Go, Yahweh will give it into the hand of the king!" *But this oracle is ambiguous* because one could just as well think of the king of the Arameans (that's the way it is to be understood!) as of the king of Israel. The best known parallel of the story is the Delphic oracle to Croesus, "When you cross the Halys, you will destroy a great kingdom!"

Gressmann's interpretation of the (reconstructed) oracle of the salvation prophets as ambiguous and of their words as objectively true allows him to conclude his exegesis in a convincing way (280):

> Yahweh and his prophet Micaiah thus have said the truth. Also the oracle which the prophets of salvation proclaimed was objectively correct. But because they were seduced by the spirit of deception, they have perverted its true meaning and so subjectively falsified it (v 12). Into the deepest secrets, however, only Micaiah has entered, and the continuation of the story confirms the report of this vision as without doubt true. Ahab let himself be deceived to fight against Ramoth, he was killed in action in spite of the precautions he took, and lost the city to the Arameans.

Gressmann's interpretation of 1 Kings 22:1–38 is impressive /8/. It is rounded and persuasively relates the two opposing human parties to each other—*sub specie Dei,* so to speak. The story is treated as essentially historical. It throws light on a stage in the history of prophecy, a stage halfway between Elijah and Amos.

Second, Gressmann's exegesis is already somewhat form-critically oriented. He does not pursue the identification of 1 Kings 20 as saga, nor does he really attempt to characterize 1 Kings 22 form critically. He says that the study of literary or oral patterns is still in its incipient stages (vi). He is interested in folkloristic parallels; his reference to the Delphic oracle is a case in point.

Third, the folkloristic interest reflects Gressmann's primary concern with the comparative study of religions, with *Religionsgeschichte*. Nevertheless, in 1 Kings 22 the internal development of Israelite prophecy is the topic, and Gressmann does not relate this phase of Israelite prophecy to comparable phenomena outside ancient Israel.

As for Kittel so also for Gressmann the interpretation of 1 Kings 22 highlights the exegete's evolutionary understanding of religious history. Thus he discusses the internal development of Israelite prophecy in categories such as traditional/original, out-of-date/up-to-date, stagnant/progressive, collective/individual, amoral/moral, and national/international. The second element of each pair eventually supersedes the first. Gressmann here clearly and openly reflects both his own and his educated readers' sentiments.

MARTIN NOTH AND THE DEUTERONOMIST

Noth's study of Joshua-Kings *Überlieferungsgeschichtliche Studien* (1943:3–110), deals briefly with 1 Kings 22. It does so redaction critically, that is, the sources are discussed and then their use by the Deuteronomist is extensively explored. Noth also discusses our text in his book on the history of Israel, *Geschichte Israels* (1956).

Noth argues that Joshua-Kings is a literarily and theologically unified piece of history writing by the exilic Deuteronomist. The work is recognized primarily by the simple, yet typical style of the redactional passages, by its comprehensive disposition, by the speeches put into the mouth of main figures, and by its brief or extensive editorials. These formal criteria are supplemented by an obvious theological feature: the philosophy of history evident especially in the speeches and the editorials. The formal and material frame of reference has allowed the Deuteronomist to bring together and to fuse a great many, varying traditions (1943:11–12):

> The Deuteronomist was not only a "redactor," but the author
> of a historiographical work. He brought together the inherited,
> rather different and differing traditions and arranged them ac-

cording to a well conceived plan. Usually he simply quoted the
sources available to him, but did so by connecting them through
his redactional passages. At times he made a reflected selection
from the sources available to him . . . The composition of the
work is thus readily understandable; its closest parallels are the
hellenistic and Roman historiographers who, using mostly
anonymous older traditions, wrote the history not of their own
but of long past times.

In the context of this redaction-critical study, what are Noth's
observations in relation to 1 Kings 22? In keeping with his approach Noth comments first on the kind of sources available to
the Deuteronomist for the treatment of the period of the monarchy: "In his presentation of the period of the monarchy the
Deuteronomist has incorporated to a large extent stories about
prophets. Here the prophets as 'men of God' appear usually as
opponents of the king—and this is the way in which the Deuteronomist wished to present them. They are the ones who starkly
confront the rulers who have fallen away or are in the process of
falling away from God, with the word and the will of God" (1943:
78). Noth here briefly discusses the clusters of the Elijah and of
the Elisha stories, also the Isaiah stories and the tradition(s) of
Ahiah of Shiloh. Then he refers to the story of the prophet
Micaiah ben Imlah and of the fulfillment of his prophetic word
directed to King Ahab in 1 Kings 22:2b–37. This story is now
connected with 1 Kings 20 through the opening words 22:1–2a.
However, 1 Kings 20 and 1 Kings 22 did not originally belong
together; 1 Kings 20 is all too different from 1 Kings 22. In 1
Kings 20 a series of prophetic anecdotes are collected and fitted
into the historical frame of the Aramean wars of King Ahab; the
names of the different "prophets," "men of God," and "disciples
of the prophets" are not given. It is quite different in 1 Kings 22.
The internally coherent story of Micaiah ben Imlah was secondarily prefaced by a collection of several smaller, different prophetic
stories which accompany a part of the history of King Ahab's
Aramean wars. At any rate, the Deuteronomist found 1 Kings 20
and 22 already fused in his sources (1943:79–80). Noth assumes
"prophetic stories" as sources for 1 Kings 20 and 22, in relation
to which historical narratives such as the Aramean war reports are

secondary; they were formulated with the prophetic scenes in mind.

On the other hand, it was probably the Deuteronomist who combined the Elijah cycle with "the Ahab and the prophets" cycle of 1 Kings 20 and 22 (1943:82–83):

> The Deuteronomist has put the Elijah story of Naboth's vineyard with the announcement of the death of Ahab (1 Kgs 21) immediately before chap. 22; then he had to move chap. 20 before chap. 21, and so put it within the Elijah cycle. (Footnote: The Septuagint has also here secondarily changed the order which the Deuteronomist had chosen intentionally; the Septuagint has connected the Elijah stories by putting chaps. 17— 19 immediately before chap. 21 . . . .)
>
> In chap. 21 the Deuteronomist has added to the announcement of the death of Ahab (v 19) in vv 21, 22, 24 and 26 of his own accord additional words which, beyond the personal fate of Ahab, take into account the fate of his dynasty. He speaks of it, as in 16:4, by using phrases that he has taken over from the Ahiah story in 1 Kgs 14:10–11. He saw Ahab (compare vv 25–26) as symptom of steadily increasing apostasy. After the prophetic story 22:1–38 there follows immediately in 22:39– 40 the closing formula for Ahab.

Thus the sandwiching of 1 Kings 20 and 22 into the Elijah cycle is probably the work of the Deuteronomist. In this case he formulated 22:38 (RSV), "And they washed the chariot by the pool of Samaria, and the dogs licked up his blood, and the harlots washed themselves in it, according to the word of the Lord which he had spoken," in order to connect it as fulfillment to Elijah's prophetic announcement in 21:19b (RSV), "Thus says the Lord, 'In the place where dogs licked up the blood of Naboth shall dogs lick your own blood.' " On the other hand, Noth also considers the possibility that 22:38 is older and so predeuteronomistic; in this case "one has to assume that the narratives of 1 Kings 20 and 22 were connected with the Elijah stories already before the Deuteronomist" (1943: 83, n. 3).

In conclusion we note first the redactional horizon of Noth's approach. The notion of a deuteronomistic redaction was already known and especially 1 Kings 22:38 credited to it. In this respect

Noth has not pushed the discussion further. What he did bring to the surface was the Deuteronomist's prophetic element with its unique outlook which lets the redactor select and annotate inherited prophetical stories.

Second, Noth views 1 Kings 22:2b–37 as literarily of one cast and as "a prophetical story." He does not pursue the genre form critically; from his references to it in his history of Israel it is evident that he does not employ it directly as historical source. With reference to the age of Omri and Ahab he says (1956:215–16):

> The Israelite kings of Omri's dynasty set themselves ambitious goals, in pursuit of which they put an end to the small scale disagreements with their Judean neighbors . . . This brought the littler Kingdom of Judah into a certain dependence upon the well-led Kingdom of Israel . . . The prophetical story 1 Kings 22:2–38 shows us the Judean king as ally of the Israelite king in a campaign against Ramoth-Gilead, a city of importance only for the King of Israel . . . .

In a footnote Noth points out that he is not certain whether the Deuteronomist has assigned to this tradition its correct historical place because "in the original text of the narrative the names of the kings did not appear" (1956:216, n. 1). He later returns to these stories and comes to the conclusion that "a definite historical interpretation of what is told there is no longer possible" (1956: 222). Noth's unfinished commentary on 1 Kings shows how he interpreted, tradition critically, the sources and the redaction of the deuteronomistic work. He died when he had completed the exegesis of 1 Kings 16; thus we do not have his interpretation of 1 Kings 22.

Third, Noth's brief redactional discussion of 1 Kings 22 does not permit an answer to the question as to how Noth would have explained Yahweh's action, permitting "the spirit" to become a spirit of deception in the mouths of the four hundred prophets— an issue that greatly concerned Kittel and which Gressmann also discussed.

Through Noth's redactional study the hermeneutic focus moves from the individual text unit to its literary context, in this case, to the Deuteronomist's work. The two generations since Wellhausen had concentrated on the individual texts; Noth analyzed the metamorphosis that integrated individual texts into larger literary contexts. More than Wellhausen he is a historian of literature, concerned with the reconstruction of a text's transmission /9/.

JAMES MONTGOMERY AND THE PROPHETICAL STORY

Easily the best known commentary series in English is The International Critical Commentary. It stands as the monument of the exegetical achievement of literary-critical biblical exegesis. For 1 Kings 22 we have the relatively recent *A Critical and Exegetical Commentary on the Book of Kings,* written by James A. Montgomery before 1944 and edited for publication in 1951 by Henry Snyder Gehman. We include its discussion of 1 Kings 22 in this review.

Montgomery explores the question of the sources of the Books of Kings. After setting this historiography into its ancient Near Eastern context (par. 12; 24–30), the author discusses in par. 13 "The Chronicles" (30–38), in par. 14 "The Historical Story" (38–41), in par. 15 "The Compilation" (42–45), and then very extensively "The Chronology" (par. 16; 45–64).

In the paragraph on "The Historical Story" Montgomery discusses two kinds of sources: (a) political narratives (38–39) and (b) the stories of the prophets (39–41). Pride of place among them is taken by the Elijah cycle, followed by the Elisha stories. He characterizes the story of Jehu's revolt (2 Kings 9—10) as the most striking story in this (the Elisha) cycle; it is "brilliant political narrative" (41). He continues (41):

> Within this complex are inserted, with historical justification, two brilliant stories, connected with otherwise unknown prophets: the history of the rout of Ben-Hadad at Aphek (I.20), in which figures an unknown "prophet" or "man of God," along with "sons of the prophets" (vv 13.28.35); and (chap. 22) the dramatic scene of the contest of the lone prophet Micaiah (cf 19:10) with four hundred prophets. . . .

Montgomery concludes that "thus we possess a continuous series of prophetical documents . . . extending from I.17 to II.10"; but "the remaining prophetical stories of the North are midrash in the current sense of the word, of dubious historical value" (41).

For Montgomery the biblical story of 1 Kings 22:1–38 is of great value as historical source. He compares it with 1 Kings 18 and says (336):

> The dramatic story is matched only by that of Elijah's contest with the Baal prophets on Carmel, as rich as that in its detail, but superior in its historical verisimilitude. The appearance of an otherwise unknown Micaiah vouches for the originality of the story . . . .

Montgomery's concern with historicity is evident. He is interested, to be sure, in the history of the prophetic movement. 1 Kings 22 becomes for him "evidence of a wider range of literary composition among the sons of the prophets than might have been expected"; thus the story is "a true precedent of the visions in Amos 1—2, Isaiah 6 and warns modern study against finding too sharp a distinction from 'The Writing Prophets' " (336).

Since Montgomery exploits the story directly for the reconstruction of history, he posits as historical reality what well may have been the deuteronomistic redactor's view. Thus the four hundred prophets of 1 Kings 22 "are distinctly YHWH's devotees, representing the state religion; according to the sequel of chap. 18 the Baal prophets had been exterminated" (337). Similarly Jehoshaphat's distrustful enquiry as to whether there is not another Yahweh prophet may well have been indication that the Judean king was "suspicious of the extravagant development of prophecy in the North, unlike the simpler religion of the conservative South; the North was peculiarly exposed to the frenzied religionism of Phoenicia and Syria" (337).

In keeping with the comprehensive exegetical coverage demanded of a large-scale commentary, Montgomery briefly discusses various issues to which earlier interpreters had been sensitive. For instance, on the problem of Yahweh allowing—in fact, ordering—the deception of a human being, he comments: "The theology is primitive indeed . . . theological criticism may well be temperate. Israel's developing religion faced the dilemma of all monotheism, as between the all-mightiness and the virtue of Deity" (339).

Montgomery's commentary marks the point which the interpretation of 1 Kings 22:1–38 had generally reached in his time. The

story is taken as reliable historical source; it is literarily of one
cast, an occasional addition such as 22:38 with reference to 21:19
notwithstanding. The redaction-critical question, which Noth was
raising at the same time, is implicitly recognized by Montgomery
in his brief discussions of the compiler (42–45) but does not
affect his interpretation of 1 Kings 22.

ERNST WÜRTHWEIN AND THE CRITERION OF THE PROPHECY

Würthwein contributed an analysis of 1 Kings 22 to the Rost
Festschrift, "Zur Komposition von I Reg 22 1–38" (1967). He
sets himself the task of examining whether the text is literarily of
one cast, and should the unit prove to be literarily composite, of
exploring the character of its composition.

Würthwein notes that, on the whole, scholarship has viewed the
unit as literarily of one cast, not reckoning such clear deuteronomistic additions as vv 1, 2a, 28b, 35bB and 38. He mentions a
few exceptions, such as the 1964 (first) edition of Gray's commentary where the possibility of literary compositeness is briefly
mentioned but not further pursued (Gray: 395) and the earlier
discussions of the secondary character of vv 19–25/10–13 by
Schwally and of vv 19–23 as later interpolation by Volz (20–21).
But Würthwein notes that the possibility of literary compositeness
of the unit has never been consistently explored; the results of his
analysis suggest to him that 1 Kings 22:2b–37 is indeed composite,
that it cannot be considered a historical narrative, and that the
layers of the unit strikingly highlight the continued search for the
criterion of true prophecy.

What is Würthwein's literary analysis? He notes that vv 2b–4
and vv 29–37 are literarily a consistent unit and of one cast in
content, while the intervening verses 5–28 interrupt that story.
Hence he discusses first only vv 2b–4/29–37 and notes that its
outlook militates against the view that it is a historical narrative
pure and simple (248):

> The main motif is rather that he who wants to save himself by
> deception will perish, while the one endangered by the decep-
> tion saves his life. In other words, this is the motif of the de-

ceived deceiver. It has been argued, to be sure, that the story
extols Ahab's valor and perseverance until death. In other
words, that the story shows him in a very positive light in
comparison to the Elijah story and the judgment of the
Deuteronomists. I think that this is a misunderstanding. The
king does not stay of his own accord in battle but merely because in the battle tumult his charioteer is unable to carry out
his master's order to take him out of combat. Furthermore,
such a positive view of Ahab ignores that the king is really dis-
loyal to his comrade-in-arms because he must have foreseen
that this stratagem endangers the King of Judah. Finally, the
stratagem shows him rather as coward than as hero.

Thus Würthwein can characterize the story as negatively dis-
posed toward the king of Israel. It is told from a Judean viewpoint
and reflects the historically accurate memory that at one time the
Judean kings were vassals of the kings of Israel and obliged to
accept their orders—ancient Oriental vassal treaties give ample
evidence that such was the duty of the vassal. This also explains
why King Jehoshaphat of Judah accepted without protest the
order of the king of Israel to go into battle in his royal robes while
the overlord disguised himself; as vassal he had no choice but to
do as bidden. Würthwein concludes his discussion of the ancient
story in this way (249):

> Certainly such stories were told in Judah with great delight to
> the detriment of the kings of Israel. As far as the form is con-
> cerned, it is a saga with a fairy-tale motif. Historical conclu-
> sions can of course be drawn from it only in relation to its
> general setting. It is no accident that the king of Israel is never
> mentioned by name. What is told here is not typical for just one
> king of Israel, but for the type "king of Israel," seen from a
> Judean perspective.

This leaves "the Micaiah story" (vv 5–28) to be considered.
It is set into the Jehoshaphat-King Ahab's vassal story and is itself not of one cast. Rather than reproducing in detail Würthwein's
argumentation, I abstract his summary of the analysis (251–52).
There are three successive layers: The oldest layer is vv 5–9,
13–17 (18?), 26–28; the second layer comprises vv 10–12 and vv
24–25; while the final component is vv 19–22 (with v 23 as a
transitional verse added later). Each of these three layers is in-

ternally consistent, but the second and the third are dependent on those that precede them.

The oldest layer is quite extensive and a fully developed story. It contrasts four hundred court prophets with the one prophet Micaiah ben Imlah whom the king has put into prison until he returns safely—an event which the prophet affirms will not happen. "Evidently the rule formulated in Deut 18:22 is thought to obtain here: 'When a prophet speaks in the name of the Lord, if the word does not come to pass . . . , that is a word which the Lord has not spoken.'" Würthwein quotes von Rad who said in a commentary on the passage: "Is it really to be assumed that in a serious case the question of the legitimacy of a prophet could be left in suspense until it was eventually evident whether his announcement had come true?" (89). Würthwein continues (252):

> Well, here in 1 Kings 22 it really remains in suspense until the prophet of doom is proven right or wrong. This means that for the purpose for which the inquiry was originally made of the prophet, it has lost all meaning. In other words, this is a literary creation which is far removed from historical reality, that is, far from the inquiry of the prophet as practiced in ancient times in holy war and which at that time had decisive significance for the situation itself.

Thus the oldest version of the Micaiah story contrasts the prophecy of the success of the king, uttered by the four hundred anonymous Yahweh prophets without express recourse to a divine revelation, with the doom prophecy of the single and named prophet, uttered with express recourse to the divine revelation as its source.

The old Micaiah story is expanded in vv 10–12 and vv 24–25 through the introduction of an individual and named counterpart of Micaiah, namely Zedekiah ben Chenaanah. Both were prophets of Yahweh, as the names indicate. Now the possession of the spirit appears as the criterion of the prophet: he who has the spirit is the true prophet. Micaiah agrees, as his answer to Zedekiah in v 25 implies: he who really has the spirit will be recognized when in the future evil shall befall Zedekiah. The true prophet as possessed by the spirit is recognized by the coming true of that which is announced.

It is striking that this second layer assumes the coming disaster to be more inclusive than the first layer. There it is only the king who dies while the people survive and will be safe (17); here only one member of the people, Zedekiah, will flee from room to room to escape (v 25).

Also vv 10–12 and especially Zedekiah's role portrayed there are secondary in relation to vv 5–9, both literarily and in content. In short, the first expansion of the Micaiah story is the second layer; there (252)

> Zedekiah ben Chanaanah is introduced and thus opportunity given to characterize the ecstatic behavior of the salvation prophets. They are subordinate to a leader who, possessed by the spirit, utters the lead word for their proclamation . . . An individual message is not proclaimed by them. Furthermore [v 24] makes clear that they claim the possession of the spirit for their activity. All this not only characterizes this particular situation but these prophets generally.

Würthwein argues that the third layer (vv 19–22), the expansion of the first expansion, deals with the prophetic claim of the possession of the spirit. It differs from the first expansion in that there false prophecy is due to not having the spirit (v 24), while here it is due to being inspired by a spirit of deception (vv 20–22) /10/. Würthwein concludes (252):

> The main question is how the salvation prophets can claim the possession of the spirit. It is answered in an extraordinarily bold fashion: Yes, they have the spirit, but it has been turned in their mouth into a spirit of deception, and this by the will of Yahweh. He wants to destroy and for that he employs deception as the tool. These are statements which go to the limit of what is acceptable for the belief in Yahweh. They reveal the extraordinary gravity of the problem of the salvation prophets which weighed heavily on Israel and was discussed, especially in the later period, time and again (Jer 23:9–32; 28–29; Ezek 12:21—13:23, and after the fall of the kingdom in Lam 2:14—4:13).

This brings Würthwein's analysis to its conclusion. He denies that the unit 22:5–28 is a real prophetical narrative. Rather we have here "the debates of the problem of the true and false prophet put into narrative form, in which the struggle to find the proper criteria becomes evident" (253). What is historical is the appearance of different and, in their announcements, contradictory prophets and the problem that this poses. In the youngest layer, "the claim to spirit possession is led *ad absurdum*" (253)—an insight which agrees with Volz's observation that the great pre-exilic prophets were negative toward the spirit and when talking about themselves never mention it as their authentication /16/.

Finally, Würthwein notes that the Micaiah story was set into the Jehoshaphat-Ahab story as its frame, without introducing there a reference to the fact that Micaiah's word did come true (253):

> That this did not happen seems to me a further argument that in [vv 5–28] we do not deal with a real prophetical *narrative* but that these verses are completely focused on the unmastered problem of the confrontation of the prophets of salvation with the prophets of doom and of the struggle for an answer to the questions as to what constitutes the true prophet. It is not the person of Micaiah that is of interest, but he as a type of the true prophet.

In other words, "the exciting struggle concerning the problem of true and false prophecy unfolds itself before our eyes in the successive formulations of the issue" (254).

Würthwein is the first interpreter who consistently analyzes the internal literary character of 1 Kings 22:1–38. He comes to the conclusion that the passage is literarily composite and that the components can be isolated on literary grounds. He finds his analysis confirmed by the resulting coherent picture of the issue that gave birth and kept alive the tradition which eventually crystallized literarily in 1 Kings 22:1–38.

ALEXANDER ROFÉ AND 1 KINGS 22:1–38 AS EXAMPLE STORY

The last interpretation we consider is entitled "The Story of Micaiah ben Imlah and the Question of the Genres of the Prophetical Stories" (Hebrew), written by Alexander Rofé and published in *Reflections on the Bible* (1976:233–44) /12/. Rofé stands broadly within the hermeneutic tradition with which I am here concerned; two of his earlier articles deal with related matters and indicate this too (1970, 1974).

Rofé's paper is divided into two parts: a general discussion of interpretive principles in relation to prophetical stories, and a specific interpretation of 1 Kings 22:1–38. In the general part he briefly refers to two principles inherent in historical research on biblical stories: (1) The date of the story's composition is not known; it may have been written immediately after the event to which it refers, it may also have been written a shorter or a longer period afterward; (2) the story must be assumed to be historical, but the variety of genres of historical traditions must be kept in mind when the story is exploited for historical reconstruction. Today's biblical historian must first ask: What is the genre of the story and of what kind are the sources used in the story? Then he must reflect on the use he as biblical historian can make of the biblical story.

Rofé outlines the four types of prophet stories: legend, historiography, biography, and parable/paradigm. He briefly comments on each, stressing that legend and historiography are the older types.

While the legend has a sign character as story about a holy man, designed to evoke the people's admiration, historiography deals with events of public national character and is realistic in its approach (in this respect it is the opposite of the legend). It is concerned with the relation of events to each other and with their causes. Prophetic historiography is somewhat different in that it singles out "the word of the Lord" as the cause of history.

Biography and parable/paradigm are two younger genres. The biography is a realistic description of the prophet's life; it neither evokes admiration like the legend nor offers insight into causes and interrelations of events like historiography. Biography is interested in the person and the personality of the central figure; Jeremiah 28 or 37—38 are examples.

The parable does not relate to anything that happened. It is the least historical and the most philosophical of all the genres of prophet stories. The Book of Jonah is an example. Naturally, the first generations of disciples of a prophet told stories about their admired master (legends), but what could later generations of prophetic disciples do? "They philosophized about the character of prophecy and clothed their reflections in the form of parabolic stories!" (236).

Rofé describes the paradigm as the sister of the parable. He adopts Aristotle's suggestion (*Rhetoric*) that while the parable invents the story or recasts a traditional story, the paradigm makes use of a historical tradition, real or thought to be real. Thus Nathan's story of the poor man's lamb (2 Sam 12:1b-4) is a parable, but David's reference to Abimelech's death (2 Sam 11:21) is a paradigm—that is, a historical tradition introduced and recast so as to teach a lesson.

This brings the first part of the paper to a close; Rofé suggests that 1 Kings 22:1-38 be seen as a late paradigm, composed by disciples of the classical prophets.

In the second section of the paper Rofé explores 1 Kings 22:1-38 in the light of this identification. The question of literary layers, basic for Würthwein's analysis, is touched upon incidentally; thus Rofé thinks that vv 17-18 are a secondary addition by an early reader who wished to eliminate the "satanic" character of Yahweh's deception of Ahab. He thinks that the rest of the story is of one cast, yet is not without difficulties.

One serious difficulty is Jehoshaphat's dissatisfaction with the four hundred prophets. He notes that already early rabbinic interpreters tried to cope with this problem, but the difficulty remains: What is the difference between them and Micaiah (239)?

> Micaiah himself insists on the fundamental difference between him and the four hundred. He, Micaiah, has seen and heard in the heavenly council (v 19 . . .), he has participated in it as a witness, and now he leaks information on highest authority . . . On the other hand, the four hundred have not been there. They only received "spirit" who proceeds from there and in whose power they prophesy. Zedekiah ben Chenaanah, as he approaches and strikes Micaiah, merely confirms in his own words that he prophesies in the power of the spirit (v 24 . . .), but is naively persuaded that all prophecy is mediated by the spirit.

Is then the difference one between two different sources of prophetic speaking? Yes! On the one hand, there was collective prophecy, enthusiastic in nature; its revelations were music related, accompanied by song, dance, racing, frenzy and eventually disrobing. It is ultimately of Greek origin and is described in 1 Sam 10:5–13; 19:20–24. Rofé continues (240):

> Now it is clear to us why Jehoshaphat was not satisfied: he ob-
> served the enthusiastic prophets but did not believe them. Thus
> becomes evident what the storyteller wished to convey to us
> through the mouth of Micaiah: There are two grades of
> prophecy. The superior one is the one of the prophet who sees,
> hears and proclaims the word of the Lord. This sort of prophecy
> is trustworthy without a doubt. Less trustworthy is enthusiastic
> prophecy, the prophecy "in the spirit of the Lord." It is some-
> times true—not always is the spirit of the Lord a spirit of de-
> ception—but at other times it is misleading prophecy, as a
> means of deception which the Lord chooses to bring to fall
> whomever he wills. The story of Micaiah ben Imlah offers in-
> struction concerning the criteria for the evaluation of prophecy;
> thus it belongs to the genre of the parable or of the paradigm.

Rofé then compares his findings with what is known of the history of prophecy generally and of the authentication of the prophet specifically. He comes to the conclusion that the criteria of true prophecy were typical for classical prophecy, especially of Jeremiah's time, and not for the ninth and eighth century prophetic protest against Baal worship. The parallelism of Jeremiah's and Micaiah's roles and of those of their opponents is noteworthy. "These similarities are hardly accidental. It is obvious that the story of Micaiah ben Imlah is a didactic story from the heyday of classical prophecy and that it was composed under the impact of the words and of the personality of the prophet Jeremiah, maybe by a disciple of his, that is, in the 6th century B.C.E." (242).

Of course, the composer used historical traditions. But the details of the story cannot be exploited for the historical reconstruction of the period of Ahab. The office of the son of the king is an office known from the last period of the Kingdom of Judah, but the treaty between Ahab and Jehoshaphat, sealed by the intermarriage of the two royal families, and Ahab's attack on Ramoth-Gilead are historical.

In conclusion Rofé argues that since the story uses and recasts ancient historical traditions and is not composed freely to illustrate a principle, it is not a parable, but rather an example story, a paradigm. The dividing line between the two types is a fine one (243–44):

> The parables instruct by way of describing the erroneous action of the prophetic hero of the story, such as Jonah or "the Man of God" of 1 Kings 13, while the paradigms, since they are attached to a great historical personality of the past, present their hero as an example worthy of imitation; so the Abraham of Genesis 24, the Micaiah ben Imlah of 1 Kings 22, and the David of the outstanding paradigm of his duel with Goliath (1 Samuel 17).

If we now return to the original question of 1 Kings 22 as historical source, we must say that as paradigm it cannot be used for information about historical detail of the time of Ahab. But it is a first-rate source for the theology of classical prophecy. This observation marks the end of Rofé's essay.

Rofé does not base his exegesis on a thoroughgoing literary analysis. He takes the biblical text as a unity and sees its climax in vv 19–22, that is, in the very passage which Würthwein's literary analysis identified as the last (and, in a way, climactic) interpretation of the tradition. Würthwein's analysis comes broadly to the same result as Rofé's in relation to 1 Kings 22:19–22, but his more differentiated literary approach allows him to cast light on earlier forms of the ancient issue as well.

EPILOGUE: DISTANTIATION, DECONSTRUCTION, AND RECONSTRUCTION

Our review of the seven historical-critical interpretations shows that Wellhausen and Noth are primarily historians of oral and literary traditions; Kittel, Gressmann, and Montgomery are chroniclers of religious evolution; and Würthwein and Rofé are analysts of past theological debates. The degree of their hermeneutic sophistication determines how directly they use the text to accomplish their goals. In all cases their reading of the text is not an end in itself; it is a means to an end. This is obviously true of Wellhausen and Noth as literary historians and of Würthwein and Rofé as theological-historical analysts; it is also true of Kittel, Gressmann, and Montgomery as chroniclers of religious evolution, even though they perceive themselves and their audiences still to be involved in that evolution, insofar as their own religion is in some way based on earlier stages which they discern in the biblical texts and which they have now transcended. All these exegeses move into a positive but critical distance from the text, for the sake of literary deconstruction and literary and/or historical reconstruction.

The seven interpreters write for scholarly or at least well-educated audiences. They themselves hold positions in departments of Bible in universities and carry out the kind of exegetical work demanded in that setting. They do not need to state this explicitly; it is evident in the type of their publishing houses and of their commentary or monograph series, in their demanding and often highly technical style, in the assumed level of their readers' sophistication and formal education, and in the spirit both of detachment from and engagement in the ancient texts which binds readers and authors into a common enterprise. Here the scholars of the nineteenth and twentieth century Western university speak to one another, certainly not in any exclusive or arcane fashion, but on *their* level, in *their* categories of thought, and in the framework of *their* humanistic ideals. This constitutes the community to which they belong, whose members read and appreciate one another's publications and who support one another mentally, morally, and to a certain extent, financially.

On the other hand, these interpreters see themselves as servants and educators of society at large and are aware of the tensions which their mission may create. The pioneers of the "comparative study of religions" approach, Hugo Gressmann and Hermann Gunkel, were especially sensitive to this dimension of their work. Gressmann intends to bring the biblical stories close to his audience; his commentary does not turn the uninitiated away through "scholarly" language and technical analyses, nor does he become apologetic when text or interpretation may be objectionable to the readers. He makes his audience aware of the temporal-spatial gap between them and the world of the biblical stories, yet he tries to bridge this gap and to bring his readers to an intellectual-aesthetic appreciation of the ancient texts.

Thus Gressmann can speak of the "mighty feeling of exaltation

which must have enthused men" who could claim for themselves
to have stood in the heavenly council, and of the "delightful
naiveté" of the scene described in 1 Kings 22:19–22 (280). He
would have agreed with Gunkel who discussed the role of heightened literary forms in relation to religion in his book on the fairy
tale in the Old Testament. There Gunkel said (1917:6):

> Religion and poetry are by nature closely related to each other:
> religion at its heights seeks poetic expression, poetry finds in
> religion its most exalted themes. Thus the poetic narrative is
> more able than sober historiography to become the bearer of
> religious thought. The reader who finds such considerations ob-
> jectionable we counsel to close this booklet now—why does he
> wish to become angry? We others, though, remain persuaded
> that the claim that this or that story found in the Old Testa-
> ment has been invented, is not disrespectful or even a judgment
> of unbelief, but rather a judgment born of deeper insight and
> better taste.

Here exegesis is related to the level of sophistication of author
and reader. This level suggests the horizons, the frame of reference, and the degree of ability to cope with tensions. On the level
on which reader and author find each other, exegesis becomes
their conversation with the past and with each other. They strive
to grasp the past—their past—comprehensively, plausibly, and to
their satisfaction. If this enterprise clashes with the sentiments of
the readers who do not share the author's outlook, further communication is at this point not possible. The spurned interpreter
rests himself with his accepting and appreciative audience in the
persuasion that his and their judgment is based on *deeper* insight
and *better* taste. If the interpreter's work does not lead to intellectual and aesthetic advance of the audience, his approach and its
negative reception by some serve to redraw the lines which mark
two different constituencies.

This is confirmed by a glance at commentaries written for rank-
and-file readers and not for the biblical specialist. Here "apologetic" or "moral" considerations understandably call for comment
by the authors.

Thus J. Mauchline (374) notes that the four hundred prophets
were really not to be blamed; they had been seduced and so became mere tools in the execution of a heavenly plan:

That it should be said that God enticed Ahab to his doom and used prophets for the purpose, is evidence of *immature theology and an unethical conception of prophecy*. The exigencies of a monotheistic faith had made the one God the author of both good and evil in such a way that men ceased, in such a case as the one here, to be moral agents and became unwitting and, hence, inculpable instruments (italics added).

R. C. Dentan is more cautious in his value judgment yet straightforward in drawing a lesson from the text (69–70):

Especially interesting [is] . . . that false prophecies are not necessarily the result of a prophet's intention to deceive, but may come from a power outside himself—even from the Lord. The last is a possibility to which *we, as Christians, could hardly assent*, but *the problem* of explaining the fact of true and false prophecy and of distinguishing between them was undoubtedly a *serious one* to the ancient Hebrews *and, in a sense, remains so* . . . (italics added).

While no test for distinguishing them is infallible, the best is the one suggested by this story: a false prophet usually tells his audience what they *want* to hear, while a true prophet tells them what they *ought* to hear . . . (italics in original).

P. F. Ellis, in his contribution to a one-volume commentary on the whole Bible, does not move beyond sympathetic explanation of literary and philosophical aspects of the passage (197):

[1 Kings 22:] 19–23. The whole vision is a *literary artifice* to dramatize the dreadful message . . . 20–23. The personification of the lying spirit of the false prophets as an angel is Micaiah's way of showing that God is in complete control of events and that even man's lies come under his causality. The prophets did not philosophize about the causality of evil in relation to a good God. They simply accepted God as the ultimate cause of all things, good and evil.

These interpreters, mindful of the more church-oriented readership of one-volume or lay commentaries, consciously bridge the gap between the world of the biblical traditions and their intellectually or morally more confined constituencies. Mauchline does so on the basis of an evolutionary perspective similar to that of Kittel and Montgomery and so can speak of the "immature theol-

ogy" of the passage and its "unethical conception of prophecy."
Dentan solves the difficulty by contrasting "the ancient Hebrews"
with us "as Christians," while Ellis stands close to Noth, Würthwein, and Rofé in his characterization of 1 Kings 22:1–38 as "a
literary artifice to dramatize the dreadful message."

I conclude with an exploration of three related questions which
might be raised in relation to 1 Kings 22.

Is the positive but critical distancing, which characterizes the
seven historical-critical exegeses characteristic of this approach
only? A literary view might suggest that the narrator of 1 Kings 22
increases his distance from the prophet Micaiah. It is striking that
the seven interpreters I have discussed also distance themselves
from the text in order to interpret it. Is this coincidence? I suggest
that the distancing which a literary critic might observe in the
ancient narrator is a natural and expected interpretive stance,
when for reasons of time, space or conviction the narrator cannot
or will not identify with one of the actors in the story. The distancing allows the narrator to gain his own perspective, a viewpoint not identical with that of any of the actors in the story but
uniquely that of the narrator.

In other words, this distancing is the result of the narrator's
sense of both discontinuity in relation to the inherited tradition
and of engagement in it. Through this device the hearer achieves
his or her own standpoint in relation to the tradition and so becomes a respondent and a renarrator.

Thus the critical but positive distancing of modern exegetes is
consistent with an interpretive movement evident already in the
stance of the biblical storytellers. The modern interpreter, though,
seeks to be conscious of the adopted interpretive stance; this is a
difference in degree, not in approach in relation to the biblical
writers. The correspondence calls for exploration.

What happened when the story of Micaiah the prophet was written down for the first time and so became *literarily* fixed? Then it
became available to literate interpreters who claimed for themselves the right to read and respond, to interpret and retell it.
They could do this simply by reading the story (within or without
its literary context). This they did from *their* perspective, within

their horizons, and in the light of *their* questions. Unless we rule out all but one of the various readings of the story of the prophet Micaiah offered in the history of interpretation, the story must be understood as "polyvalent," that is, capable of different readings. Does this mean that each and every reading is acceptable? Or are there degrees of acceptability?

How is historical-critical interpretation related to the community out of which it rises? The nontraditional, at times iconoclastic character of historical-critical exegesis seems beholden to no constituency, especially when compared with rabbinic exegesis or traditional ecclesiastic interpretation which both are functions of clearly defined religious communities. This essay, however, has demonstrated that historical-critical exegesis is related to a community, however loosely defined. This community constitutes itself when author and reader meet and find each other. Their encounter is based on a broadly conceived dynamic-evolutionary and/or existentialist understanding of life. It occurs when the reader perceives the interpretation of an ancient text as illumination of a facet of past or present life. The reader's horizon is widened, his or her understanding of life deepened and his or her aesthetic appreciation heightened. The reader thus practices an expansive and impansive hermeneutic and is open toward the new which the encounter with the interpretive text brings, but is also confined by his or her horizons of perception.

On the other hand, a reader-respondent will not be able "to hear" a text interpretation which is offered within a different horizon, no matter how familiar the text itself may be to the reader; it will merely serve to reconfirm the reader's perspective. The statement of Gunkel quoted above supports this observation. However, if the horizon is different from the reader's but capable of being incorporated or dialectically related to his or her perspective, the two horizons may melt into each other or move into creative tension with each other. This will happen on a broad scale if the different horizons and their constituencies find themselves also socially in the situation where opening themselves to each other is not threatening anymore, to a degree that negates or endangers one's own persuasion.

NOTES

/1/ All quotations from non-English publications have been translated by the author.

/2/ For a discussion and appraisal of Wellhausen's literary-critical method and historical reconstruction see Perlitt: 153–243.

/3/ Quoted by Perlitt: 166, from Wellhausen's review in *Göttingische Gelehrte Anzeigen* 159 (1897): 614.

/4/ In fact, Johannes Hempel said of Rudolf Kittel that he was "Wellhausen's opponent" (78).

/5/ Hempel: 85. The eulogy concentrates first on R. Kittel's text-critical achievements (80–85), then on his historiography (85–90).

/6/ For a fuller appraisal of Rudolf Kittel's hermeneutic see Hempel: 85–90.

/7/ See Gressmann's introduction to the commentary (section 4) and comp. Sellin: xii.

/8/ Sellin (page xii) characterized Gressmann's interpretive work well when he said in his eulogy: "The burning desire to bring the sacred texts close to modern human beings through modern means and perspectives, is evident on every page. Obvious is also the loving care with which the author deals with the kind of naive religion which is mirrored in the texts and which was that of a people which was still in many ways primitive."

/9/ Noth's tradition-historical study of the Pentateuch, *A History of Pentateuchal Traditions* (1948), is consciously tradition-critical in approach; that is, Noth follows the transmission of a given tradition from its earliest recognizable form in oral lore all the way to its incorporation into the literary composition of the Pentateuch. See also Bernhard W. Anderson's introduction to his English translation of Noth's *A History of Pentateuchal Traditions,* for an appraisal of Noth's traditio-historical approach and its hermeneutic assumptions. He says by way of summary: "It appears that Noth stands between two worlds of scholarship. On the one hand, he is like Wellhausen in that he makes full use of the method of literary criticism and works primarily within the context of the Old Testament, though rejecting any simple developmental scheme. On the other hand, he is like Gunkel in that he builds upon form-critical analysis and emphasizes the creativity of the pre-literary period, though rejecting a romantic conception of history which fails to do justice to the uniqueness of Israel's historical experience" (xxii–xxiii).

/10/ Würthwein here adopts and quotes the argumentation of Volz, *Der Geist Gottes,* 20.

/11/ Würthwein refers to Volz, *Der Geist Gottes,* 62ff.

/12/ Professor Rofé of the Hebrew University kindly supplied me with an offprint when informed of the writer's projected essay.

Chapter 8

Micaiah ben Imlah: A Literary View

David Robertson

I

I would like to begin with a parable that I want to use to set my comments in a context that helps me, at least, make sense of what we are about in this volume. The parable will also help me to establish a framework for commenting on the two preceding essays, and will finally lead to the point where I can offer one kind of literary reading of the passage under discussion, that is, 1 Kings 22.

To begin with the parable: once upon a time a scientist invited a photographer to take some pictures by electron microscopy, and the photographer did so. The scientist took the pictures into his laboratory and inspected them for what information he could glean. After he was finished, the photographer came for the pictures and placed them in a museum, where people came to view them as art. It so happened that the scientist heard about the showing and also came. By chance, photographer and scientist began to discuss the question, "What are these photographs?" Are they scientific documents for laboratory use? Or are they works of art? They each gave their own point of view. They continued to discuss the issues long past the time when the rest of the people had gone home. Finally, having resolved nothing, they too retired for the evening.

I would like to make two comments on this parable. The first is that texts are always given in context, analogous to the laboratory and museum. Unfortunately, the contexts that are given with biblical texts are not so obvious. They are not structures built in time and space, and we do not have the feeling of going out of òne of them and over to another one. Nevertheless, they are always there. In scholarly discussions we have said time and again, let us consider the text in its *own* terms. In terms of my own parable, however, it is clear that such a statement has no rational meaning. No text has one meaning that is its own, or real, meaning, any more than the above mentioned photographs do. All texts are placed into contexts by readers and interpreters. Conclusions as to a text's own meaning are statements of our biases and, as such, may be very useful. At least they indicate to others our starting point.

If it is true that texts are always given in contexts like laboratories or galleries, then there is no difference between traditional interpretations and modern interpretations. It may seem to us that modern interpretations are freer and operate within a less restrictive system. But I suspect that this feeling on our part is illusory, and that future generations will point out to us precisely how restraints operate on us just as we find it fairly easy to point out how restraints operated on the rabbis. We may not be in exactly the same boat as the rabbis, but we are in another boat. It is not a question of not being in a boat.

And now for the second comment: I strongly suspect that the choice of a context by anyone of us is arational or prerational or the like, and that debates between ourselves over the choice of frames of reference are bound to be futile. Frames of reference are starting points from which we ask questions, compile evidence, and draw conclusions. Rational argument within the context of a frame of reference is meaningful, but the choice of the frameworks themselves, is, at least in my mind, not rational and negotiable. Imagine our artist and our scientist trying to decide what the photographs really are. I think in that case it is abundantly clear that they would not get anywhere. It is not a rationally arbitrable matter, as if at the end of all this debate they could say, "Ah ha! This is it!" Just as futile are our arguments over whether Deuteronomy is sacred Scripture, history, literature or the like.

So what are we doing when we discuss these issues, if we are not engaging in rational argument? I suspect that our discourse on these issues fits into a well-known, well-defined genre of speech, namely, witness or testimony; that is, we are really testifying to each other about our deepest convictions, and that is the reason why our talk so easily becomes impassioned and rhetorical, why we so easily resort simply to restating the case with greater and greater emphasis. This is not a criticism of what we are doing. I think that we do not have any choice in the matter and I think that it is very good that this is so. If we think that we are going to arbitrate these things rationally, we are liable to come away from interdisciplinary discussions rather frustrated, because nobody seems to have moved. If, however, we see what we are doing in different terms, that is, as *testifying,* then we do not expect to solve the issues; they are not resolvable. We can gain understanding, appreciation; we can experience at least in a surrogate sort of way what it is like thoroughly to put ourselves within frames of reference that are not our own, and that I find extraordinarily exciting. I find trying to see the Bible as the rabbis saw it fascinating and a great deal of fun. (I should note here that in some sense my conviction that frames of reference are not rationally arbitrable is in itself a kind of presupposition, a kind of frame of reference, and that therefore we have circles within circles within circles.)

II

Now, what I also have tried to do in these remarks is establish a context in which I can say something about the two preceding papers. It seems to me that Professor Roth's assembling these seven different interpretations is extremely helpful, because it is easy to see, as you read from one to the other, what the basic frames of reference of their respective authors are. As for Professor Goldenberg's paper, I would like to comment on two or three passages within it. First, a comment on the part where he speaks about the text in its own terms. It is implicit in such remarks, it seems to me, that we know what the text is trying to say in its own terms, and I do not think it can be emphasized too much how deceptive that language is. It fools us into thinking that we know what the text says in its own terms and that the rabbis missed it. Another comment refers to the paragraph that begins: "I think this entire investigation has in the end taught us very little about the Bible. The talmudic sages were using the Bible to achieve purposes of their own. . . ." Yes, indeed, the entire investigation has taught us little about the Bible in terms of *our* frame of reference. They have purposes of their own and we have purposes of our own. We can imagine some gathering in the year 3001, and someone there presenting a paper on nineteenth and twentieth century historical-critical interpretation of the Bible. That person might conclude: "Historical-critical interpretation of the Bible is very interesting, indeed, but we can learn little about the Bible from it. They were using the Bible to achieve purposes of their own."

And now for a final comment. Professor Goldenberg has written "The line of questioning in a sense was simple. Given that the ancient rabbis were no less intelligent than I, and no less capable of making sense of a text, why should they have distorted these in so striking a manner?" Briefly put, it is not clear to me that the rabbis distorted the text, given their frame of reference. I think it is meaningful to talk in terms of textual distortion within a given frame of reference, just as it would be meaningful for scientists to debate what it is they learn from photographs of chromosomes dividing. They could come up with several theories and one or more of them would be wrong. However, our artist should not go over into the laboratory and, as artist, claim that the scientist is misinterpreting his photographs. To talk that way, the artist must leave his occupation as artist and become scientist. Only after we have thoroughly begun to swim in rabbinic waters can we say that the rabbis have distorted the text. From my point of view, Professor Goldenberg seems to remain too much within a modern point of view to make this judgment. It is not all that clear to *me* that they have distorted the text.

III

All this talk raises the question about validity of interpretation and, while I think it is meaningful to talk about wrong interpretations, I am much more comfortable in talking about adequate or inadequate interpretations, complete or incomplete interpretations, and imaginative or unimaginative interpretations. This leads me then to a literary reading of 1 Kings 22. In that connection, I would like to put myself in a literary frame of reference and give one kind of literary reading of the passage. The burden is on literary criticism to show whether it has anything imaginative to say about the Bible. The rabbis are in an enviable position. They have said some extraordinarily imaginative things about the Bible. The historical critics are in an enviable position; they have also said some extraordinarily exciting things about the Bible. Literary criticism of the Bible seems to be in its infancy. There are many of us who have tried our hand at it, and I am quite excited about much of what we have done. But compared to what the rabbis did and compared to what the historical critics have done, we have not done very much yet. Are literary critics going to have some exciting and imaginative things to say?

To put my reading in this context is, in one way, very pretentious, as if I am going to reveal to you something very exciting. I really do not mean it that way. Nevertheless, it seems to me that this burden to interpret the texts, all of them, within a literary frame of reference cannot be shirked. We must get down to the job and produce some material, and let it be looked at, and criticized. So, then, we should look at the interpretation I am about to give and ask, "Does it merely say over again what we already knew about the text? Or does it till ground heretofore left fallow? One caveat is certainly mandatory here: what follows is only one way of reading the text literarily. If we were to go to an English department at almost any university, we would find as many different points of view about what is literary criticism as we find views about what the Bible is among scholars. Literary criticism is not monolithic, to say the least.

With regard to 1 Kings 22, I want to ask about the basic plot. This seems to be a story about prophets and kings, about a false prophet who says one thing and a true prophet who says another thing, and a king who does not follow the advice of the true prophet and therefore comes to his destruction. There are other stories in the Old Testament with this basic plot and theme. Presumably there are parts of the narrator's story that the narrator cannot change without making it an entirely different story. He must have a king, he must have two kinds of prophets, he must have the king march into battle and be killed, and so forth. There are other aspects of his story that the narrator can manipulate in order to make his own point. It is those items that I want to look at. The basic story line determines the genre, and it sets up certain expectations in any reader who is familiar with it. The narrator is in the position of ringing changes on this genre and, thereby, communicating his meaning.

I am going to choose only three aspects of the text for the sake of brevity. The first of these is the introduction of Jehoshaphat. Obviously Jehoshaphat is not absolutely necessary to the story. The point could have been made by having Ahab talk to someone else. He could continue, for example, talking to his officers. But having him talk to Jehoshaphat solves a problem for the narrator: Jehoshaphat has the status to ask Ahab to consult prophets and has the status to ask if there is not another prophet. Thereby the narrator can get Micaiah into the story. The introduction of Jehoshaphat is freighted with other kinds of overtones. For example, it sets up expectations that this story might have as one of its overtones a critique of the kings of Israel as opposed to the kings of Judah. The narrator seems to want us to think so, but then he does not follow through. The story is really not in praise of the kings of Judah or Jehoshaphat, because Jehoshaphat demands to hear what Micaiah says and then ignores it. He goes right into battle with Ahab, showing himself no better than Ahab on that point.

The second group of plot modifications by the narrator begins in v 13. The narrator introduces a messenger to fetch Micaiah. Again this solves a very practical problem: we need to get Micaiah on the scene and the messenger accomplishes that purpose quite satisfactorily. The messenger does not need to say anything to Micaiah, however, yet he does so anyway. He says, "Behold, the words of the prophets with one accord are favourable to the king; let your word be like the word of one of them, and speak favourably" (RSV). Why did the narrator have the messenger say this? One reason, obviously, is to increase tension. Micaiah needs to know the stakes back there, and this is a way of informing him. The main reason, however, is to elicit from Micaiah the follow-ing statement: "As the Lord lives, what the Lord says to me, that will I speak" (RSV). That statement sets up the expectation that this story is a story about true versus false prophets. Micaiah, then, comes to the king and the king asks, "Shall we go, or shall we not go?" Micaiah replies, "Go up and triumph, the Lord will give it into the hand of the king" (RSV). Now this reply, this sarcastic reply, is also unnecessary. He does not need to say that to complete the basic plot line. Why does the narrator introduce it? Probably for various reasons. Possibly to set up one very interesting juxtaposition. Micaiah says, "I am going to speak only what Yahweh tells me," and he proceeds to do precisely the opposite. This increases the narrator's distance from Micaiah and begins to indicate to us that his task is not to tell a story about true and false prophecy. More interesting even than this is the effect Micaiah's statement has on Ahab. Notice that, given the genre, Ahab is the villain. Micaiah's sarcastic remark, however, prompts Ahab to respond, "Look, Micaiah, tell me the truth," a response that brings a great deal of credit to Ahab. But praise for the villain is not in keeping with the type of story we are presumably reading. We are not supposed to sympathize with the evil Ahab, and the irony is that Micaiah's own sarcasm brings it about. Another addition to the bare bones of the plot is, of course, Micaiah's report of his eavesdropping on the divine assembly. Why is it included? Perhaps one of the reasons is to put in sharp juxtaposition Ahab's concern with the truth over against Yahweh's decision to lie. The effect of this juxtaposition is, again, to direct our attention to the praiseworthy aspects of Ahab's character.

Finally, the last aspect that I would like to comment on is Ahab's decision to disguise himself. The narrator could have reported the outcome of the battle without mentioning this at all: Ahab went into battle and was killed. What is the point of mentioning the disguise? It seems that this might be in order to make a subtle commentary on Yahweh's behavior. Ahab decides to disguise himself, that is, play a trick. He lies, as it were, except now in appearance rather than in word. The outcome is disastrous for the liar. Previously, Yahweh lied. But, of course, since Yahweh is in control of the entire situation, his strategy works whereas Ahab's does not.

Two general conclusions: the narrator uses genre to set up expectations within the reader that he does not fulfill in any straightforward way. The difference between what we expect and what we get is one of the ways of finding meaning, at least within a literary context. We expect Jehoshaphat to follow the advice of Micaiah; he does not. We expect Micaiah to tell the truth; he does not, at least not at first. We expect Ahab not to press for the truth; he does. We expect Yahweh to tell the truth, and he does not. Now what then is the point of the story? I confess that I am not sure that I know, but one thing seems clear: the narrator, by the way in which he tells the story, effectively distances himself from all the characters, Yahweh included. His is a rather dramatic sort of presentation. It is almost as if he said, "Here they are, acting out their parts; now you draw your own conclusions." And whatever conclusions we draw, they will surely not be unambiguous. I suspect that seeing such ambiguity may be one of the results of approaching the Bible from a literary point of view.

One last word. Let us return to the basic problem of frame of reference. Whether or not my analysis is in fact imaginative or exciting, it does show that the literary frame of reference is different from a rabbinic frame of reference and is different from a historical-critical frame of reference. You ask different questions, you go about amassing the evidence in different ways, and you are liable to draw very different conclusions. How different is this frame of reference? How radical a shift in perspective is this, and what does it portend for the future of the Bible in our society? It is, I think, a very significant shift in perspective. If you take an African mask sculptured in order to be used in a specific ritual within a specific African tribe, bring it to Western Europe and put it in a museum, you have certainly made a drastic alteration in the way that object is seen. I suspect that literary criticism is doing precisely that to the Bible.

Part IV

Dialogue Between Traditions

Anthony J. Saldarini
and
Dan Ben-Amos

Michael Fishbane
and
Geoffrey Hartman

Chapter 9

Interpretation of the *Akedah* in Rabbinic Literature

Anthony J. Saldarini

The *Akedah,* the story of the binding of Isaac in Genesis 22, has stimulated profuse discussion and comment in rabbinic and modern literature. Both Jewish writers (Spiegel, Levi, Schoeps) and interpreters of the New Testament (Vermes, Le Deaut, Daly) have elaborated on this theme for itself, for its contribution to the theology of sacrifice, and for its insight into the relationship of humans to God. In this presentation I shall not attempt to cover the full range of rabbinic comments on the *Akedah* nor shall I attempt to determine the chronological development and interrelationships among the *Akedah* traditions. Rather, I shall review several longer and relatively early treatments of the *Akedah* and elicit from them the major interests of the commentators, the points of tension to be explained in the story, and the theological use to which the story is put. The purpose of this review is to make the main approaches and perspectives of rabbinic literature available for comparison with other treatments of the story. It should be noted that several later collections have even more extensive treatment of the *Akedah,* but the profusion of traditions makes them hard to control and elucidate (*Tanhuma, Wayyera* 18–23, ed. Buber 108–15; *Pirqe de Rabbi Eliezer* 31; *Yalqut Shimoni; Midrash Ha-Gadol*). After the rabbinic texts have been presented, four relatively early, Palestinian sources which had contact with rabbinic traditions will be treated: the Book of Jubilees; Pseudo-Philo; Josephus; and the Targumim. These sources serve here merely to reinforce the centrality of the themes associated with the *Akedah* in rabbinic literature.

This study will examine first the brief mentions of the *Akedah* in *Mishna-Tosepta,* and then turn to longer passages in the Palestinian and Babylonian Talmuds and in *Genesis Rabbah* and finally to scattered references in two of the halakic midrashim, the *Mekilta de Rabbi Ishmael* and the *Sipre Deuteronomy.*

RABBINIC LITERATURE

Rabbinic comments on the *Akedah* cluster about four main points: the person of Abraham (and to a lesser extent Isaac); the actions of God and the explanation for them; the future good effects of the *Akedah* for Israel; and the relationship of the *Akedah* to Jewish worship, especially feasts and sacrifice.

Many comments stress that Abraham acted voluntarily and was indeed enthusiastic and meticulous in his obedience to God's commands. His admirable character and extraordinary behavior as well as other positive qualities are detailed and praised. Isaac's voluntary participation in the sacrifice is also mentioned a few times. Some attention is given to the difficulty of the test Abraham faced, its impact on him, the "unnatural" demand made by God and even Abraham's resistance to God or insistence that he be tested no more.

Often the rabbis reveal a need to explain why God tested Abraham in this unusual and somewhat repugnant way. Various explanations of God's actions are offered, including parallels to the Book of Job and reassurances that God never meant or would dream of asking that Isaac be sacrificed. God's mercy toward Abraham and his availability in prayer both to Abraham and subsequently to Israel are occasionally noted.

The future good effects of the *Akedah* for Israel are often mentioned. Various acts of redemption and salvation by God in the past and expected salvation in the future are attributed by the rabbis to the merit gained by Abraham through his willingness to sacrifice even his son, at God's command. This is part of the larger doctrine of the merits of the fathers (Moore: 539–41; Schechter, 1961: 170–98; Marmorstein: 149).

The *Akedah* is connected in various ways to Israel's worship. Sacrificial language and ritual are applied to the binding of Isaac.

The place, Moriah, is identified as an ancient holy place and as the place where the Temple will later be built and sacrifices offered. The ram and his horns lead to mention of the shofar and a connection with the feast of *Rosh Ha-Shanah*; Passover and its blood of the lamb is cited once. The *Akedah* is also discussed in connection with its use in Jewish prayers.

The variety of comments clustered around these themes will be indicated for each of the texts presented in this study; many minor interpretations must be omitted. A listing of all rabbinic comments would be both exhausting and bewildering. The following summaries and observations attempt only to open up the major concerns and perspectives brought to the story and drawn from it by the rabbis.

MISHNA-TOSEPTA

m. Ta'an. 2:4. During a time of fast six benedictions were added to the usual eighteen, the first two of which were taken from the feast of *Rosh Ha-Shanah* ("Remembrance" and "Shofar"). The concluding formula to the first of these six blessings alludes to the binding of Isaac: "May he that answered Abraham our father on Mount Moriah answer you and hearken to the voice of your crying this day" /1/. This formula implies that Abraham prayed for Isaac's deliverance or that Abraham's obedience to God provoked a response from God which resulted in Isaac's deliverance. Abraham is the central figure and his actions on Moriah were judged to be efficacious for Israel in a later period. On the basis of what happened at the *Akedah,* requests can later be made of the same merciful God. Note that the mention occurs in a liturgical context and that the specific blessing which the formula concludes comes originally from the feast of *Rosh Ha-Shanah* /2/.

t. Soṭa 6:5 (Zuck. 304). *m. Soṭa* 5:4 teaches what Akiba said about the original reciting of the Song at the Sea (Exodus 15) and *t. Soṭa* 6:2–5 comments on that passage. At the end of 6:5 is one sentence changing the subject of the saying to the *Akedah*.

> The same angels who said, "What is man that you are mindful of him (Ps 8:5)" /3/, said to them (the rest of the angels?):

Come and hear (lit. "see") the song. When they saw Israel, they also began to sing (*pthw . . . w'mrw*) a song, as Scripture says: "Oh Lord, our Lord, how majestic is your name in all the earth." (Ps 8:10) And Rabbi Simon ben Eleazar says: This section was said only (because of Isaac, son of Abraham) on account of the *Akedah*" /4/.

The dignity of humanity is based on the Song at the Sea according to the main part of the passage and on the *Akedah* according to Simon ben Eleazar. In the variant, emphasis is put on Isaac himself /5/. The general context is a discussion of Biblical songs used in liturgy.

Summary: The evidence found in *Mishna-Tosepta* is slim and in both cases attached to a discussion of liturgy. This indicates that the *Akedah* was a familiar subject in both worship and discussion. The binding of Isaac has present effects and contributes to defining the relationship between God and humanity or Israel.

TALMUD

p. Ta'an. 2:4 (65d). Several complex currents of interpretation run through this passage (see comments on text #1 above) which seems in any case to be composite /6/.

Rabbi Bibi Abba in the name of Rabbi Johanan: Abraham said in the presence of the Holy One, blessed be he, "Master of the universe, you know clearly that at the time you told me to offer up Isaac my son, I could have responded and said to you, 'Yesterday you said to me: "For through Isaac shall your descendants be named." (Gen 21:12); and now you say: "Offer him there as a burnt offering." (Gen 22:2). It is unthinkable!' I did not do that, but rather I suppressed my natural impulse and did your will. So let it be your will, Lord my God, when the sons of Isaac my son experience persecution and have no one to argue for their defense, that you become their defense attorney."

Adonai Yireh, may you remember the finding of Isaac their father for their benefit and be filled with mercy for them.

What is written after this: "And Abraham lifted up his eyes and looked and, behold, behind him was a ram . . ." (Gen 22:13). What does behind (*'ahar*) mean? Rabbi Judan, son of Rabbi Simon said, "After all the generations (in which) your

descendants will fall into the clutches of sin and become vic-
tims of persecution, they will be redeemed by the sacrifice of
this ram, as Scripture says: 'The Lord God will sound the trumpet and march forth in the whirlwinds of the south.' " (Zech
9:14). Rabbi Huna in the name of Rabbi Hinana, son of Isaac,
said, "All that day Abraham saw the ram caught in this tree,
get loose and go free; caught in that bush, get loose and go free;
caught in this thicket, get loose and go free. The Holy One,
blessed be he, said to Abraham, 'In the same way your
descendants will fall into the clutches of sin and become vic-
tims of empires from Babylon to Media, from Media to Greece,
from Greece to Edom (=Rome).' Abraham said to God,
'Master of the universe, will it be this way forever?' God answered him, 'In the end they will be redeemed by the sacrifice
of the ram; "The Lord God will sound the trumpet and march
forth in the whirlwinds of the south." ' " (Zech 9:14)

In the first part of the passage Abraham points out to God the
extraordinary nature of what he did in binding Isaac and how he
willingly went against his natural inclination. Using that as a basis
Abraham requests that God protect Isaac's descendants. Abraham,
his voluntary obedience, and the difficulty of what he did are seen
as affecting subsequent relations between God and Israel. The
brief prayer for God's mercy based on the name of the place (Gen
22:14) is not found in the parallels in *Lev. Rab. and Pesiq. Rab
Kah.* It conveniently separates the two parts of the passage.

In the second part the grammatically odd *'aḥar* and the presence
of the ram caught in the thicket cause the rabbis to connect the
ram's fate with that of Israel and Israel's salvation with the sacrifice of the ram. Further, Zech 9:14 is cited because a trumpet is
mentioned there and it is associated with the ram's horn which is
sounded at the New Year. The ram's horn and Zechariah both
imply salvation coming from God. Further, in *Lev. Rab.* and
Pesiq. Rab Kah. the context is a discussion of *Roš Haššana* and
specifically Lev 23:24, "In the seventh month." Redemption de-
rives from the events on Mount Moriah against a liturgical background and with specific reference to a sacrifice of an animal
(Vermes: 206, 213–14).

Summary: Abraham's willingness and the extraordinary nature
of what he did are stressed in the first part of *p. Ta'an.* Because
of this Israel is seen as having a claim on God's protection. This

latter theme is developed in the second part where God is seen as saving Israel and this salvation is associated with the New Year ram's horn.

Just three texts will be treated from the Babylonian Talmud, one from *Roš Haššana* which connects the ram and the *shofar* (the ram's horn), one which discusses Isaac's ashes, and one which is an extended comment on the *Akedah*.

b. Roš. Haš. 16a. In discussing the New Year's blessing *Shofarot,* the Talmud connects the efficacy of the sounding of the ram's horn with the binding of Isaac. Isaac's relationship with his descendants is strikingly communicated in a comment by Rabbi Abbahu: "Why do we blow the ram's horn? The Holy One, blessed be he, said: 'Blow on the ram's horn before me so that I remember on your behalf the binding of Isaac, son of Abraham and credit you as if you bound yourselves before me.'" The voluntary nature of the act, its connection with *Rosh Ha-Shanah* and its continuing efficacy are all stressed.

b. Ta'an. 16a. Another liturgical custom is related to the *Akedah.* In a discussion of putting ashes on the ark and on one's head (*m. Ta'an.* 2:1) one opinion insists on ashes and not dust because the practice is so that God "may remember for our sake the ashes of Isaac." The binding of Isaac is seen as so real and efficacious that reference may be made to *Isaac's* ashes. *P. Ta'an.* 65a and Sipra, *Behuqqotai* (ed. Weiss 112c) speak of the ashes of Isaac "as if they were piled on the altar." This seems to be a Palestinian tradition (*Lev. Rab.* 36:5; *Gen. Rab.* 49:11; 94:5; Vermes: 205; Spiegel: 42).

b. Sanh. 89b. and *m. Sanh.* 11:5–6. Here it is taught that a false prophet is to die by strangulation, and likewise he who disregards the words of a true prophet. The next question, naturally enough, concerns identifying a true prophet and Abraham is cited as an example of a well-established prophet; how else could Isaac have listened to him at Moriah? This introductory comment solves the practical questions associated with the shocking command given to Abraham by seeing him as a prophet who knows the word of

God, obeys it and is recognized as an authoritative source by others.

An independent discussion of the binding of Isaac follows. First, the fact that God tested Abraham is explained by a story that Satan accused Abraham of not duly honoring God because he did not offer sacrifice at the feast celebrating Isaac's weaning. God defends Abraham by saying that he honors God so much he would even sacrifice Isaac if commanded. The obvious parallel to Job is marshalled here as an implied defense of God and explanation of how such a command or test could be given.

A second explanation of God's actions depends upon the list of the ten trials of Abraham, found in *'Abot de Rabbi Nathan,* Versions A and B (Schechter, 1887: 94–95; Goldin: 132; Saldarini: 213–14) and *Pirqe de Rabbi Eliezer* 26–31. This tenth and ultimate trial is necessary to show that Abraham's fidelity in the previous nine was real. God, however, realizes what he is asking of Abraham and entreats him (*-na'* in Gen 22:2). In both explanations of God's actions Abraham is considered to be an extraordinarily strong and faithful man, despite the alleged defect in his behavior at Isaac's weaning. Yet, he is not impervious to the difficulty of God's request, for the wording of the command in Gen 22:2 is stretched out into a dialogue between God and Abraham to ease the shock ("Your son." I have two sons. "Your only one." Each is the only one of his mother. "Whom you love." I love them both. "Isaac.").

On the way to Moriah, Satan is pictured as coming again to test Abraham. The words of Zophar in Job 4 are put into Satan's mouth to weaken Abraham in his resolve, but to no avail. This dialogue shows the voluntary and reflective nature of Abraham's actions, even though he does not understand why God commands him. Finally, another explanation of the origin of the trial is associated with Isaac himself and his willingness to be sacrificed. Ishmael taunts Isaac that he submitted to circumcision willingly at age thirteen, as opposed to Isaac who was circumcised as an infant. Isaac then says that if God told him to sacrifice himself, he would obey. This last tradition parallels what was said above about Abraham's willingness, but shifts the focus to Isaac.

Summary: b. Sanh. focuses on three themes: the reason for the test (with an implied defense of God), the willingness of Abraham and Isaac to give all to God, and the stature of Abraham in resisting Satan and accepting God's command.

GENESIS RABBAH

Genesis Rabbah, a major and relatively early commentary on Genesis, has three sections on the binding of Isaac (Theodor and Albeck: 55–57). A wealth of materials is obtained in these sections and many passages have parallels elsewhere in rabbinic literature. With a limited purpose I shall divide the commentary into six sections which fit the flow of the action and I shall bring out the major concerns and themes which the rabbis struggled with and which were collected in Genesis *Rabbah*.

Gen. Rab. 55:1–6: The Test (Gen 22:1). In 55:1–3 various explanations are offered for why God tested Abraham. Ps 11:5 (RSV), "The Lord tests the righteous," is applied to Abraham and the fact that Abraham became so famous and wealthy is characterized as a reward for his enduring the test. As in *b. Sanh.* the rabbis seem eager to explain God's reason for this frightening test of Abraham. In 55:4 the angels are said to accuse Abraham of not honoring God at Isaac's weaning (as Satan did in *b. Sanh.*) and the dispute between Isaac and Ishmael is also recounted. At the end of *Gen. Rab.* 55:4 (in Theodor and Albeck) the author applies Mic 6:6, "Shall I give my firstborn for my transgression?" to Abraham, rather than Mesha, who sacrificed his firstborn (2 Kings 3:27); the terrible choice facing Abraham is emphasized along with God's rejection of such worship (see Mic 6:7). In 55:6 Abraham is praised because of his obedience. The reflective voluntary nature of his decision is emphasized by a comment of Rabbi Akiba: "He tested him unequivocally, that people might not say that He confused and perplexed him so that he did not know what to do." Reference seems to be made to the three-day journey during which Abraham had time to realize what he was to do.

Summary: In introducing the story of the *Akedah* the commentators in *Genesis Rabbah* strongly emphasize Abraham's voluntary obedience, his other positive qualities, and the greatness of what he did. They explain why God acted as he did and at this point show no interest in the future effects of the binding of Isaac.

Gen. Rab. 55:7-8: Instructions, Setting Out (Gen 22:2-3). Emphasis is placed on Abraham's self-denial and his corresponding merit all through this section. The dialogue between God and Abraham (cf. *b. Sanh.*) is here interpreted to mean that Abraham was made to realize just how beloved Isaac was to him. God gradually reveals what he wants Abraham to do and this uncertainty increases Abraham's anticipation, involvement, and merit. Abraham's love even causes him rather than his servant to saddle the ass; love upsets the natural order. But from Abraham's actions correspondingly good results are expected. "As a reward for the two cleavings wherewith our father Abraham cleaved the wood (plural form) of the burnt offering, he earned that God should cleave (divide) the sea before his descendants." (cf. *Mekilta*, Text #13).

The mention of Moriah brings with it a series of comments marking out Moriah as a holy place and as the site of the future temple. Also Isaac's sacrifice is seen as similar to the later Temple sacrifices and precise sacrificial language begins to be used.

Gen. Rab. 56:1-4: Arrival at Moriah. (Gen 22:4-8). The account of Abraham's arrival is filled with two themes that stand in tension: Abraham's uncertainty about what will happen and reassurances given by the commentator that Isaac will be saved. In connection with these themes, stress is laid on the sacrificial nature of what is being done; " 'And they went both of them together' (Gen 22:6): one to bind and the other to be bound, one to slaughter and the other to be slaughtered." The temple and worship are also mentioned. Salvation on the third day is paralleled to and connected with the third day on which Abraham bound Isaac. Abraham's knife causes all the eating which Israel enjoys now. In 56:4 Samael tempts Abraham and Isaac both and Abraham resists and helps Isaac resist, a mark of their unity of spirit and willingness.

Summary: In Texts 8 and 9 above, attention is focused on Abraham's exemplary behavior and its subsequent good results. Frequent connections are made between Abraham's and Israel's sacrifices and the commentator evinces anxiety to show that God will save Isaac.

Gen. Rab. 56:5–8: The Attempt at Sacrifice (Gen 22:9–12). Abraham's attempted obedience to God's command is said to provoke vigorous activity within heaven. The angels protest the act as unnatural and later it is said that the tears of the angels dissolved the knife. The words of the messenger who tells Abraham to stop are interpreted to mean that Abraham was emphatically told not to harm Isaac in any way. These several comments strongly imply that God would not allow human sacrifice to be carried out and we get a sense that such a thing is repugnant in heaven.

At the same time, Abraham's care and willingness are stressed. He is said to have hid Isaac so that Satan would not render him unfit for sacrifice. (This implies that Satan, knowing the good effects the act would produce, sought to thwart it.) Abraham is said to have thought of strangling Isaac when the knife dissolved. He is so obedient that 56:7 concludes "I ascribe merit to you as though I had ordered you to sacrifice yourself and you had not refused." (Traditions of protest have not been lost. *Gen. Rab.* 56:8, in Theodor and Albeck, contains a protest to God by Abraham, the very protest which *b. Sanh.* says that Abraham did not make. God defends himself by saying that the command *ha'alôt* did not mean to sacrifice, but literally to take Isaac up, a command which Abraham has fulfilled.) The good effects of Abraham's actions are briefly noted. The angels of evil nations were bound in heaven, though later released by Israel's sinfulness; Abraham's actions with the knife instruct Israel how to conduct sacrifices (56:6).

Summary: In this central section of the *Akedah* story the commentators squarely face the problem of the *Akedah*: Would God let this happen? They answer that question negatively through the medium of several comments. At the same time, the positive side of the *Akedah,* Abraham's response and the good effects issuing from it, are reaffirmed.

Gen. Rab. 56:9–11: The Sacrifice of the Ram and the Return

(Gen 22:13-19). Several themes are reinforced in the discussion of the sacrifice of the ram. The commonplace connection of the ram to the ram's horn of New Year and to redemption is repeated, as is the entanglement of the ram and its release from the thicket as symbolic of Israel's future history. The significance of the sacrifice is emphasized by the prayers put into Abraham's mouth which equate the sacrifice of the lamb with that of Isaac: "Look upon the blood of this ram as though it were the blood of my son Isaac . . . ." Abraham points out (as in *p. Ta'an.*; Text #3) that he did not protest to God when he might have and that God should therefore help Israel. The place of the sacrifice is identified as a holy place and connected to the Temple. Abraham is presented as making God promise not to test him again after this greatest test. Finally, Gen 22:19, which says that Abraham returned and fails to mention Isaac, is interpreted to mean that God sent Isaac to study Torah (in paradise) with Shem. (Spiegel: 5-7; Ginzberg: 5:254-55, n. 255). Isaac is not present to mourn at Sarah's death (Gen 23:2) and only reappears at the end of Genesis 24. Gen 22:19 was later interpreted to mean that Abraham had actually gone through with the sacrifice of Isaac (Spiegel: 4 and chap. 7). The theme of sacrifice brings out a rich group of theological considerations and problems which both elucidate the nature of the story and relate it to Israel.

Gen. Rab. 57:1-4: Subsequent Action and Reflection (Gen 22: 20). Immediately after the story of the binding of Isaac, Gen 22: 20-23 informs us that Abraham's brother had eight sons and that the last son was the father of Rebekah who became Isaac's wife. The midrash interprets this to mean that, while on Mount Moriah, Abraham was informed that Isaac's future mate had been born; presumably this is to console or reassure Abraham. But a second midrash interprets the verse in a more negative light, stating that Abraham was going to marry Isaac to a woman not of his people. Since Isaac would have died and had no children anyway, the ancestry of his children could not be important. The authors of these midrashim seem to be struggling with the consequences of the events on Moriah for Isaac, Abraham and Israel. In 57:4 the author struggles again with the negative side of God's test of

Abraham. Abraham is presented as fearing further suffering and God reassures him by informing him that Job has already been born and will receive all further tests. There follows a long discussion of Job, including this striking comment by Simeon ben Lakish: "Job never existed at all." This is interpreted to mean that Job never was exposed to the sufferings recounted in the Book of Job. Simeon ben Lakish cannot accept that God would allow the events recounted in the Book of Job to happen to anyone. *Summary:* The final two sections of *Genesis Rabbah* (Texts #11 and 12) bring out the value of sacrifice and also the fears and difficulties associated with it. The extraordinary test God gave Abraham and his exemplary behavior in response to the test provoke discussion, some of it an oblique defense of God and some of it a working out of the consequences for Abraham and Israel.

HALAKIC MIDRASH

The *Mekilta* of Rabbi Ishmael and *Sipre Deuteronomy* contain only a few mentions of or allusions to the binding of Isaac. Some comments and applications are, however, striking.

Mek. (Text #13). All the passages are connected with the Passover materials in Exodus 12—14, rather than with *Rosh Ha-Shanah* and the ram's horn as in materials previously studied. The *Akedah's* future effects are seen in the redemption of Israel from Egypt; the blood of the passover lamb is connected to the blood of Isaac. Exod 12:13, "When I see the blood," is united to "'*Adonai yireh*," of Gen 22:14 and interpreted to mean "I see the blood of the binding of Isaac." (Lauterbach: 1:57). No explanation is given of the shocking phrase, the *blood* of the binding of Isaac, but traditions concerning the spilling of some of Isaac's blood or that Isaac is considered as if sacrificed must be presumed. *Mekilta de Rabbi Simeon* to Exod 6:2 connects the redemption from Egypt to the fact that a quarter of Isaac's blood was left on the altar (Spiegel:46).

Three comments focus on the activity of Abraham. Abraham's harnessing of the ass counteracts the harnessing by Balaam and

Abraham's stretching out his hand to take the knife counteracts
Pharoah drawing his sword (Exod 15:9) (*Mek.* to Exod 14:6;
Lauterbach: 1:199). A comment by Rabbi Banaah links the opening of the sea to the cleaving of the wood: "Because of the merit
of the deed which Abraham their father did, I will divide the sea
for them. For Scripture says: 'And he cleaved the wood for the
burnt offering.'" (Gen 22:3) (*Mek.* to Exod 14:15; Lauterbach:
1:218). A final comment connects Abraham's rising early in the
morning (Gen 22:3) with the prayers of the righteous being heard
in the morning (*Mek.* to Exod 14:24; Lauterbach: 1:237–38). In
each of the comments some one of Abraham's actions is viewed as
so meritorious that it has some future effect on Israel.

Sipre Deuteronomy. Here the binding of Isaac is mentioned only
twice. *Sipre Deut.* on Deut 6:5 interprets "with all your heart" as
referring to Abraham and "with all your soul" as referring to Isaac.
Of Isaac it says: "Like Isaac who bound himself on top of the
altar." Isaac's voluntary participation in the sacrifice is very
strongly communicated by the image of him binding himself (#32;
Finkelstein: 58). The reference to Abraham is not explained, but
another passage in *Sipre Deut.* stresses that Abraham's giving of
Isaac means that he would have given his eye and his person; also
it stresses that Isaac was very beloved by Abraham and so the
sacrifice was that much more meritorious (#313; Finkelstein:
355).

RELATED TEXTS

The *Akedah* is interpreted in other Jewish literature preceding
and contemporary with the rabbinic literature. We shall briefly
explore major themes in Jubilees, Pseudo-Philo, Josephus and the
Targums in order to gain further awareness of the literary and
theological interpretations swirling around the sacrifice of Isaac.
All the sources chosen are Palestinian and relatively early.

Jubilees (second century B.C.E.) connects the sacrifice of Isaac
to the Feast of Passover and places it on Mount Zion. The tradition of associating Abraham's act with a festival sacrifice and with
the Temple is shown to be very old. An explanation is also given

for why Abraham is tested: a voice in heaven (God?) proclaims him faithful; then an angel (*Mastema*) challenges this, and the test (as in the case of Job) is on. Finally, the liberation of Israel from Egypt is connected to Passover and stressed by Jubilees; by implication the *Akedah* also causes this liberation. Three of the four major themes found in rabbinic literature (explanation of God's actions, future good effects and connections with Israel's worship) are found in Jubilees (17:15—18:19; Charles: 2:39–40).

Pseudo-Philo's Biblical Antiquities does not treat the binding of Isaac in place, but in speeches given at important moments in Israel's history, a phenomenon which stresses the theological import of the *Akedah* (Harrington et al. on 32:14; 18:5; 40:2–3). Both Abraham and Isaac are presented as voluntary participants. Stress is laid on the extraordinary nature of what is done. The reason for God's action is cryptically given as the jealousy of the angels. Sacrificial language is used and reference is made to cult sacrifices. The worthiness of humans to be sacrificed is noted. Mention is made of Isaac's blood. Finally God will remember the sacrifice for Israel's well-being. Each of these themes found concentrated in Pseudo-Philo is found in the rabbinic sources studied.

Josephus in his *Antiquities* retells the story of the binding of Isaac according to his own biases and purposes (1:13 [222–36]). Josephus sees the *Akedah* as an example of God's providence at work in history, with a special instance of that being Israel's history and here the *Akedah*. Abraham responds properly with faith and so is rewarded (Attridge: 71–107). Woven into Josephus's retelling of the story are themes found in rabbinic literature: the voluntary obedience of Abraham and Isaac, the use of sacrificial language, location of the act at the site of the later Temple, the merit gained by Abraham and Isaac (though no mention is made of future effects on Israel), and a defense of God who explains to Abraham that he would never take human life.

The Targums, which probably contain material early and late, have a number of comments about the *Akedah*. The motifs are summarized by LeDeaut as a connection of the *Akedah* to Passover, an emphasis on Isaac (in contrast to the rabbinic emphasis on Abraham) and the effects of the *Akedah* on the future of Israel (178).

CONCLUSION

Given the nature of our sources we cannot arrive at *the* rabbinic interpretation of the binding of Isaac. The typical and relatively early sources which have been examined are collections of comments and observations. Within them we may discern some concerns and problems and the rabbinic responses to them and these interpretative materials guide our reading and understanding of Genesis 22. Some generalizations can be made. The story provokes both positive and negative responses. Admiration is expressed for Abraham (and Isaac), especially because of their extraordinarily generous obedience to God. The negative response is somewhat muted because it would involve criticism of God, God's command, or Abraham's intentions toward his own son. The horror which may underlie the texts is muted into explanation of God's testing Abraham, of God's motives, and of Abraham's experience.

The paradoxical and shocking command given by God is exploited to pierce the depths of God's impact on human life, his care for humans, the basis of human dignity and proper human attitudes toward God. The fact that Abraham has the strength to obey, the fact that a human is worthy of this interest from God, and the fact that Isaac can be a sacrifice, are used to establish the value of humans before God and become the foundation of the praise and honor heaped on Abraham by God and humans. A careful balance is made between God's sovereignty in making his demand on Abraham and his mercy in saving and honoring Abraham and his descendants.

The story of the binding of Isaac is a powerful story and its power is seen at work through all Israel's history to the present. The original redemption of Israel from Egypt is attributed to the *Akedah* in some rather early traditions. The later redemption of Israel from hostile nations is associated with the New Year and other fall festivals and the blowing of the ram's horn. God's accessibility in prayer and at critical points stems from the *Akedah* and Abraham's total self-giving. Although the story is unique in the Bible, it is firmly bound to Israel's experience in prayer, festival and interpretation of historical events.

EPILOGUE

The discussion of this essay at the Ottawa Biblical Studies Symposium in 1977 made explicit several points which elucidate the nature and limits of the texts studied. The theological concerns which emerge from the rabbinic discussion—theodicy, redemption, ritual and human-divine relations—all belong to a highly referential, closed system characteristic of Jewish culture in the first half of the first millennium. Allusions and common understandings are as important in comprehending the *Akedah* as are the explicit references to it in these texts. The brilliant essay by S. Spiegel best presents the full range of material, early and late, on the *Akedah* in all its richness and diversity. For the early period studied in this paper the allusions and citations of the *Akedah* in the Targum are extremely important and have been presented by Vermes and LeDeaut.

The modern literary critic will be interested in the actions of the characters in the story. Rabbinic comments give some attention to this, but their attention is preeminently focused on the relations of God and humans. Abraham's thoughts and feelings are developed somewhat; Isaac's role is made active in some interpretations of the story; and Sarah, totally absent in the biblical story, plays a role in some later versions of the story. Beyond these rudimentary observations, the rabbis give little thought to story as story and to a self-conscious reflection on its working and structure. A more thorough analysis of these matters awaited later generations. Nevertheless, the rabbis' struggle to understand the *Akedah* within a highly referential system directed their attention to the dynamics, impact and implications of the story for themselves and their understanding of the world. On this ground the rabbis and modern literary interpreters meet.

NOTES

/1/   *m. Ta'an.* 2:4 contains seven, not six, concluding formulae. For a discussion of this problem, see *b. Ta'an.* 16b; Albeck (2:492–493).

/2/   *m. Tamid* 4:1 uses the verb *'qd* and the noun *'qydh* but the words refer to the binding of the lamb of daily sacrifice and not to the binding of Isaac.

/3/   This clause presumes that the reader knows the story that the angels opposed the creation of humans. See *Pesiq. R. R.* 14 (ed. Friedmann, 59b); tr. Braude, 272–73 and *Tanhuma, Wayyera* 18. For a recent treatment of the whole question, see Schäfer (85–89).

Lieberman (1973: *Nashim,* Pt. 8:669) says that the Erfurt manuscript is an abbreviated version and elsewhere (1973a: 184–185) he prints the Vienna manuscript next to Erfurt with the reading: "When (humans) sprouted forth, the ministering angels who composed an accusation before the Holy One, blessed be he, said . . . ."

/4/   The Vienna manuscript lacks a page here. Lieberman prints the editio princeps which has the name Simeon ben Menasia and concludes "because of Isaac son of Abraham on account of the Akedah." Zuckermantel lists the addition to Erfurt in his apparatus.

/5/   See the treatment of Pseudo-Philo 32:1–4 below; Vermes: 201. Ps 8:6 is used in 1 Cor 15:27 to speak of the relationships among God, Christ and humanity.

/6/   The names in this text are problematic. See the notes with the parallel passages in *Lev. Rab.* 29:9–10 (ed. Margoliot, 682–84) and *Pesiq. Rab Kah.* 23:9 (ed. Mandelbaum, 342–43; tr. Braude, 358–59). All these sources are Palestinian and fifth century or soon after.

The Akedah: A Folklorist's Response

Dan Ben-Amos

The *Akedah* is a central theme, image, and metaphor in Jewish literature and thought. Direct exegesis comments upon its significance in the postbiblical period, but reveals only part of its meaning. In order to fill the gaps and to obtain a more comprehensive view of the concepts of and attitudes toward the *Akedah,* it is necessary also to examine indirect references, coded allusions and propositions that state the relations of the *Akedah* to other biblical and historical events.

Saldarini correctly states the absence of a single rabbinical doctrine about the *Akedah.* During the rabbinical period there were diversified notions of this narrative that changed in time and differed according to schools of biblical interpretation. Saldarini examines these variations on the basis of a literary thematic analysis, deliberately omitting questions of chronological development. Since an important aim of this volume is to wed modern literary criticism with biblical scholarship, it would have been appropriate, in this case, to bring the historical dimension into this alliance.

There is a need to inquire whether the increase in references to the *Akedah,* from the slight mention in the Mishna and Tosepta, to the wealth of material in *Genesis Rabbah* is only literary or also historical? Has the *Akedah* gained in significance with the passage of time and changes in history? Is it possible to explain, historically as well as literarily, the shifts from purely liturgical and theological concerns that Saldarini finds in the Mishna and the Tosepta, to the focus on the sacrifice, the fears associated with it, and Abraham's exemplary obedience that dominate later sources? What

166

is the historical background for the shift in the image of Isaac from a naive victim to a conscious martyr (Spiegel, 1950)? Geza Vermes (198) finds that Isaac was already a model martyr in the Maccabean period. Has this view been submerged during the decrease in religious persecutions to reemerge in a later period when the acts of martyrdom were on the increase? In other words, literary analysis cannot supplement; it can only complement historical examination of rabbinical sources. Although the focal point of investigation could, and often should, be of literary nature, there is a necessity to examine texts in their relationship to the culture, ideas and events of distinct historical periods.

The literary-historical analysis of the *Akedah* would account not only for thematic variations, but also for formal, generic changes and structural relations. Literary genres offer contexts for interpretations (Hirsch: 68–126; Ben-Amos 1976, 1976a) and enable speakers to convey ideas in ways that their listeners will understand them. The consideration of the roles of narrators and their audiences adds a social dimension to this analysis.

Thus, focusing on the literary-historical and social dimension of the *Akedah* will reveal the dynamics of change in the conception of the *Akedah,* not only as an idea, but also as a narration, image, or metaphor, and will indicate the social basis for such variations. Such research will further Saldarini's theme of the lack of a single rabbinical doctrine of the *Akedah* and will reveal the diversity of opinions and literary expressions that existed at that period.

Chapter 10

"A Wretched Thing of Shame, A Mere Belly": An Interpretation of Jeremiah 20:7–12*

Michael Fishbane

⁷ You have enticed me, YHWH, and I've been had:
You have overwhelmed me and prevailed;
 I am mocked all day long,
 Everyone reviles me.
⁸ Whenever I speak or shout; I cry: "violence
and plunder!"
 The word of YHWH is become my daily shame
 and reproach.
⁹ And whenever I would think: "I will not mention Him,
 Nor speak in His name ever again"
Then His word burned me up like a consuming fire
locked in my bones;
 I have tried to contain it but to no avail.
¹⁰ Surely I have heard the slander of many—terror
 on every side:
 "Let us denounce him but good!"
Even old friends and sidekicks have said:
 "Perhaps he may be enticed—then we'll prevail
Against him and get our revenge!"
¹¹ But YHWH is with me like a mighty warrior,
Therefore my pursuers shall stumble and not prevail;
 They shall be sorely abashed for lack of success,
 With an unforgettable, permanent shame.
¹² O YHWH of Hosts, who tests the righteous and sees
 the innermost heart,
Let me see your revenge on them
For I have revealed my case to you.

Jer 20:7–12 is one of many lay prayers in the Hebrew Bible not found in the Book of Psalms. A common feature of these prayers is their spontaneous character and immediate relationship to a situation of personal crisis /1/. Indeed, in contradistinction to the first-person laments recited in ancient Israelite shrines (e.g., Psalms 7; 28; 35; 109) /2/—and with which Jer 20:7–12 and his other laments have features in common /3/—first-person laments not found in the Psalter are inextricably linked to a specific individual. Thus, however much a later idealization of Jeremiah's suffering may have affected the editorial decision to include Jeremiah's private prayers in a collection of his public oracles (with the result that these prayers could become spiritually paradigmatic), the relationship between Jer 20:7–12 and the prophet is primary /4/. Every effort must be made to locate the singular characteristics of Jer 20:7–12 within Jeremiah's life history as a messenger of God.

But it is just here that a number of problems confront the latter-day interpreter. What indications does the text provide for precise historicization? At first glance, the contextuality of the prayer is presumptive: on the one hand, there appears to be a historical and situational relation between 20:7–12 and the preceding scenario in 20:1–2, where Jeremiah is described as having been physically abused by his enemies after a prophetic denunciation. On the other hand, there is a specific phraseological link between the two passages. Jeremiah's oracle against his persecutor Pashhur (vv 3–4) pivots on a reinterpretation of the latter's name as *māgôr missāvîv,* "terror on every side," an expression used by Jeremiah in v 10 to characterize his own distress. But, despite these conjunctions, any actual nexus between the events of vv 1–6 and the prayer of vv 7–12 is not certain /5/. In fact, it is more likely that it reflects a redactional conceit. This assumption is reinforced by what appears to be an editorial doubling-up of prayers in 20:7–18; for the somewhat hopeful conclusion reached in the first prayer (vv 7–12) is immediately undercut by the suicidal cry of anguish in the second (vv 14–18). Given these considerations, and the fact that 20:7–12 presents Jeremiah's plight as something recurrent in his biography, it may be prudent to approach the prayer as a heightened expression of Jeremiah's inner history as a prophet of God, and not feel constrained to locate its external *Sitz im Leben.*

The foregoing methodological difficulty—that of finding in Jer 20:7–12 textual indicators sufficient to establish its historical locus —has its corollary in the difficulty of finding in Jeremiah's prayer formal directives fully adequate to a confident understanding of its inner logic and progression. As the received prayer is full of nonparatactic juxtapositions—connections between phrases (v 8a, b and c) and among units (v 10 and vv 11–12) are often missing or obscure—an interpreter is required constantly to make sense of these instances of syntactic underload of meaning. And because Jer 20:7–12 is now a literary artifact, a canonical transcription of a spoken event, no audible tones or breath sequences linger to inspire confidence. What will be produced, by way of interpretation, is a reflex of the dialectical relationship between Jer 20:7–12 and one reader; what will be achieved is but one public testimony of the inner life of this prayer as resurrected, through an interior performance of it, by an interpreter (cf. Fish).

Jeremiah's words are addressed to God: tormented by his enemies, he feels anger and accusation, betrayal and hope commingled in him. The experiences and consequences of his prophetic destiny are revealed as a "case" (*rîv*) before the Lord /6/. In his vulnerability Jeremiah turns to God, and says: "*You* have enticed *me*"; "*You* have overwhelmed *me*"; "*I* have revealed my case to *you*." This language of direct encounter frames the prayer, bracketing and counterpointing the references to God as "Him" and "He," and the citations of the enemies' plots against "him" (Jeremiah). Such rapid shifts of subject and object, and of other-directed and self-directed address, constitute one of several stylistic features in Jer 20:7–12.

The general ring structure to the prayer, just indicated, may be more fully delineated:

A   stanza 1 (v 7) direct speech to God ("you")
B   stanza 2 (vv 8–9) self-reflection; indirect reference to God ("He")
C   stanza 3 (v 10) recollection of enemies' plots against "him"
B′ stanza 4 (v 11) self-reflection; indirect reference to "the Lord"
A′ stanza 5 (v 12) direct speech to God ("you")

This chiastic form also serves to diagram the inner transformations of Jer 20:7-12. The framing stanzas (A and A') address God directly, whereas the internal ones move on a more reflective plane and incorporate the "case" presented to God. These internal stanzas are not, however, of a piece: stanzas 2 and 3 develop the claims put forward in stanza 1; whereas stanza 4 is separated from 1-3 in terms of mood, theme, and tense /7/. In stanza 4 the speaker returns to the present moment and switches from balanced lines to an extended prose assertion. The bursting forth of hope in stanzas 4 and 5 confirm the force of God's presence upon the prophet referred to in the opening sections. In a sense, stanzas 1-3 are Jeremiah's attempt to restrain the words of prophecy and release the tensions he feels by means of a protest prayer directed to God. But the shift toward hope in stanzas 4-5 indicates that God's presence could not be long suppressed in him, and that prophetic words would again burst forth from Jeremiah's lips.

The entire prayer moves from despair to hopeful assertion; from psychical disintegration to spiritual wholeness. As Jeremiah's sense of destiny and vocation are restored in the course of his prayer, a growing confidence emerges. Indeed, Jer 20:7-12 is a verbal record of a religious sufferer who is transformed in and through the language of his prayer—offered to God for His judgment and verdict. But these matters anticipate our discussion.

The first unit of Jer 20:7-12, v 7, opens the prayer with an expression of anger and impotence. Jeremiah accuses God of having taken unfair advantage of him; *pittîtanî*, he says, *vā'efāt*, "You have enticed me . . . and I've been had": *hizaqtanî vattûkal*, "You have overwhelmed me and prevailed" (v 7a). This incriminating broadside seems to point beyond specific moments in Jeremiah's life and include the very roots of his prophetic destiny, concerning which two levels can be distinguished: Jeremiah was foreordained by God to be a prophet while yet in the womb (1:4), and was confirmed in this destiny upon reaching majority (vv 5-8). In his present protest (20:7), which refers to his ineluctable fate, Jeremiah undoubtedly felt, on the one hand, that God took unfair advantage of him before his will was formed; and, on the other, that he had been beguiled by God, against his conscious—though timid—will, for God had told him not to fear, saying: "I will be with you to protect you . . . I have made you forthwith as a protected fortress, a pillar of bronze, and walls of iron; [people] will contend against you, but they will not prevail, *lō' yūklû lāk*" (1:8, 18).

Jeremiah felt that all such blandishments of support had proved worthless; for if his curse of his birthday in 20:14–18 most fully expresses his anger at his prenatal destiny, vv 7–10 most fully indict God for leading him on time after time—such that he suffered persecutions for His sake. As if to provide a physical correlative to his sense of being forced, Jeremiah expresses himself with terms (*pittîtanî*, "You have enticed me;" *hizaqtanî*, "You have overwhelmed me") which elsewhere refer to sexual seduction and rape (see Exod 22:15 and Deut 22:25, respectively) /8/. It is furthermore striking that a true prophet is described in Ezek 14:9 as one who is *yefuttê*, induced or set upon, to speak the word of God; and that in 1 Kings 22:22 the true prophet Micaiah reports his vision wherein God instructed an evil spirit to speak lies through the mouths of the prophets of King Jehoshaphat with the words: *tefattê vegam tūkāl*, "You will traduce and prevail." Conceivably, these several interpenetrating overtones of the verb *pittâ* were present to Jeremiah's consciousness as he voiced his protest. They nevertheless permit the modern interpreter, aware of the inner-biblical semantic field of the verb, a fuller sympathetic penetration into the conflicting feelings which ravaged Jeremiah's heart. The prophet is felt to be a person at once overwhelmed by God's choice of, and control over, him as a prophet; and as one with an acute sense of having been duped, if not actually "had"—for Jeremiah goes on (v 7b) to describe his life as a prophet as an unbroken series of torments.

The relationship between v 7a and v 7b is cumulative. Jeremiah's opening outburst about the impact of divine power over him is concretized in the succeeding depiction of his victimization at human hands. For the prophet, a void of anguish lies between the pressure of divine power and the pain of human scorn; indeed, the net effect of the second clause (v 7b) is to strip the earlier references to divine power (v 7a) of any providential dimension. Jeremiah feels possessed and abandoned.

What has collapsed for Jeremiah is his trust in God's promised protection. How is God a bulwark for him in the face of such daily disdain? As the contempt of the community to whom he speaks invades his soul, and as he senses the collapse of his inner strength, Jeremiah believes God to be absent from him and cries out in despair and protest. True, others in similar circumstances found solace in memories of divine care:

> Woe, I'm a worm and not a man,
> Shamed by men and condemned by the crowd;
> Whosoever sees me, reviles me . . .
> But you it was who guided my bursting forth at birth,
> Who placed me trustingly at my mother's breasts.
> I've been cast before you since birth;
> From my mother's womb you are my God.
>   (Ps 22:7–8, 10) /9/

Not so Jeremiah, who felt himself doubly deceived: before birth he was conditioned with a God-given destiny, and from adolescence on (cf. 15:20) he was beguiled by God and His promised protection.

The next section of Jeremiah's prayer, vv 8–9, deepens the opening verse and extends its thrust. Detailed reflections replace and justify the initial charge. Verse 8 (victimization by men) develops v 7b, and v 9 (vulnerability to God) develops v 7a, thereby replicating on a smaller scale the chiastic structure of the prayer as a whole. In v 8 Jeremiah reports his case to God: how he rebuked the people for injustice and violence, but himself became a victim; how he exposed the plunder on every side and spoke the prophetic "word of YHWH." The tone is despairing and indignant. The prophet focuses on the personal consequences of his words and speaks resentfully of his task. In fact, internal ambiguities in the syntax of v 8 give this resentment an unexpected irony. For when Jeremiah cries "violence and plunder" it is unclear whether he is exposing the injustice of his fellowmen, or whether he is reacting to the violence done to him as a result of his speaking and shouting /10/. A recent opinion has even proposed that the sense of v 8 is that whenever Jeremiah *shouts* prophetic words to the people, he *cries* to God for the *violence* which He has done to him in forcing him to speak /11/. All this and more; for it is even possible that the opening phrases in v 8 must be construed: "whenever I speak, I shout, and cry"—a reading which rhythmically underscores the fitful nature of Jeremiah's prophetic speech. In sum, the network of syntactic ambiguities in v 8 is truly complex; but it does not seem necessary to affirm one resolution at the expense of any other. Indeed, such rich ambiguity suggests simultaneous levels of protest and distress raging within Jeremiah— each one struggling for life expression.

As remarked earlier, v 9 extends the issues of v 7a. Jeremiah's constant speaking (*middēy 'addabēr,* v 8) of the prophetic word (*dābār*) is juxtaposed to the decision not to speak (*lō' 'addabēr,* v 9) God's words again. The rabble reviled him with contempt and frightened him with plots; they conspired that "his name (*shemô*) would never be mentioned (*yizzākēr*) again" (11:19). As a result, Jeremiah thought to reject his task, to refuse to "mention Him (*'ezkārennû*)" or "speak in His name (*shemô*) ever again." But this was impossible. He could not banish God's controlling voice within him. Paradoxically, it is only this prayer, with its brief assertion of private mind space, which gives Jeremiah temporary respite. But even so, even within the very course of this brief protest, the prophet is constrained to admit: "I have tried to contain (*kalkēl*) [God's word] but to no avail (*velō' 'ûkāl*)." The verbal and thematic link with v 7a ("you have overwhelmed me and prevailed, *vattûkāl*") is obvious. Indeed, the reemployment of the same verbal stem serves to dramatize Jeremiah's spiritual crisis. He can neither reject his task nor control his fate (*velō' 'ûkāl*); whereas God is fully and forcefully in control (*vattûkāl*) of him.

Comparable portrayals of the internal and physical dimensions of prophetic experience are found elsewhere in the Book of Jeremiah. At an earlier point in his life, Jeremiah knew that he was unable to withhold God's words of doom. He felt the need to speak them long before they broke the barrier of his lips:

> O my pain, my deep, inward pain!
> My heart bursts its walls,
> My being strains and breaks.
> I cannot keep silent.
>
> (4:19–20)

Now, again, Jeremiah is filled with the unyielding prophetic word of "fire" (*'ēsh* v 9)—an image he elsewhere used to distinguish the force of authentic prophetic speech from the slick-styled lingo of prophetic pretenders: "For is not my word (*devārî*) like fire (*'ēsh*), oracle of YHWH, like a hammer smashing stone?" (Jer 23:29). The true prophet, he stresses, is consumed by the scorching power of his uncontainable task and bellows forth words which sear the security of the nation. "Behold," said God to Jeremiah, in a rephrasing of the commission language of 1:9, "I am making my words (*devāray*) in your mouth as fire (*'ēsh*); and this people are like wood which it will consume!" (5:14). "Can grain be compared to chaff?" (23:28)—even so can the self-induced fantasies of false prophets replace the true word of God.

> My heart has crashed within me,
> All my bones sway;
> I am like a drunkard,
> Soaked with wine
> Because of YHWH,
> Because of His holy words!
>   (23:9)

Thus Jeremiah knew himself seduced and filled by divine words of fire (20:9). Much as his frequent wish that he had died unborn in his mother's womb (15:10; 20:14–18) is undisguised anger at the natural source of his destiny, his present attempt to stifle the prophetic word incubating within him is, correspondingly, an attempt to act out this anger on his own body. Perhaps because of the prenatal (1:5) and adolescent (1:9; 5:14) factors in his prophetic biography, Jeremiah recurrently expressed his experiences with images of interiority (e.g., 4:19–20; 15:10, 15–16; 20:9, 14–18; 23:9) /12/.

He knew in his bones that he could not reject his prophetic destiny. But he could not accept it, either. And so, just here, lay Jeremiah's tragic paradox. Like Thamyris of old, Jeremiah was hounded by divine demands. But when Thamyris tried to inhibit his inspiring divine voices, the gods crippled him with a more awesome silence (*Iliad*: 2.594–600). Jeremiah, by contrast, could not for a moment restrain the divine words which consumed him. He felt himself—in the mocking words once spoken by the Muses about their prophetic mediums—a wretched thing of shame, a mere belly /13/.

Verse 10 deepens the reality of Jeremiah's torment. The mocking and derision referred to in vv 7b and 8b is now fully expressed
through two quotes. The prophet presents new evidence of his
"case," of his being a constantly reviled messenger. Jeremiah tells
God how he has heard the scheming of his enemies: they hope to
trick him and do him in; they have encircled him—"a terror on
every side" (māgôr missāvîv) /14/.

Several elements in Jeremiah's characterization of his enemies'
threats against him have ironic resonances. It will be recalled that
the phrase "terror on every side" picks up the language of Jer
20:3–4, where Jeremiah told Pashhur that he would henceforth be
called māgôr missāvîv (v 3)—for God would bring "terror,"
māgôr, "upon you and all your compatriots." Since Jeremiah had
also used this phrase to announce the invasion of the enemy who
would actualize the divine punishment against Israel (6:22–25),
his present use of it to express his own sense of personal māgôr
(20:10) underscores the irony of Jeremiah's prayer in relation to
his oracles, and his sense of being a victim of attack and siege.

Additionally, when Jeremiah remarks that his enemies have
plotted against him and cites them as saying: "Perhaps he may be
enticed (yefuttê)—then we'll prevail (nûklāh) against him," his
words echo those spoken by Jeremiah to God at the outset of the
prayer (pittîytanî . . . vattûkal). This intratextual loop is also
ironic in the extreme, and suggests a structural analogy with
Jacob, who contended with God and man and prevailed (vattûkal,
Gen 32:29). By contrast, Jeremiah struggled with God and men,
but was prevailed over by both: a victim of heaven and earth. This
is the deep anguish of his situation.

But now a change occurs. Without warning, the prayer shifts
gears (vv 11–12). What has been implicit throughout—namely,
Jeremiah's inescapable commitment to God—is now made explicit.
With renewed confidence the prophet affirms, "But YHWH is with
me like a mighty warrior." The negative, recriminatory tone of the
opening stanzas is abruptly replaced by this positive assertion of
divine providence—as much hoped for as experienced. With this
shift in mood, it would seem that Jeremiah has regained his com-
posure, and that the crisis of confidence has been abated. Picking
up on the enemies' hope to prevail against him (nûklāh, v 10),

Jeremiah rejoices that his enemies will no longer prevail (*yukālû,* v 11). This recurrence of the verb "to prevail" reminds us that each stanza of the prayer has used variations on the stem *yakal* ("to be able;" "prevail"), such that it underlines the thematic transformations and progressions in Jer 20:7–12 as a whole. Seen thus, the prayer moves from God's power over Jeremiah and Jeremiah's corresponding impotence, to the enemies' will for power over Jeremiah and his corresponding spiritual triumph.

The thematic significance of the stem *yakal* in Jer 20:7–12 is complemented by its tonal dimensions as well. The phonemes /k-1/, together with the allophonic variations /q-1/ and /g-1/, produce an alliterative network of sounds which thicken and unify the intensity of the prayer /15/. Accordingly, diverse verbs and nouns are coordinated on the basis of their euphony with the root stem *yakal*. In this way the tone of struggle inherent in the key verb prevails throughout the prayer, as the following transcription makes clear:

v 7.   *vattûKaL hāyîtî LeshōQ KoL hayyôm KuLLōh Lō'ēG Lî*

v 8.   *hāyâ . . . Lî Leherpâ ûLeQeLes KoL hayyôm*

v 9.   *niL'ētî KaLKeL veLō' 'ûKal*

v 10.   *Kî . . . KōL . . . 'uLay yefuttê venûKLāh Lô veniQhāh niQmātēnû*

v 11.   *'al Kēn . . . yiKāshLû veLō' yuKāLû . . . Kî Lō' hisKîLû KeLimmat 'ôLām Lō'*

v 12.   *bōḥēn KeLāyôt vāLēv . . . Kî 'ēLêKâ GiLLîytî 'et rîvî*

The preceding does not exhaust the alliterations found in Jer 20: 7–12, but it does underscore its prevalent tonalities /16/.

However, attentiveness to the phonemic sonority of Jeremiah's prayer does more than underscore its tonal unity or orchestrate new combinations of its dominant thematic stem (*yakal*). It also enables one to shift critical attention away from the representational character of speech and towards non-representational aspects of language /17/—most pertinently, to the relationships between sound, sense, and silence. In the process, a reader becomes a listener, sensitive to and appreciative of the way silences create or modulate linguistic meaning /18/. As a "speechless want"

(Merleau-Ponty) gives birth to tones rhythmically deployed, enjambments of sound clusters and silence presume to express a speaker's heart and mind; just this is the paradox and miracle of speech. For speech organizes the hylic swirl of indiscriminate sounds and silence, and creates a world—a cosmos—with words /19/. But when, however, these resonant tones, inspired and animated by human breath, fade into a new silence, the speaker is left with the echo of his hopes. Sensitivity to these dialectics of sound, sense, and silence deepens our literary and human appreciation of Jeremiah's prayer. For this prayer is not only a heightened expression of linguistic dynamics generally, but comments on a dialectic of sound and silence all the more awesome: the word of God in the resisting heart of man.

But although Jer 20:7–12 has a tonal and linguistic unity, the sharp transition from v 10 to v 11 still begs explanation /20/. What explains the abrupt transition from Jeremiah's remonstrations of injustice to his assurance that God will judge justly? A double process may have been at work. On the one hand, we have noted that the language of Jeremiah's restatement of the plots of his enemies: "Perhaps he may be enticed (*yĕfuttĕ*)—then we'll prevail (*nûklāh*) against him" (v 10), harks back to his opening protest that God had enticed him (*pittīytanî*) and prevailed (*tûkal*). While these references to being enticed reinforce the sense of victimization which pervades the prayer, they may also have had a dialectical effect. Jeremiah was presumably stimulated to realize that such domination was also a sign of God's presence in the life of a true prophet (cf. 23:9, 29). Such a realization would serve to restore Jeremiah's confidence in his task. "YHWH is with me," he exults, "like a mighty warrior."

Repetitions of the verbal stem *yakal* may also have helped trigger Jeremiah's inner transformation. Not only could the sense of being prevailed upon have produced a reaction similar to the foregoing, but the stem *yakal* could also have served to remind Jeremiah of God's promise of protection in his original commission to prophecy: "And they will contend against you, but will not prevail (*lō' yuklû*) against you; for I am with (*'et*) you, oracle of YHWH, to save you" (1:10). Thereby reconfirmed in his destiny, Jeremiah boldly took up the words of this promise in his exultation and wish: "YHWH is with (*'et*) me," he shouts; but as for his enemies, let their fate be as promised long ago: *lō' yukālû,* "let them not prevail" (v 11).

Although Jer 20:11 (stanza 4) does reflect the prophet's new resolve, it does not conclude the prayer. Closure is found in v 12 (stanza 5) /21/, where the successive alliterations of the preceding verses (*k/g-l*) reecho with a summative effect /22/: *rō'ê KeLāyôt vāLēv . . . Kî 'eLêKâ GiLLîytî 'et rîvî.* At first glance Jeremiah's appeal for divine revenge against his enemies merely serves to pull together the preceding charges of injustice. But, in fact, the conclusion completes the transformation of Jeremiah's religious consciousness begun in v 11. The prophet speaks to God as one who "tests (*bōḥēn*) the righteous (*ṣādîq*)." Such a phrase is an ironic reversal of Jeremiah's God-appointed task as a "tester" (*bāḥôn*; cf. 6.27). It also reflects Jeremiah's revised perception regarding his suffering. He does not refer to God as a righteous (*ṣedeq*) judge or tester, in continuity with his own and other biblical expressions /23/, but as the one who tests him, Jeremiah, who is *ṣādîq*: a justified or righteous person. Jeremiah has presumably come to realize that his torment is but a test, and that he has never been abandoned. He therefore trusts in God's avenging justice.

Yet Jeremiah's new personal truth, which retrospectively annihilates his past pain as something wrongly seen, raises new questions. If God put His own word in Jeremiah's heart (*libbî,* v 9), and can see (*rō'ê*) the innermost heart (*lēv*) of man (v 12), what need is there for testing? And further what need is there for Jeremiah to reveal his case to Him whose knowledge comprehends all?

The logic of such a closure would thus seem to undermine the very pathos and necessity of Jeremiah's prayer. But not entirely. For it is the very process of prayer whereby the prophet has achieved his new knowledge. What Jeremiah achieves by revealing his case to God is to see his life in a new way. In the process, he recognizes himself as a tested sufferer—one whose physical and emotional torment does not invalidate the divine promise of protective providence. God's protection is spiritualized: It is the confidence He gives His servants that their heart and service are seen and accepted. This realization, as the others, would seem to underlie the transition from despair to hope in vv 11–12. Jeremiah's final appeal for violent recrimination against his enemies reflects his new confidence—with all the venom of *resentment*: you "who *sees* the innermost heart, let me *see* your revenge . . ."

This remarkable prayer reveals a tragic moment wherein a prophet despairs but cannot fully rebel. Jeremiah struggles to suppress God's voice within him. But his realization that God's word is in his bones, and his recognition of divine protection in v 11, point to the reunification of his will with God's. For Jeremiah's spiritual restoration lies in the full acceptance of his unique task in the world: to be a faithful and trusting divine messenger.

No word of God comes to build or confirm Jeremiah's hope and confidence, as happens elsewhere (11:21–23; 12:5–6; 15:19–21). But we know, nevertheless, that Jeremiah will again speak in His name, for he quickly added—or are these the words of another?—the following hymn (v 13).

> Sing to YHWH;
> Praise YHWH;
> For He has saved a needy soul from his enemies!

NOTES

*A slightly different version of this essay appears in my book *Text and Texture; Close Readings of Selected Biblical Texts* (Schocken Books, N.Y.: 1979).

/1/   For lay prayers not found in the Psalms and Prophets, see A. Wendel. On biblical prayer in general, see Y. Kaufmann (499–506; English abridgement: 309–311).

/2/   These laments were classified by Gunkel as "Klagelieder des Einzelnen," in H. Gunkel and J. Begrich (172–265).

/3/   The close formal and linguistic relationships between Jeremiah's prayers and psalms of individual lament has been demonstrated by W. Baumgartner (48–51, 63–67). The recent attempt to establish a communal basis for Jeremiah's prayers by H. Graf Reventlow has been effectively refuted by J. Bright (1970:189–213).

/4/   Cf. the remarks of S. Blank (1974).

/5/   A recent discussion on Jer 20:1–6, with pertinent literature, can be found in W. Holladay (1972). He also discusses the meaning of the phrase; and see the discussion below, n. 13. The name Pashhur is of Egyptian origin, and is found elsewhere in the Bible and on extrabiblical artifacts; see S. Ahituv.

/6/   For the overall legal background of the "cases" of Jeremiah, as well as a suggested breakdown of their component parts, see S. Blank (1948).

/7/   A review of recent attempts to separate vv 11–12 from the original prayer, especially because of the call for revenge (!), can be found in Blank (1974:116–118). Attempts to dismiss vv 10ff. as secondary have recently been countered by D. J. A. Clines and D. M. Gunn (1976).

/8/   Medieval commentators like Rashi and Kimhi understood the foregoing verbs in terms of aspects of the prophet's original commission. In light of the larger issue as to whether Jeremiah's prayers were recited publicly or privately, S. D. Luzatto, basing himself on this verse (Jer 20:7), suggested in his commentary that Jeremiah spoke them publicly so as to convey to the people that he spoke by *force majeure*—not because he wished to criticize them. In this way he hoped to bring them to repentance. This last point has been reiterated, apparently independently, by Clines and Gunn (1976:401–2).

/9/   For the assessment that Jeremiah was actually aware of Ps 22, and that it informed his prophetic self-consciousness, see W. Holladay (1964: esp. 156, 159, 164).

/10/   In divergence with the common medieval tradition, R. Joseph Kara understood Jeremiah's cry of violence as voiced about himself. See his *Perush Yirmiyahu*.

/11/   Clines and Gunn (1978).

/12/   The dialectics of inner and outer space, both private and public, are quite varied in the Book of Jeremiah. A suggestive probe into this typology can be found in J. Starobinski (1975).

/13/   The original phrase from Hesiod's *Theogony* is: "wretched things of shame, mere bellies" (1.26). Shelley has poignantly expressed the impossibility for a poet to restrain the fire of inspiration within him:

> A man cannot say, "I will compose poetry." The greatest poet even cannot say it; for the mind in creation is as a fading coal, which some invisible influence, like an inconstant wind, awakens to transitory brightness . . . and the conscious portions of our natures are unprophetic either of its approach or its departure.

See his essay (1957) and compare Milton's remarks on divine dictation in *Paradise Lost* 9:21–24. More recently, Julian Jaynes has discussed many structural similarities between prophets, poets, and schizophrenics; and he has compared the "mental organization" of hallucinatory echolalia to the phenomenon of biblical prophets who articulate their commanding voices (424).

/14/   The meaning of *māgôr* has long been a matter of debate. The Targum, followed by Rashi, does not derive it from the stem *gwr*, meaning "fear" (as does Kimhi). They translate "gather" and apparently assumed here the homologous stem "to dwell." Be this as it may, the Septuagint has a verb which assumably translates the stem *'agar*, "to gather," as noted by A. W. Streane (162).

māgôr missāvîv appears in v 10 without parataxis. The New English Bible deletes it as extraneous; but if the phrase is not simply a subjective clarification of Jeremiah's experience, a more intriguing possibility has been suggested. In slightly different ways, and apparently quite independently, Ehrlich (221f.), W. Rudolf (121), and J. Bright (1965:132f.) regard the phrase as a quote spoken in mocking derision to Jeremiah—something like: "there goes old (i.e., the one who always says) *māgôr missāvîv.*"

/15/   On related matters, see K. Burke and also D. Hymes.

/16/   Other examples: *PiTTîyTanî VāʾePPāT* (v 7); *ʾAṢuR be ʾAṢmōtay* (v 9); *HaGGîDû veNaGGîdennu* (v 10); *NiQḥāh NiQmātēnû* (v 10).

/17/   See the discussion of M. Bloomfield.

/18/   Cf. L. Bloomfield, who devotes attention to "significant" phonetic distinctions. The Russian formalists have considered "word-boundaries" an important factor in the perception of a poem. See V. Erlich (216).

/19/   I have found the essay by G. Hartman most instructive.

/20/   Although Jeremiah's prayer and its transition to trust does follow a pattern commonly found in psalms of lament (cf. Baumgartner, and see C. Westermann: 64–81), I am disinclined to reduce the shift in Jeremiah's praying consciousness to such formal considerations because of the intensely spontaneous nature of his cry. Adequate attention must be given to Jer 20:7–12 as the expression of a unique moment of prayer with its own dynamics. All this is not to deny, of course, that traditional literary factors may have helped organize Jeremiah's mental and emotional response to his particular situation.

/21/   I have found Barbara H. Smith's book stimulating in thinking about closure in Jer 20:7–12.

/22/   For this expression, see Hymes (118).

/23/   See Jer 11:20, 17:10; 1 Chr 29:17; and cf. Ps 11:5, 7. The Septuagint and Targum understood "righteous judge" here, as did R. Joseph Kara.

Jeremiah 20:7–12: A Literary Response

Geoffrey Hartman

As a respondent, I would first like to make some general comments on literary criticism, and only then turn to Michael Fishbane's paper. A question can be raised concerning the relation of homiletic interpretation and literary criticism and there I shall begin.

I

Literary interpretation is not a pure or autonomous form of interpretation. Some might say that interpretation is always the same but that its language changes according to the context, both the polemical context and the literary context. There is such a thing as a text milieu; new texts are generated and these become part of our awareness. It may be also that interpretation itself changes; but that remains an open question. What I do know is that literary interpretation is never pure, never anything like a science or an autonomous discipline. One might, therefore, go so far as to say that it is midrash despite itself, or midrash not linked —and here is the negative that has to accompany any definition to make it at all precise—midrash not linked to the Torah lections, not subordinated in a discernible way to a religious calendar and everything (the polemic, the disputation) that surrounds that calendar.

I want to focus for a moment on the relation of commentary to subordination. Is literary interpretation simply an unsubordinated midrash? Wherever a canon is established, do you not also get a commentary, or one kind of commentary, that proves to be insubordinate? If so, when the subject of that commentary is the Bible rather than a secular classic, how does it deal with the possibility of profanation that resides in its liberated or virtuoso character? You might say this is where the individual has to either come forward or else hold his peace. It is a matter of witnessing, of the individual stepping forward and confessing, of taking the chance of being profane. I do not think that the question of profanation can be totally avoided. Even should we compare biblical interpretation with biblical scholarship rather than with midrash or rabbinical exegesis, the situation is not radically changed.

Biblical scholarship, while it is not one thing any more than rabbinical or patristic exegesis is one thing, must also consider the problem of redaction. Its hermeneutics of suspicion questions the unity of biblical passages conceived as a generic unity. The appearance of unity in the Bible or parts of the Bible is not necessarily due to single-author composition, in this view. But what unity is there then? Can we still talk of unity? Is the process of redaction a tendentious harmonization or reconciliation of different authors and sources? Is it also perhaps inspired by so-called "literary" considerations?

With respect to this line of inquiry the literary theorist ventures to say the following. The concept of the unity of the work of art is derived mainly from some hints in Aristotle's poetics on the difference between epic and dramatic action. Tragedy does not depend, Aristotle says, on the unity of the hero whereas epic does depend on it, because epic, unlike tragedy, allows itself a certain episodic largesse. Considerably revised, this concept of the unity of the work of art did not dominate our view of art until the seventeenth century and the revival of classical or pseudoclassical standards, especially in French criticism; and it was already being questioned by the end of the eighteenth century. It lost force with the rise of interest in folklore and oral traditions, and also with a rise in our knowledge of medieval contamination literature (that is, the way stories were built up by fusing different stories with one another). Even biblical higher criticism may have drawn something from this questioning movement coming from the later eighteenth century. Today psychoanalysis has intensified our sus-

picions concerning the unity of art by suggesting that the unity of
the person is at best synthetic or adaptive and more likely to be
multiple and self-divisive. The more vigorous the person, you
might argue, the more multiple or self-divisive he or she is. And
finally, what unity there is in person or art tends to come about by
a process of self-revision and self-interpretation. This process,
while intrapsychic, is not unlike the more external-seeming redactional process. What we are left with, then, if this cursory sketch
can be trusted, are the following issues:

1. The issue of the historical relation of commentary to the
text, that is, to the sacred or institutional work of written art. That
historical relation would include the rise and multiplication of
literary commentary. If we complain today that there are too many
interpretations, that needs to be considered as a historical fact.

2. The issue of the intrinsic, not now historical but generic,
relation of commentary to the institutionalized or sacred word.
God needs man, God demands man or demands of man. The text
needs, the text demands interpreters, and this would have an intrinsic or generic component, not only an historical one.

3. The process of institutionalization—let us call canonization
part of such a process—should be considered as it affects the
classic work, secular or sacred. The process of institutionalization
should be considered because we have had centuries of commentary; and Judah Goldin pointed out /1/ that in some sense midrashic commentary was like the commentary on Homer, though
with at least one important difference. But we have centuries of
commentary, so by now the latter should be considered an activity
in its own right, one that argues a need in us for the permanent
revision of institutionalized texts. Commentary itself, moreover,
has often experienced institutionalized moments of closure just
like the texts it refers to. Is it possible that when we are as far
from the twentieth century as it is from the seventeenth, we may
seem in retrospect to have passed through a period of *closure* in
the commentary process? We have seen, in our period, a semi-
conscious transfer of criteria of unity from works of art, or classi-
cist notions of them, to the work of commentary itself.

Let me add a codicil. There is a kind of threat in the air, the threat of radical exegesis. This threat, as I understand it, is related to our dissatisfaction with the commentary process, its institutionalization, or our failing attempts to close it. Radical exegesis may try to solve the whole problem by foreseeing the disappearance of the text.

One already feels it in Hegel who was a very strong if protestant-minded interpreter, in whom the movement of internalization—internalization of the code or of the historical process—produces that revel of thoughts which is described in his phenomenology of mind and which marks the end of the internalization of history. Of course, we don't quite know what that revel consists of. It is a revel of thoughts, but thoughts are different from words or quotations, and I wonder what is really looks like in that philosophic belly or mind—whether Hegel is not ventriloquizing, whether his mind has not become the belly at that point.

Leaving that aside, I see a movement toward a point where the text is felt to be dispensable, where one moves by interpretation beyond the text. I think this possibility has always been part of the enmity between philosophy on the one hand and literature on the other. Philosophy by now has its own primary texts, its own secular canon. Still, within it there continues to be a movement beyond text dependence, because it is a dependence. But we as people of the book are dependent on certain texts. It is almost as if there were an evolutionary or educational process of which the far-off and divine event would be a freedom from the words of others. Even in the Book of Jeremiah there is a famous passage that seems to point toward a new covenant which is totally internalized. I would call this a movement toward radical exegesis; and in a modern philosophy like that of Jacques Derrida, a new word, "dissemination," evokes a state in which the interpreter makes the text so much part of the writing or thinking process that we can't say that this is *our* text, or this is *the* book, or this is a masterpiece. Derrida is not against the text: for him the ideal commentary makes the text escape the status of thing or fetish. "Dissemination" may nevertheless come close to radical exegesis. What has to be rethought is the dependence of humanists, our dependence, on the text.

II

I now come to my formal task as a respondent. I agree with what Mr. Fishbane has found in the text in terms of *formal* structure. I see the same patterns he does. I might have put before you certain refinements, but in terms of the chiastic structure of vv 7–12 I follow him. In terms of the stems and the play with stems I also follow Mr. Fishbane. I agree with the way he states the problem of linking the second part of this prayer to the event that seems to give it rise, the way he brings in the generative matrix or the life situation of the prophet.

I am with him, then, up to the point where he stops formal analysis, even though he does not admit to doing so. He crosses over from formalistic to what he has called on another occasion /2/ nonformalistic matters. It is not that I disagree with what he does but it would take me much longer to cross over and perhaps I would see the proper task of the interpreter to stay in the transitions, in the cross-over, a longer time. Towards the end of his essay, Mr. Fishbane has already left formalistic analysis behind several times, but he has carefully leaped back; he is a very agile interpreter. This crossing over is understandable, however, since Mr. Fishbane knows that interpretation is not simply pattern hunting. In the integration of formal patterns with something else, the nature of the something else, the ideological nature of it—is it a higher form, is it a different thing—is the vital question. And toward the end of his essay, he suggests the following which has long been foreshadowed. It has to do with the nature of prayer. He has previously discussed the prayer and he has made striking comments on prayer as a genre; but now he ventures to say that one can feel within the structure of the poem itself the effectiveness of prayer on the one (Jeremiah) who prays.

Technically, Mr. Fishbane is referring to the anastrophe. In Jeremiah's prayer you don't have the downturn or catastrophe because it's already there; so you convert the soul, you turn the soul around, you make it move back, you turn it up. This anastrophic turn he then interprets as the result of the movement of prayer itself, or as somehow effected by the prayer on the one who prays. Now if he had stated this as a formal consideration "there is here a movement from catastrophe to anastrophe," we might be disappointed. After all, one has to go somewhere: one either stays where one is or goes down or goes up, and most prayers do tend to go up. In Jeremiah, of course, one starts all over again for there is the additional problem that after v 13 a sudden new lamentation is heard. Mr. Fishbane, however, focuses mainly on the extracted structure of the main prayer: the paradigm provided by vv 7-12.

How are we to understand that self-expressive catharsis, the effect of speech, of Jeremiah's speech on Jeremiah? To derive the formal fact from the psychological matrix, we would have to say that only prayers with this kind of upturn were written down, circulated as a public type. Mr. Fishbane does not put it that way; he thinks that Jeremiah's prayer has affected Jeremiah, that there has been some action of the self on the self. In short, he goes from the formal feature to a psychologistic premise, but does not show how the psychological feature might have resulted in a formal genre.

Moreover, and this is my second reservation, Mr. Fishbane goes too quickly from considerations of form to the nonformalistic area. He tries to catch the relation between what he calls generative logic and tone, the relation between the sequence of verses and the psychological state of the speaker. His essay is certainly rich in psychology. He talks about anger, he talks about resentment, he talks about pathos, and he often talks about tone. Tone here, as I understand it, does not mean simply a formalized level of style, but really tone of speech. Although, as he says, we do not hear Jeremiah actually enunciating and breathing, he courageously suggests that we must, as modern latter-day interpreters, infer a psychic breathing within Jeremiah. My second question then is whether the psychologistic thesis is tenable. Has Mr. Fishbane earned the right to cross over so quickly, even if he replies that as a modern reader he must do this?

And my third hesitation is perhaps the hardest to express. Toward the end Mr. Fishbane talks about silence. What he implies, although he expresses it in formalistic terms having to do with boundaries (the boundary of speech and silence, and certain semiotic considerations), is that Jeremiah has a *psychic* difficulty in speaking to one who already knows. Mr. Fishbane implies that if this prayer is addressed to a god, it is a god who already knows, who is omniscient; therefore the thought arises, how can I have a *riv*, a case, or how can I prosecute that case? *Why talk at all?* He must know what's going on in me. *He* knows. Hence a tension in the very succession of the words.

In literary terms we could point to the "orderly confusion" which became a characteristic of the great ode of the seventeenth and eighteenth centuries. This feature regularizes the irregularity of quick transitions between states of mind. In Jeremiah such a transition is between subjective and objective as well as the god-addressed and the self-addressed. The formal feature of orderly confusion is understood by Mr. Fishbane in nonformalistic terms as expressing a desire to keep silent because silence is faith and obedience rather than *riv*. Thus, while I am in considerable agreement with the formal analysis, my hesitation comes when the interpreter crosses over toward nonformalistic considerations. It is in that crossover that the hermeneutic task is most sensitive.

III

That is what I now wish to show. Jeremiah being a prophet, the status of language or of the cry is at least as important as the genre concept of prayer. Formal analysis can type vv 7–12 as a prayer. But if there were a genre called "the cry," surely we would consider it at least as fitting. I do not mean psychologically that Jeremiah cries from the depths of his soul; I mean something like "whenever I speak, I shout" or "I cry violence and plunder." In these verses Mr. Fishbane has shown a careful patterning of direct speech, a patterning which is chiastic and which, I would add, culminates in a movement of direct speech within direct speech "I shout and cry violence and plunder." Now in one of the most prophetic portions of the Book of Job, the sufferer says, "I cry out violence and nothing happens." This raises in my mind the question which perhaps only the historical scholar can answer, whether "I cry out violence" had any kind of legal or ritual implication, just as a policeman is supposed to cry "halt" two times before he fires. Had Job or Jeremiah remained silent, not gone into the street and cried out "violence," would they have had a case? Maybe there is a legal implication, or the metaphor of one.

Even when there is a note of self-reflection, that is, when we seem farthest from cry or direct speech, and the poet is not addressing God but himself, the theme makes the Yahweh-crying emphatic. "It was in me as a consuming fire locked in my bones, I have tried to contain it but was unable." After that we have direct speech in terms of the "I" returning, and *māgôr missāvîv*, "terror on every side," reappears, as a nexus between lines 1 and 6 and the prayer of lines 7 following.

The name, *māgôr missāvîv*, returns as a phrase and this convertibility again raises a question as to the relation of naming to speaking, or the most direct form of languaging (naming) to the more indirect elaboration of language by way of syntax, etc. In v 11 you get the quietest verse of them all, the only verse, perhaps, which is quiet; yet it is also assertive, a verse of constatation; so the name is still there, the direct address is implicitly there, but in the least direct form. There is a counterpoint between the mode of statement and the thematic assertiveness of "they shall be bitterly abashed."

Finally, v 12 returns to the mode of direct address similar to that of v 7, and the entire sequence ends with "let me see your revenge on them, for I have revealed my case to you" (one version has at this point "but oh, Lord of hosts that triest the righteous, that seeth the reigns and the heart, let me see thy vengeance on them"). I would pick up the doubling of the word "seeing" at that point because when Job cries violence he also says "I will come to see God" or "I will try to see God face to face." Directness of the wish to see relates to the directness of the burning impulse to speak out. Job has his "riv" too. I want to see my accuser, he pleads. I want to make my case directly to him and so be justified. Jeremiah's cry, as a whole, is an extraordinary pattern of the modalities of direct address.

For a literary mind what is central is the relation of direct speech to indirect speech; the relation of the cry to direct address, or to Yahweh as a name; and how this kind of directness is mediated by language. The desire of immediate justification or immediate success in seeing one's accuser, of seeing oneself justified, has to pass through the mode of language and even through words which

God has put into the prophet's mouth. It is not the desire only that is mediated but also the words themselves. The words which Jeremiah uses against God are God's own words which he uses against Judah in Jeremiah 2 and 3, and which the prophets elsewhere hear spoken by God. Israel has played the harlot, Israel has betrayed me, and so on. Is it this precarious conversion of God's words that we call prayer?

Certainly the prayers in the *Siddur* often petition God in God's own words. God may listen to the words that he has used. So his own words are given back and made persuasive toward him. Man's petition to God in God's own words, that precarious cry, is prayer. Mr. Fishbane points out that it may not result in an immediate result, but rather in a kind of silence, however we understand the silence. To me it seems to point to a radical indeterminacy: when the poet says "you have enticed me," does he mean, "you have enticed me with those very words? I believed your words and your accusations, but now I am the one betrayed." "You have overwhelmed me," but what has overwhelmed him? I would suggest that what has overwhelmed Jeremiah is not just "terror on every side" or the man of that name who put him in the stocks; rather it is what is suggested by Jeremiah 1: "and the word of the Lord came unto me, saying . . . ."

It is the *word* that comes, and it says

> Before I formed thee in the belly I knew thee and before thou camest forth out of the womb, I sanctified thee. I have appointed thee a prophet unto the nations. Then said I: "Ah, Lord God, behold I cannot speak for I am a child."

It is not only the correspondence of Jer 1:4–6 but what comes later in Jeremiah 20, "Cursed be the day wherein I was born," which is important. These verses answer the question, by what is the prophet overwhelmed? He is overwhelmed, as prophets are, by the word of God. The simplest meaning of these opening verses is, "you were mine by election, I knew you by omniscience, I knew you were the man to do the job." But, "Before I formed thee in the belly I knew thee," is so radically figurative that a generic displacement occurs which goes toward a certain Christian idea without being Christian, toward "In the beginning was the Word," toward the seminal and inseminative power of the word. (I do not say this in order to Christianize the text, but to show that these issues arise out of texts such as "Before I formed thee in the belly I knew thee, and before thou camest forth out of the womb I sanctified thee.")

My mind as an interpreter—and you'll notice how long I am taking in this crossing—turns at this point, strangely enough, to Lacan. "Before I formed thee in the belly I knew thee" understood in the light of "In the beginning was the Word," could be an epigraph for Lacanian psychoanalysis. Lacan's concept of the "Discourse of the Other" can be understood as restating this predetermination with which it is our fate to deal.

Although Jeremiah's "Oh, Lord God, behold I cannot speak for I am a child" could be a first refusal or a scrupulous ritual step ("Oh, I'm not worthy" or "I'm not ready"), God has taken that excuse away by saying, "I have already given you prophetic speech. My word has predetermined you." Moreover, when Jer 20:7 states, "you have overwhelmed me and prevailed," it is as if God's own prophecy to the prophet were coming true. There is an internally predicted pattern to the book of life and a literary interpreter rejoices when he sees the book turning on its own axis. What is being completed is surely an inner figure of that kind.

I, too, then am haunted in Jeremiah by the correlation of voice—feeling and word. Mr. Fishbane puts it in terms of the intermixture of the subject and object, of the prophet's words and those of God. The words in which Jeremiah speaks are so forceful in relation to the divine word that there is fusion or contamination between human and divine word; and this leads to the question of prophecy or the questioning of prophecy as false prophecy. When Jeremiah says "you have enticed me" we go back to 1 Kings 22 and the enticement mentioned there; and now I think we *can* cross over to approach the topic of the psychology of the prophet. Consider the interchange of subject and object, look at the radical metaphoricity, at the fact that the second event or prayer seems to be the fulfillment of an earlier prophecy. Is the word of God a pregenerative word? How do we distinguish the words of the prophet from the divine word? Who is to separate the subjective and fallible from the authoritative and prophetic? "Whenever I speak, I shout." Why can't Jeremiah talk in a normal voice? What is the matter with him? Is he shouting because a prophet needs to shout, or because he is not being heard? Or is it a psychological condition that when the spirit breaks out he has no speech, he has only shouting? Shouting is hard to bear, for him and for us. As a literary critic I would have to say that Jeremiah's prayer is marked by the fact that it is a kind of shouting or can be classified as crying and shouting rather than speaking or the modalities of speech which we usually associate with literature. The word or a voice overwhelms the prophet. One might almost say that the word is the violence of which he complains.

I would like to add a final note, to introduce a text of what to me is sacred, yet must be classified as non-sacred literature. Michael Fishbane and I agree that the Book of Jeremiah is the cry and voice of someone under siege. On how to describe that siege we may differ. But it is the response of someone who is called, and whose problem is with the word in relation to directness and desire for the word. It is true that I see that in an anti-psychologistic manner. Therefore, I want to quote a passage from Wordsworth which actually goes in both directions: that of prophetic speech as in some sense discontinuous with normal speech, being a shouting and everything that implies; and ordinary speech, however elevated, so that, like Michael Fishbane, one can work out the psychological and affective implications. The passage I want to quote is from his autobiographical epic *The Prelude*. It refers to a period after the French Revolution has broken out and massacres have occurred. The French Revolution has betrayed itself in Wordsworth's eyes, but he does not feel it is an absolute betrayal. He was frightened by the September massacres, but he is still with the revolution. Even as he writes (this is about twelve years after the events of 1792) he still feels in sympathy with the revolution and he tries to understand why after all these years he is still a Jacobin at heart.

> But as the ancient Prophets, borne aloft
> In vision, yet constrained by natural laws
> With them to take a troubled human heart,
> Wanted not consolations, nor a creed
> Of reconcilement, then when they denounced,
> On towns and cities, wallowing in the abyss

Of their offences, punishment to come;
Or saw, like other men, with bodily eyes,
Before them, in some desolated place,
The wrath consummate and the threat fulfilled;
So, with devout humility be it said,
So did a portion of that spirit fall
On me uplifted from the vantage-ground
Of pity and sorrow to a state of being
That through the time's exceeding fierceness saw
Glimpses of retribution, terrible,
And in the order of sublime behests:
But even if that were not, amid the awe
Of unintelligible chastisement,
Not only acquiescences of faith
Survived, but daring sympathies with power,
Motions not treacherous or profane, else why
Within the folds of no ungentle breast
Their dread vibration to this hour prolonged?
Wild blasts of music thus could find their way
Into the midst of turbulent events;
So that worst tempests might be listened to.

Here also is one who, like a prophet, acknowledges the power of word and feeling that is in him, however visionary and terrible it was, and continues to be.

NOTES

/1/   At the Ottawa Conference in 1977.
/2/   At the Ottawa Conference in 1977.

Conclusion

John Dominic Crossan
Robert Polzin and Eugene Rothman

Chapter 11

"Ruth Amid the Alien Corn":
Perspectives and Methods in Contemporary
Biblical Criticism

John Dominic Crossan

The purpose of this article will be to locate different approaches to biblical studies as fully as possible within the present situation of biblical criticism and thereby to chart the probable trajectories of its history or, if one prefers, the probable transformations of its system. To render my position as clearly as I can, I shall present the argument in six consecutive propositions, each basing itself on the one before it. In biblical tradition, after six comes the rest.

First Proposition: Biblical exegesis is in a state of change as revolutionary as was the advent of the historical-critical theory at an earlier date.

I recognize full well that the term "revolution" has been invoked so often in the past of biblical exegesis that my present usage can easily be disregarded with polite murmurs about little boys and big wolves. It is true that almost every major linguistic and archeological discovery in the ancient Near East, from the Rosetta Stone and Behistun Rock to Qumran and Nag Hammadi, and most presently, to Ebla in Syria, has resulted in pronouncements of a revolutionary breakthrough in biblical criticism. But I am still ready to risk the term because I am convinced that it is the only one adequate to what is happening. I am convinced that we are now into a situation analogous to the period in which the historical-critical vision first erupted into biblical studies. In other words, a second revolution is upon us.

I use the term "revolution," then, in the precise manner in

which Thomas S. Kuhn defined it in his fascinating book *The Structure of Scientific Revolutions*. It is a change not just at the level of *data* (new materials: tablets, scrolls, codices, etc.), nor even just on the level of *methods* (from source to redaction criticism), but at the level of *theory* about the very subject itself. It is thus a change in the self-consciousness of scholars concerning their scholarship. It involves (Kuhn: 85, italics added):

> a reconstruction of the field from new fundamentals, a reconstruction that changes some of the field's most elementary *theoretical* generalizations as well as many of its paradigm *methods* and *applications*.

When the theory of the field changes, so will the methods, and thence the applications and the conclusions. It seems to me that, for the first time since the revolutionary advent of historical-critical theory, methods, applications, and conclusions, a similar change is on the horizon.

Second Proposition: This revolution may best be described as changing biblical studies from a single discipline to a field of disciplines.

If my first proposition be accepted, there is one very interesting point of comparison between the first revolution, the advent of *historical criticism,* and this second one, the arrival of *field criticism.* That former change involved reading the biblical materials not as an act of piety but as a discipline of scholarship. But where for some personality types, some ecclesiastical contexts, or some historical situations, these were absolutely disjunctive options (piety *or* scholarship), for others these were but simultaneous aspects of the same magnificent process (piety *as* scholarship). That is, there was no *necessary* disjunction between the two ways of reading the biblical tradition. So also with the second revolution, the change from biblical study as a discipline to biblical studies as a field. For some, myself included, this field necessarily includes the disciplines heretofore used in biblical criticism under the general rubric of historical research, so that I experience a both-and rather than an either-or situation. For others, this new revolution must be articulated in terms of disjunctive opposition. I am thinking especially of the bitterness which has soured relations between the more established biblical methods in Germany and the work of Erhardt Güttgemanns's Generativ Poetics group at the University of Bonn /1/. This is in strong contrast, as he himself has noted (1975: 85–86), to the more amicable situation within the American Society of Biblical Literature where the *Journal of Biblical Literature* and the *Society of Biblical Literature Monograph Series* represent the older and more established aspects of biblical scholarship while *Semeia* and its attendant monograph series, *Semeia Supplements* (now *Studies*), have been established for "the exploration of new and emergent areas and methods of biblical criticism . . . employing the methods, models, and findings of linguistics, folklore studies, contemporary literary criticism, structuralism, social anthropology, and other such disciplines and approaches . . ." /2/. Other American publications, such as the trilogy published (since 1974) by The Pickwick Press as The Pittsburgh Theological Monographs, Reprint, and Original Texts and Translations Series /3/, or Fortress Press' Old Testament Guides and New Testament Guides /4/, include both established and experimental viewpoints within the same series.

My argument is that biblical study will no longer be conducted under the exclusive or even dominant hegemony of one discipline such as historical philology or even of one discipline with two divisions, philology and archeology, but will be studied through a multitude of disciplines interreacting mutually as a *field criticism*. It is clear to you, I hope, that the field I envisage is electric with creative tension rather than pastoral with bleating sheep.

This *field criticism* process is being greatly facilitated in America by three indigenous factors. First, as biblical criticism moved from a theological seminary to a religious studies department in a college or university (actually or nostalgically denominational; privately or publically supported), something happened to it which should have but apparently never did in the major divinity schools long associated with great universities. Second, the problem of teaching *about* the Bible in the public schools has effected a self-consciousness about biblical scholarship in dialogue with other areas of study and pedagogy on all levels. I am thinking, for example, of the work of the Public Education Religion Studies

Center at Wright State University in Dayton, Ohio, and of the publications stemming from the fact that "in 1969 the Indiana University Department of Religious Studies received the first of three grants from the Lilly Endowment, Incorporated, to conduct a series of summer institutes for secondary school teachers of English who wanted to develop or improve courses or units using the Bible in their literature classes" /5/. Third, the creation of Scholars Press by Robert W. Funk at the University of Montana gave scholarship a forum for experimental publication (in both senses) which the general presses and even (or especially) the university presses could not furnish at a price possible for its audience.

When biblical studies are conceived as a field of disciplines with no single discipline transcendentally dominant, certain conclusions will immediately follow. It is always possible, of course, to practice such rhetorical terrorism as Walter Wink's declaration that "historical criticism is bankrupt" (1973). And all such statements have a certain therapeutic value. But, in itself, it seems to me that the future of biblical studies involves incorporating our earlier methods into a wider framework rather than simply junking them for alternative methods. The only absolute disjunction is where any one discipline denies the scholarly integrity of another or forbids it either access or participation within the field of biblical studies. An individual scholar will certainly maintain within this field the discipline one prefers (for example, archeology or textual criticism) but it would be naive to think that the simultaneous presence of a plurality of disciplines will not necessitate a general knowledge by each of the major results from all and a definite creative interreaction (welcomed or not) by all upon all. We are dealing, I repeat, with a field of force, not a field of sheep.

Third Proposition: The present influx of anthropological, sociological, and literary methods can best be seen as establishing this field conception of biblical studies.

In support of this proposition I will simply adduce some examples and I admit that they are but the ones that come most readily to mind. Nobody should be either unduly flattered by inclusion or unduly offended by exclusion. You will probably be able to think of many more for yourself.

A most important factor in this entire process is that we seem to be dealing with two-way traffic. Not only are scholars formally trained in biblical studies (in the older sense) using social and literary methods and models but those specifically trained in the social sciences and literature are investigating biblical texts just as they would those others available to them.

1. Social Sciences. Two very interesting examples of anthropologists discussing biblical texts are the studies by Mary Douglas on Leviticus 11 (1966) which were, for me, the best I had ever read on the biblical dichotomy of clean and unclean animals /6/, and the work of Edmund Leach (1976), which studies sacrifice in Leviticus 1—10 and Exodus 28—30 as a major and paradigmatic case study in an undergraduate introduction to social anthropology.

As an example, going in the opposite direction, that is, from Bible to sociology, but with no less interesting results, there is the recent work by John Gager on primitive Christianity (1975).

2. Literature. Again we are confronted with a two-way process. Herbert N. Schneidau, professor in the English Department of the University of California, has traced the fertile alienation and sacred discontent of our western tradition back to its biblical roots in the Old Testament (1976).

From the opposite direction, and working more with the New than the Old Testament, there are the recent books by Robert C. Tannehill, Robert W. Funk, Dan O. Via, Jr., and my own trilogy on the language of the historical Jesus /7/.

Any one of these books might be discussed and dismissed as an interesting activity on the margins or fringes of biblical studies, works which in no way change the critical self-awareness of mainline biblical scholarship. But there are too many of them not to indicate that something rather profound is underway. So many swallows make a summer /8/.

Fourth Proposition: The twin axes of biblical studies as a field are the historical and structural methodologies.

This proposition means that we are dealing with two basically distinct but inevitably intertwined methodologies. By this term I intend the entire complex of philosophy, theory, method, application, and conclusion operating along each axis. These twin methodologies, about whose separate identities and mutual relations scholarship will no doubt differ quite widely, will also tend, of course and increasingly, to appear within each separate discipline involved in the field of biblical studies. These twin axes of the historical and the structural establish, then, the vast grid upon which biblical criticism will hereafter unfold.

At this point I would draw your attention to the opening comments in an article by John Collins where he points out that the biblical texts have been studied genetically so that the "historical sequence facilitates explanation in terms of cause and effect" /9/. (It may be noted in passing that biblical scholarship has all too often tended to confuse sources and causes.) Over against this quite legitimate diachronic emphasis, he contrasts the structural approach whose "main emphasis falls on the synchronic view of the internal relationships within a system." One might simplify to say that historical methodology disciplines the study of units claimed to be in direct, genetic, or causal relationship with one another, while structural methodology disciplines the study of units claimed to be in indirect but significant relationship with one another, in a systemic but not a genetic contact.

Indeed, we would probably have to admit that heretofore the area of biblical studies occupied itself almost exclusively with the *prehistory* of the text, with all that led up to its final fixation and ignored as outside its realm what happened thereafter, namely, the *posthistory* of the text. (These terms may stand for the moment but obviously they are part of the problem rather than the solution.) I do not deny that independent religious or ecclesiastical traditions have developed and studied the posthistory of biblical texts. In many ways such traditions and institutions *are* that posthistory itself. But what about all and any such multiplicity and plurality of interpretation as a problem for biblical study itself, and not just for polemics, apologetics, dogmatics, or ecumenics? This refusal to consider posthistory as part of biblical studies by relegating it to dogmatics or homiletics, to denominational or ecclesiastical history, formed the problematic for a symposium at Ottawa's Carleton University in fall, 1977. There the rationale was described as follows: "The very historical-critical impulse that is at the heart of modern biblical studies suggests that we who for so long have looked at the Bible and worked *backwards* to its origins might profitably study it by working *forwards* towards ourselves, through its successive traditional interpretations."

My fourth proposition claims that as well as historical study involving both the prehistory and the post-history of the biblical texts, there must also be what could be called their *parahistory,* an investigation of significant parallels, wherever found and from whatever time and on whatever level—an investigation carefully disciplined by structural methodology. I envisage, in other words, the grid in Figure 1 as the future of biblical studies:

FIGURE 1.
FIELD CONCEPT OF BIBLICAL STUDIES

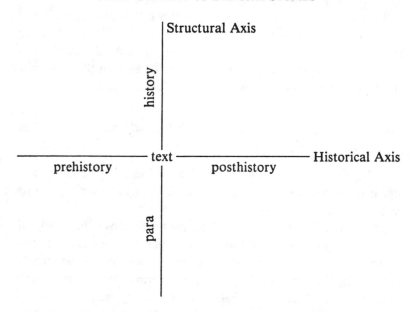

You will notice that I have slipped the term "history" onto both axes by inventing the word "parahistory" on the structural line. This is quite deliberate because, recalling John Collins's citation of Lévi-Strauss, "everything is history" /10/, so also and with equal truth, everything is structure. History is the transformations of structures, which means, I think, that structure is logically prior to history. But structure without history is chess without players, and history without structure is chess without rules.

An example of this biaxial phenomenon, and by no means an innocently chosen one, may be taken from language itself. There competence demands a simultaneous move along two axes: one of choice *and* one of contiguity; one of selection *and* one of sequence; one, as Roman Jakobson might say, of metaphor *and* one of metonymy (1956: 76–82). The simplest sentence demands simultaneous and conventionally approved activity of both vocabulary (as it were, the structural axis) and of syntax (as it were, the historical axis, with its before and after). Similarly, I would argue that a biblical text is only fully and adequately studied when it has been fixed along both axes and biblical criticism only comes to competence when historical and structural considerations operate simultaneously within it.

This means, I would suspect, that the full study of a biblical text, either by the same or different scholars, will demand in the future as much use, for example, of James Pritchard's magisterial collection *Ancient Near Eastern Texts/Pictures* as of Stith Thompson's equally magisterial *Motif-Index of Folk-Literature*.

Fifth Proposition: Structural analysis is logically prior to historical analysis.

This proposition is not a hidden plea for hierarchy and superiority. It intends no more than it says. Two examples may explain its meaning.

The first is from the New Testament. Suppose the work of William Farmer and his followers so sapped the Two Source consensus that redactional work on its presupposition became quite impossible. But suppose also (and if the former happened, I think this latter would as well), that no other theory was ever able to gain a like consensus (once bitten, twice shy). What would redaction theory have to do? It could no longer read Mark, Matthew, and Luke in historical and genetic relationship, but it could still read them in structural or systemic relationship. That is, it could compare the deep, intermediate, and surface structures of the three synoptic Gospels as independent variations on the same theme and then interpret accordingly. Thus, the structural level underlies the historical because A cannot derive from B unless the structures of B allow A so to transform them. If one begins, with proper logical priority, on the level of structural comparison, one can later move to questions of genetic contact, but failure to establish this second level does not render study fruitless *if* one has correctly investigated the structural or systemic context in the first place.

The second example is from the Old Testament. I am going to offer you a story you probably have not read before. As you read it I ask you to be very conscious of your reactions, of the questions that start through your mind, and especially of the order of such questions.

In the ancient times there was a mother-in-law and her daughter-in-law. Because the father-in-law and husband had died, the mother-in-law said to the daughter-in-law, "I am old. Because you are still young you get married again. How about it?" The daughter-in-law replied, "Although I am young I will truly not marry another. I will certainly live with my old mother-in-law." The mother-in-law again exhorted her thus, "Young people must not be deceived in this way. Won't it be all right to marry another?" The daughter-in-law said, "I cannot marry anyone like that."

Later the mother-in-law again said, "Because you will not marry away, I can get another to be my son (and your husband). Will that be all right?" The daughter-in-law also said, "According to this, I request mother to be very careful." When the mother-in-law heard these words, she could hardly think out a plan. So when on that day she saw a beggar standing in a cave, she returned home and told her daughter-in-law. The daughter-in-law said, "That is good." The mother-in-law asked, "Why is a beggar good?" She replied, "Because he is a poor man, on the one hand I can live with my mother (in-law) and on the other hand I can assist a poor person without relatives. This is my mind." Her mother-in-law said, "Tomorrow I will bring him here."

The next day the mother-in-law brought the beggar to be her son and the husband of her daughter-in-law. On the third day the old mother-in-law gave him a tael of silver to buy rice for breakfast with. When he saw the silver he asked the mother, "Is this silver?" The mother said, "Yes." He said, "If that is so, every day in the cave I saw a lot of white silver. I don't know how much rice it would buy." He led her to the cave, and she saw the cave filled full of white silver. The wife and the husband then carried it away during the whole night. The next morning the old mother got up and saw it, and was truly very happy. From this time the husband and the wife and the old mother were very rich people.

If I may presume to guess what you have been thinking, I suggest both a combination of structural and historical reactions but I would also suggest the priority of the former. How soon did you think, Ruth! I gave you no historical information—maybe, for all you know, I made up the story myself. But as you watched the story unfold, noting the structural (not just thematic) parallels and differences between it and the biblical narrative of Ruth, historical considerations begin to arise: the stories are so similar that there must be some contact . . . ; they are so different that there is none . . . ; but, it makes the point of rewarded compassion without any of the possibly polemical details which scholars have suggested were added later to the Ruth story . . . .

The story was collected in the period 1921–1934 along with about 750 others (quite a few about mother-in-law and daughter-in-law relationships, but only one other about a very loving daughter-in-law, most being about cruel mothers-in-law) by Daniel C. Graham (262–263), Curator of the West China Union University Museum of Archeology, Art, and Ethnology, from among the Ch'uan Miao, an ethnic group of about 150,000 in (mid) Western China. A comparison of this story from China with that of the biblical Ruth could easily begin with historical questions, either prehistorical (did Ruth come from it), or posthistorical (did Ruth influence it). Such a study would probably end up quite negatively and the investigation be judged a waste. Yet a structural comparison of this tale against its own sociological background and then of these against Ruth and its own biblical background should come first and would certainly be far from fruitless, no matter what conclusions were later accepted concerning historical and genetic relationships. And suppose, for example, that the Chinese story had been unearthed in Moab rather than China. Could the historian make any compelling genetic conclusion without knowing whether similar mother/daughter-in-law stories were found all over the narrative world?

Sixth Proposition: Biblical theology, that is, a theology taking the Bible as its creative matrix, must proceed along both structural and historical axes simultaneously.

I intend this final proposition to be almost exclusively programmatic, to be asserted rather than defended.

We know how often the excellent studies of the biblical texts' prehistory have been all that biblical studies would furnish the reader. All else, thereafter, was denominational or ecclesiastical. If one tried to move from the past of the text's canonical fixation (pun intended) to the present of the reader's concerns, one was asked to take huge existential leaps across the chasm of two or three thousand years. But what was in between all that time and all that space?

I would suggest that what was in between were the structures of language, the laws of story, the genres of communication, and the rules of semiotics. All of these link our linguistic and narrative world to theirs and link it as a vast three-dimensional grid. Biblical theology will have to work out how the multilevelled and hierarchically constrained structures of the biblical text intersect with our own textuality today, at what place and on what level. We may still need some existential leaps, but beneath our leaps is the net of language and of text, of genre and of story, of human convention, signification, and communication.

This means, I suppose, that the phrase "Ruth amid the alien corn" can stand not only as a title for that Chinese folktale, for biblical Ruth among the alien Chinese, but also as a metaphor for the future of biblical studies. We are going to find ourselves like Ruths agleaning in strange and alien fields, in places we have not seen before, among companions we have not met before, but with gains we have not known before.

NOTES

/1/   E. Güttgemanns (1971, 1971a). He founded and edited the journal *Linguistica Biblica,* since 1970–71, and its monograph series, *Forum theologiae linguisticae,* since 1972. *Semeia* 6 (1976) is an edited (N. R. Petersen) translation (W. G. Doty) of some of his key articles.

/2/   The journal since 1974 and the monographs since 1975. The first general editor was Robert Funk. That position has now been assumed by J. D. Crossan. The editorial process for the journal is also experimental in that individual associate editors (S. Berg, R. Detweiler, C. Exum, W. Green, R. Jewett, B. Kovacs, D. Patte, N. Petersen, R. Polzin, M. A. Tolbert, C. Winquist) take responsibility for creating volumes around a common theme. The quotation is from the journal's inside cover. The board for the monograph series is Dan O. Via, editor, and William A. Beardslee, associate editor.

/3/   See Nos. 3, 9, 11, 13, 18, 19, 20, 23 in *PTMS,* and No. 3 in *PRS.* These include published and promised volumes. *PTMS* 19 is a projected translation of E. Güttgemanns (1971).

/4/   Recent publications are D. Patte (1976, *NTG*), D. Robertson (1977, *OTG*), and N. Petersen (1978, *NTG*).

/5/   The quotation is from Gros Louis (7). This work is in a series called "The Bible in Literature Courses" and "is the first in a series of resources for teachers of literature" (9).

/6/   Her other works are (1970) and (1975). There is a very fine analysis of her work's implications for religious studies in Sheldon R. Isenberg & Dennis E. Owen.

/7/   R. C. Tannehill, *The Sword of His Mouth* (Sem Supp 1. Missoula, Mont.: Scholars Press/Philadelphia: Fortress Press, 1975); R. W. Funk, *Jesus as Precursor* (Sem Supp 2. 1975); D. O. Via, Jr., *Kerygma and Comedy in the New Testament* (Philadelphia: Fortress Press, 1975); J. D. Crossan, *In Parables* (New York: Harper & Row, 1973); *The Dark Interval* (Niles, Ill.: Argus, 1975); *Raid on the Articulate* (New York: Harper & Row, 1976).

/8/   For other discussions of this phenomenon, see N. Perrin (1976); Robert Detweiler (1978), and Robert M. Polzin (1977).

/9/   *Biblical Research* 22 (1977): 19.

/10/   *Biblical Research* 22 (1977): 20.

Chapter 12

The Mosaic Revisited

Robert Polzin and Eugene Rothman

In order to begin the necessary process of assessment, we want now to review the confrontation of perspectives that constitutes this volume. If we appear to preempt the necessary and valuable assessment that belongs to our readers, it is because our experimental confrontation involves no easy answer to questions like, Who won? or Who lost? Indeed, as David Robertson perceptively indicated, the scholars involved in this volume confront one another not in a struggle to overpower, but rather in an effort to understand the cherished convictions concerning which each of them has witnessed before his colleagues. As editors of this volume, it is now our turn to testify concerning our own convictions by formulating a statement of understanding. This statement will involve an attempt to correlate the various perspectives embodied in the preceding essays and to assess the importance of this correlation with respect to the past, present, and future study of biblical literature. We will no doubt raise fundamental questions more often than we will provide important answers. To gain insight into the first four textual studies of this volume, we will discuss the rabbinic and philosophic perspectives of chapters 2 through 5 in relation to one another.

The philosophic positions apparent in the papers of Gold and White succeed in suggesting many of the important issues highlighted by our experiment in mutual testifying. What is the relation of synchronic to diachronic analysis of the biblical text? Do we know what a text's apparent meaning is, or can we understand a text in itself? What is the function of distancing in the formation and interpretation of a text? How does the concept of frame of reference help us understand what we do when we interpret? How fundamental or fanciful are semiological themes supposedly discovered within the Bible? How do we relate the playfulness of language with seriousness of academic purpose? Can we relate the rabbinic distinction of *peshat* (the simple meaning of a text), and *derash* (the interpretative, fanciful, or derived meaning of a text), to the results of modern rabbinic, biblical and literary scholarship? All these questions and more swirl around in our minds as we reflect upon the changing perspectives of the biblical mosaic.

White is a biblical critic trained in historical criticism, yet deeply involved in structuralist research. Gold is an eminently persuasive literary critic venturing a tentative foray into the muddy waters of modern biblical exegesis. Yet their papers are united by a similar semiological purpose. White proposes that the structure of the Genesis narrative mirrors the semiological process whereby an open human signification replaces a closed one. Gold argues that the Book of Deuteronomy witnesses the emergence of a Mosaic monotheism that is coincident with a crucial stage in human evolution: man's emerging awareness of the centrality of language in his life. These semiological theses about the fundamental implications of two biblical books are similar, but nevertheless have divergent nuances. White's semiological process of prohibition to promise, and of closed to open signification, is a "synchronicized" statement drawn from a sequential story. On the other hand, Gold's semiological process remains diachronic since Deuteronomy represents for him an actual stage of human evolution insofar as language is concerned. Also, White's semiological scheme seems to emphasize a universal human paradigm; Gold's is particularistic, if not nationalistic, in emphasis.

In their semiological concerns both run the risk of being charged with interpreting the Bible in such a way as to substitute the worship of language for the worship of God. This charge would appear to us to be too simplistic a response to their valuable essays, since their common semiological frame of reference reflects an important and unavoidable aspect of present-day humanistic concerns. If it is clear that their interpretations tell us as much about key hermeneutic assumptions of the present day as they do about biblical perspectives of the past (and we believe that this is so), then perhaps that is as much as we can expect from any seriously proposed interpretation. If one has reservations about the transformation of familiar biblical themes into abstruse semiological theses, such reservations are understandable if unfortunate. For example, one might wonder whether the Book of Genesis would have survived for millennia had God demanded that Abraham sacrifice not, in so many words, "his son Isaac," but in White's words, "the denotative content of his fulfilled promise" as a test of faith? Yet who is to say that the story of the *Akedah* may not be translated and proclaimed in such a way as to provide solace to the ears of many modern humanists?

The suitability of particular frames of reference is intimately connected with questions of literal versus metaphoric and apparent versus fanciful interpretations of a text, and of all the other dichotomies that may be used to represent this particular problem of interpretation. In view of the important contributions of the rabbinic scholars in this volume, perhaps we may be allowed to discuss this problem by using the terms *peshat* versus *derash*. When Gold or White offer us a semiological interpretation of Genesis or Deuteronomy, do they offer us a *peshat* or a *derash* of a biblical text? Is the meaning they uncover literal or metaphoric, apparent or fanciful? It appears to us that one way to counter the terminological and mental vertigo that results from trying to correlate the diverse perspectives of the combined essays in the present volume is to propose tentatively that such dichotomies as *peshat* and *derash* are important heuristic devices rather than absolute categories. In other words one should be careful to apply a distinction like *peshat/derash only within one frame of reference at a time.* What is *peshat* in a rabbinic frame of reference may be *derash* in a historical-critical one; what is apparent in a semiological frame may be fanciful in a literary frame, and so on.

Once we take Robertson's counsel to heart and remain conscious of the frame of reference in which or about which we speak, then it is possible to be much more receptive to the insights available in unfamiliar or in so-called "fanciful" approaches to the biblical text such as are represented by the essays of Gold and White. For example, Gold's reminder that in reading the Deuteronomist "I am necessarily also reading myself," and his perceptive remarks about how the Bible has already become a part of our cultural perception before we ever come to interpret it, are strongly reminiscent of the phenomenological insights of Heidegger as they, for example, have been further refined by the "effective historical consciousness" of Hans Georg Gadamer. It is because of such hermeneutic considerations as these that the semiological approaches which are coming more and more to be read and heard in biblical journals, books and conferences should be listened to seriously as a possibly valuable interpretation of the biblical text. In so reading the Bible we are reading ourselves and our own age. And within a literary-semiological frame of reference, reverence for the text and emphasis on the centrality of language are strong guarantees that we are not just solipsistically reading ourselves; we are also continuing to read the Bible in a committed way, as countless generations before us have.

(We will deal with other issues, raised by the Gold and White essays, such as distancing from the text, and playfulness in language and in interpretation, as we make our way through the subsequent essays.)

The rabbinic perspectives of the papers of Silberman and Heinemann involve us in two questions. First, what kind of interpretation do these scholars give us of rabbinic texts? And second, given Silberman's and Heinemann's help, what kind of interpretation do these rabbinic texts afford us of the biblical text? The following seems clear and obvious to us as an initial response to these questions. Partly because of the relative brevity of the homilies they present to us, and partly because of the nature of the concrete literary—rather than broadly semiological—questions they ask of their respective texts, Silberman and Heinemann have produced close literary-critical readings of their rabbinic texts that are much more like the avowedly literary analyses of Jeremiah offered us by Fishbane and Hartman, or of 1 Kings 22 offered us by Robertson, than like the overarching literary analyses of Genesis and Deuteronomy by White and Gold. That is to say, if we consider the broad semiological themes of Gold and White as representative of one kind of literary frame of reference, then we seem to have in

these four papers two convenient extremes on the broad spectrum
of the practical literary criticism of the day: at one end interpretation aimed primarily at broad theorizing, and at the other end
interpretation aimed at a close reading of the text. Leaving aside
the ideological implications of calling Gold's and White's papers
"deep readings" as opposed to Silberman's and Heinemann's "surface readings," the latter scholars are much more obviously atten-
tive to and illuminating about the microscopic details of their
textual object than are the macroscopic interpretations of Gold
and White. The latter appear to be one more step removed from
their texts than Silberman and Heinemann are. Gold and White
have *distanced* themselves from their text to a greater degree than
have Silberman and Heinemann.

If we look to our second question, that is, about the nature of
the rabbinic homilist's interpretation of biblical texts, some helpful correlations of our four papers may result. Silberman shows in
detail how the artful skill of his rabbinic preacher produced a
brilliant collage-like homily in which he could pleasurably persuade and convince his hearers "that the overriding meaning of
Shabuot is not *hag-ha-bikkurim,* the festival of first fruits, but
Mattan Torah, the giving of Torah at Sinai." Heinemann, with an
abundance of internal evidence, argues that his rabbinic homilist
composed his example of "the rewritten Bible" in order to "give
encouragement and comfort to his audience, who have suffered yet
another fall and upon whom lies the cruel yoke of a hated foreign
power." They, in so doing, have provided us with detailed examples of the distancing involved in the production of ancient
midrash, a distancing that allowed both the inversion of what we
might today call the "apparent" meaning of the biblical text, as
well as its extensive reordering, for religious, ritual or theological
purposes. What Heinemann and Silberman are clearly doing in
each of their papers is presenting a *peshat* of the *midrashim* they
write about.

On the other hand, Gold's and White's papers, by their emphasis more on arguing for a valued semiological or humanistic thesis
than on constructing a close, completely detailed interpretation of
their biblical material, remind us much less of the *peshat*-like
explications du texte of Silberman and Heinemann than of the

brilliantly creative *midrashim* of the two homilists so superbly interpreted by their modern masters. These homilists, as Heinemann
says, attempt to deal with textual and contextual issues, "by way
of creative philology and historiography." It seems to us that
White and Gold do precisely in their own literary frame of reference what ancient midrashists did in *their* frame of reference, be
the latter called religious, theological, liturgical or whatever.

The important point is that if Gold, White, Silberman and
Heinemann may be understood as operating within a wide
scholarly frame of reference, and if that frame may even be further
specified as literary, then we may be justified in correlating their
offerings in this volume as respectively two *peshatim* of rabbinic
texts, followed by two *midrashim* of biblical texts. Far from im-
plying a value judgment on the adequacy or inadequacy of their
interpretations, this characterization of their hermeneutic efforts
looks rather to the degree of distancing they exhibit with respect
to their textual object.

Obviously the question is not so simple as we have suggested
in this preliminary sketch. For one thing, Heinemann's extraordinary historical command of rabbinic literature enabled him to remind us that the genre of his *pisqa* points to a rather late literary
creation that "disappears utterly from talmudic-midrashic literature . . . . Apparently the Rabbis conceived a danger that the public might take such freely treated accounts of the Bible for authentic reflections of the text itself."

The clear import of this information is that among *midrashim*
themselves the rabbis found it necessary to distinguish between
authentic reflections and freely treated accounts of the biblical
text. Even, therefore, within the original rabbinic context out of
which arises the *peshat/derash* distinction, the complicated problem of degree of distancing did not allow any facile or absolute
application. We should not be surprised if this is also the case in
modern applications as well. It then follows, if one may characterize literary interpretation as "midrash despite itself" (Hartman) that modern (literary) midrashim (that is, even interpretations within the same literary frame of reference), may run the
gamut from so-called "authentic" reflections of an interpreted text
to "freely treated" accounts of it, from *peshat*-like attempts to

derash-like ones. After all, for solid and extensive knowledge of the text itself and for extremes in reverent but creative playfulness of interpretation, the ancient rabbis are at least the equals of brilliant literary critics like Barthes and Hartman, both before and after these moderns "cross over" from formal to nonformalistic analyses of their textual object. We shall soon see from Roth's essay that most modern historical critics of the Bible can be shown often to have distanced themselves in their exegetical reconstructions as much as their rabbinic predecessors and their literary-critical contemporaries. It will soon appear that the concept of "distancing" itself is ambiguous.

Another issue raised by the correlation of the first four essays is the problem of interpreting redacted material. If we are to believe what historical critics tell us about the complicated and extensive redaction of the Pentateuch, and what Silberman and Heinemann argue as to the largely unredacted nature of the rabbinic homilies they have interpreted, then we should ask ourselves whether these factors have any bearing on the nature of their respective interpretations and our assessment of them. It is precisely here that one's views on the operational priority of synchronic over diachronic analyses, or vice versa, may be relevant. Are we to follow Gold who, in his approving quotation of Norman Perrin, apparently sees "historical criticism as the essential first step in coming to understand any text . . ." or should we heed Crossan whose fifth proposition categorically states "Structural analysis [that is synchronic, literary, agenetic analysis] is logically (that is, operationally) prior to historical analysis."

To follow Gold and Perrin would be to render, paradoxically, Gold's and White's semiological forays vulnerable to criticism from the historical-critical camp, since neither obviously bases his interpretation upon historical criticism. Indeed Gold and White can be accused of not taking important source, form, or redactional-critical considerations into account in proposing their views on Genesis and Deuteronomy. On the other hand, to follow Crossan's scheme would be to allow Gold and White to have their say first, before having them relate their theses to relevant historical-critical study. At least one of the editors is convinced of the wisdom of Crossan's proposition, yet there is a third alternative

implied by Hartman in his essay when he comments on the unity
of the Bible. Hartman suggests that all texts, regardless of their
origin and by reason of our greater understanding both of the
gradual development of folklore and oral traditions and of intrapsychic factors, can be considered to be the result of processes
that are "not unlike the more external-seeming redactional process." If this important suggestion of Hartman's be taken seriously,
then the redactional or non-redactional nature of a particular text
may not be so relevant to the question of priorities in synchronic
versus diachronic study of the Bible and to our assessment of
Gold's and White's proposals.

Before going on to the three essays concerning 1 Kings 22,
there is one more issue not arising directly from the essays under
consideration but suggested by John A. Miles at the Ottawa Symposium and reiterated by Robert Alter in his closing talk there.
Miles had suggested that one way in which traditional exegesis is
different from modern critical exegesis is in the way each answers
the question, For whom was this passage written? He writes, "Traditional exegesis answers the question . . . existentially: This
passage and every other passage in the Bible were written *for
you* . . . . Nontraditional exegesis, in contrast, never says that this
passage was written for you. It presumes rather that it was written
for some third party, or a series of third parties." Alter then went
on shrewdly to suggest "that the modern literary critic stands in a
middle ground, or potentially in that middle ground in relation to
the text."

It seems to us that Alter's insight here is considerable. If we
apply Miles's and Alter's criterion to the first four interpretations
of this volume, they all clearly lie between the extremes posed by
Miles. The sympathetic reverence with which Silberman and
Heinemann treat their homilies and the distanced concern for
their audience so apparent in the style and tone of their essays
approaches the existential concern they show to be central to their
homilists' intentions. Similarly, one of the most obvious aspects of
Gold's and White's papers is the clear intensity with which they
illuminate the existential implications of the Deuteronomy and
Genesis narratives for their humanistic colleagues, many of whom
might be unable otherwise to identify with many of the dilemmas

inherent in Moses' and Abraham's lives. The biblical narrative, they believe, still has something to say to those who, for whatever reason, are not personally concerned with the implications of divine promise and prohibition.

The issue, therefore, of traditional versus critical exegesis is an important one in terms of modern scholarship's self-understanding. Alter's perceptive comments concerning literary criticism are all the more welcome when we realize that much of modern historical criticism understands itself as fitting the "third-party" response to Miles's question about the audience of a biblical passage. It is because of modern insights into the nature of the hermeneutical task, represented in a classic manner in Gadamer's magisterial *Truth and Method,* that Roth's helpful survey of modern historical-critical exegeses of 1 Kings 22 with their profoundly distanced perspectives takes on the importance that it so richly deserves.

The papers of Goldenberg, Roth, and Robertson on 1 Kings 22 provide us with perhaps the sharpest focus upon the important issues already raised in the preceding essays. The theoretical lines are already sharply drawn by Goldenberg who claims that rabbinic interpretation differs from modern scholarly interpretation precisely by the addition of existential concerns that "forced the rabbis in this case to sacrifice plausibility for mere defensibility as their criterion in accepting the interpretation which they did. In the absence of any such dependence, the modern academic scholar is under no such compulsion." But when we come to Roth's key survey of modern historical-critical interpretations of 1 Kings 22, it becomes immediately obvious, as Roth is the first to point out in his suggestive epilogue, that "In all cases their reading of the text is not an end in itself; it is means to an end. . . . All these exegeses move into a positive but critical distance from the text, for the sake of literary deconstruction and literary and/or historical reconstruction." Perhaps with Goldenberg's views on the absence of existential or communal constraints upon modern scholars in mind, Roth takes pain to emphasize precisely those audience-related constraints which impel the historical critic to distance himself just as they had compelled the ancient biblical narrator in the first place: "Thus the critical but positive distantiation of modern exegetes is consistent with an interpretative movement evident

already in the stance of the biblical storytellers. The modern interpreter, though, seeks to be *conscious* (emphasis added) of the
adopted interpretative stance. . . ." Here Roth clearly takes issue
with Goldenberg and may have the better of the argument. In our
opinion, what needs to be inserted into Goldenberg's scheme are
precisely those existential constraints which modern scholars operate under and which despite a different frame of reference are
similar to those of their ancient rabbinic counterparts.

Roth has focused our attention on precisely that area of modern
day hermeneutics that separates, say, the stance of E. D. Hirsch
from that of Hans Georg Gadamer. The question is not whether
one can or should reconstruct the past, or whether the ancient
rabbis could or could not do so; rather, as David Couzens Hoy
has recently written (167–168), Heideggerian insights have enabled
Gadamer to argue

> that the attempt to reconstruct the past on its own terms is in
> fact an important moment of hermeneutical reflection. It is only
> a moment, though, and one that is (perhaps in an unconscious,
> but preferably in a conscious way) mediated by awareness not
> only of present interests but also of the intervening tradition
> of the work's influence . . . . Our consciousness of the past, as
> well as that of the present, necessarily involves an awareness of
> the influences and effects that past events or works have had
> (or failed to have) and will be colored by prior interpretations
> of this past and its intervening effects.

The awareness of which Hoy writes, and which Gold has also emphasized in his essay, necessitates the distantiation so obvious in
Roth's modern historical critics and in Goldenberg's ancient midrashists. In fact, Gadamer argues persuasively that such distantiation is necessary precisely because the classic threefold scheme of
the hermeneutical problem (understanding, interpretation, application) really demands that each of the three elements be united
in the hermeneutical operation not in a sequential but in an integral way. It follows for him, therefore, that *application,* that
hermeneutical aspect directly related to the communal and existential constraints about which we have been presently concerned, is
part and parcel of every exegetical enterprise. As Roth points out,
the principal difference amongst interpreters, be they ancient or
modern, resides in the degree of consciousness each has of the

applied aspects, the *distanced* aspects, of his interpretative offering.

Robertson's literary critical essay bolsters Roth's position on this crucial hermeneutical point. The former's theoretical views accept application as a necessary part of every interpretation ("We may not be in exactly the same boat as the rabbis, but we are in another boat. It is not a question of not being in a boat") and his practical interpretation results in a biblical narrator as much bound by constraints and moved toward distantiation as subsequent interpreters of the biblical text. There is evidence of distantiation present in the interpreters so far who have written or were written about in the present volume. Gold's and White's overriding semiological concerns placed them at the forefront of explicit modern application of the biblical text just as Heinemann, Silberman, and Goldenberg show the ancient rabbis to be centrally concerned with an ancient application of the biblical text. Robertson presents us with a biblical narrator who is distanced from his story in 1 Kings in much the same way as are the modern historical interpreters of 1 Kings 22 presented to us by Roth. At the same time, whether the modern scholarly interpretations of Silberman, Heinemann, Gold, White, Goldenberg, Roth, and Robertson be termed *peshat*-like (e.g., Silberman, Heinemann) or *derash*-like (e.g., Gold and White), some degree of distantiation is present.

Since we have to relate these two kinds of scholarly interpretation, perhaps a tentative formulation would be to suggest that within a scholarly frame of reference *peshat*-like interpretations seem to emphasize, or represent more obviously, distantiation away from the interpreter (and his concerns) toward the interpreted text (and its concerns), whereas *derash*-type interpretations emphasize, or represent more obviously, distantiation away from the interpreted text and its concerns toward the interpreter's and his audience's needs. The concept of distantiation, however, is actually ambiguous, since "distance from the text" can be used to characterize not only ancient and modern *derash* which by definition move toward an existential and contemporary application of the biblical text, but also ancient and modern examples of *peshat,* which are more obvious attempts temporarily to move away from such existential involvement. Moreover, any one interpretation may be a combination of both movements, as when modern historical critics attempt to move away from contemporary perspectives by reconstructing an original text or context only to use their reconstructions to move toward contemporary and communal needs, as Roth rightly emphasized. Similarly, when modern rabbinic scholars like Heinemann and Silberman, and literary or biblical critics like Robertson and Fishbane produce their convincing *explications du texte,* what is immediately obvious is a *peshat*-like movement away from contemporary perspectives toward the mind set of the texts they interpret. At the same time the very context of a multidisciplinary dialogue in which their essays appear may argue for an overriding movement toward contemporary perspectives.

Whichever meaning of distantiation one chooses to discuss, there will always be included in the definition a recognition of existential biases and constraints, more or less conscious as the case may be. We may thus say for modern historical criticism of the Bible as for modern rabbinic scholarship what Alter suggests for literary criticism: it occupies a middle ground between traditional exegesis ("the text is written for you") and what we now see to be an incomplete depiction of critical exegesis ("the text is written for a third party or parties"). Consciously or unconsciously, even modern critical exegesis—be it historical or literary, *peshat*-like or *derash*-like—says, "the text was written for you."

In the dialogue between Saldarini and Ben-Amos, what is immediately obvious is the tentative and incomplete nature of Saldarini's preliminary synchronic analysis. His useful, even indispensable survey of rabbinic attitudes and interpretations of the *Akedah* is recognized by Ben-Amos to lead inevitably to historical questions of genre development. Following the lead of Crossan and such modern literary critics as Makhail Bakhtin (230) and Istvan Soter, we would see this section of the volume as an excellent example of the operational priority of synchronic interpretation and the scholarly necessity of subsequent historical investigation.

Fishbane's and Hartman's contributions bring our confrontation of exegetical essays to a satisfying conclusion. If we start with Hartman's contention that literary interpretation is "midrash despite itself" and relate this to the midrash-like characteristics Roth found in all the historical-critical interpretations of 1 Kings 22 he surveyed, we are led to the conclusion that all the scholarly interpretations of ancient texts offered in this volume are examples of modern midrash, whether they appear to deal faithfully and reverently with their texts as some kind of a literary unity (Heinemann, Silberman, Robertson, Fishbane, Hartman) or whether they appear to deal more freely or creatively with their texts (the homilists of Silberman's and Heinemann's essays, White, Gold, Goldenberg, the historical critics surveyed by Roth). Just as the rabbis of old distinguished freely treated accounts from authentic reflections of the text even within midrash itself, so too do we concerning the examples of modern midrash present in this volume. The one difference is that we, unlike the rabbis in their frame of reference, view both kinds of modern midrash as potentially acceptable within our scholarly frame of reference. We may even say that the *peshat*-like interpretations of Silberman and Heinemann are each of them superb examples of "midrash despite itself."

Hartman's reflections on redacted material further suggest that even the most unified of texts is as fragmented as the most redacted of texts is unified. If this is so, then may we not say that all scholarly interpretations of rabbinic or biblical texts, be they predominantly historical or literary, *peshat*-like or *derash*-like, are examples of "midrash despite itself, midrash not subordinated to a calendar or other religious factors"? Further, if our basic scholarly frame of reference be subdivided into literary-critical and historical-critical frames of reference, then it may be possible, for example, to characterize the predominant distancing movement of a particular interpretative effort as *peshat* from the point of view of one frame of reference and *derash* from another frame's point of view. Thus, the historical reconstructions of Wellhausen et al. may be *peshat* historically but *derash* literarily; Goldenberg's essay may be historical *peshat* but literary *derash*; Gold's and White's papers may be *derash* both literarily and historically; and Silberman's and Heinemann's essays may be *peshat* both literarily and historically. There are no absolute vantage points from which to call this or that interpretation simply *peshat* or simply *derash*;

everything is relative to a particular frame of reference and there is no fundamental or universal frame of reference. If *all* scholarly interpretation is termed midrash it is only in relation to an absolutely objective kind of interpretation that does not exist: an absolute *peshat* is the absence of interpretation.

Bibliography

Ahituv, S.
1970   "Pashhur." *Israel Exploration Journal* 20:95ff.

Albeck, Ch.
1959   *Shisha Sidre Ha-Mishna.* Jcrusalem/Tel Aviv: Bialik.

Alter, Robert
1975   "A Literary Approach to the Bible." *Commentary* 60: 70–77.

1976   "Biblical Narrative." *Commentary* 61:61–67.

Attridge, H.
1976   *The Interpretation of Biblical History in the Antiquitates Judaicae of Flavius Josephus.* Harvard Diss. in Religion. Missoula, Mont.: Scholars Press.

Bakhtin, M. Khail
1973   *Problems of Dostoevsky's Poetics.* Ann Arbor, Mich.: Avdis Publications.

Barthes, Roland
1964   *Essais Critiques.* Paris: du Seuil.

1966   "Introduction à l'analyse structurale de récits." *Communications* 8:1–27.

1966a   *Critique et Verité.* Paris: du Seuil.

1969   *Literatur oder Geschichte.* Frankfurt: Suhr Kamp.

1970   *Writing Degree Zero and Elements of Semiology.* Boston: Beacon Press.

1974   "The Struggle With the Angel: Textual Analysis of Genesis 32:23–33." Pp. 21–33 in *Structural Analysis and Biblical Exegesis.* Trans. Alfred M. Johnson, Jr., Pittsburgh, Pa.: The Pickwick Press.

1974a   *S/Z.* New York: Hill and Wang.

1975   *Roland Barthes.* Paris: du Seuil (New York: Hill and Wang, 1977).

225

Baumgartner. W.
1917   *Die Klagedichte des Jeremiah.* BZAW 32. Giessen.

Ben-Amos, Dan
1976   "Analytical Categories and Ethnic Genres." Pp. 215–242 in *Folklore Genres* ed. by Dan Ben-Amos. Publications of the American Folklore Society Bibliographical and Special Series Vol. 26. Austin: University of Texas Press.

1976a   "The Concepts of Genre in Folklore." *Studia Fennica* 20:30–43.

Benveniste, Emil
1971   *Problems in General Linguistics.* Trans. Mary Elizabeth Meek. Coral Gables, Fla.: University of Miami Press.

Bialik, H. N. and Ravnitzky, J. C. H.
1956   *Sefer ha-Aggadah.* Tel Aviv: DNIR.

Blanché, Robert
1966   *Structures Intellectuelles.* Paris: Librarie Philosophique, J. Vrin.

Blank, S.
1948   "The Confessions of Jeremiah and the Meaning of Prayer." *Hebrew Union College Annual* 21:331–354.

1974   "The Prophet as Paradigm." Pp. 111–130 in *Essays in Old Testament Ethics.* Eds. J. L. Crenshaw and J. T. Willis, New York: Ktav.

Bloomfield, L.
1933   *Language.* New York: Henry Holt.

Bloomfield, M.
1967   "The Syncategorematic in Poetry: From Semantics to Syntactics." Pp. 309–317 in *To Honor Roman Jakobson* I. Paris: Mouton.

Braude, William G.
1962   "The Piska concerning the Sheep which Rebelled." PAAJR (Proceedings for the American Academy for Jewish Research) Vol. 30:1ff.

Bright, J.
1965   *Jeremiah.* The Anchor Bible. Garden City, New York: Doubleday.

1970   "Jeremiah's Complaints-Liturgy or Expressions of Personal Distress?" Pp. 189–213 in *Proclamation and Presence.* Eds. J. I. Durham and J. R. Porter. Richmond, Va.: John Knox Press.

Burke, K.
1973   "On Musicality in Verse." Pp. 369–378 in *The Philosophy of Literary Form.* Berkeley: University of California Press.

Charles, R. H., ed.
1913   *The Apocrypha and Pseudepigrapha of the Old Testament,* 2 vols. Oxford: Clarendon Press.

Clines, D. J. A. and Gunn, D. M.
1976   "Form, Occasion and Redaction in Jeremiah 20." *Zeitschraft fur die alttestamentliche Wissenschaft* 88: 394–398.

1978   " 'You Tried to Persuade Me' and 'Violence!' 'Outrage!' in Jeremiah XX 7–8." *Vetus Testamentum* 28: 25–16.

Crossan, J. D.
1973   *In Parables.* New York: Harper & Row.

1975   *The Dark Interval.* Niles, Ill.: Argus.

1976   *Raid on the Articulate.* New York: Harper & Row.

Daly, Robert
1977   "The Soteriological Significance of the Sacrifice of Isaac." *Catholic Biblical Quarterly* 39: 45–75.

Dentan, Robert C.
1964   *Kings. Chonicles. Layman's Bible Commentary* 7. Richmond, Va.: John Knox Press.

Detweiler, Robert
1978   *Story, Sign and Self.* Semeia Supplements 6. Missoula, Mont.: Scholars Press/Philadelphia: Fortress Press.

Douglas, Mary
1966   *Purity and Danger.* New York: Praeger.

1970   *Natural Symbols.* New York: Pantheon.

1975   *Implicit Meanings.* London: Routledge and Kegan Paul.

Driver, S. R.
1895   *A Critical and Exegetical Commentary on Deuteronomy.* International Critical Commentary on the Holy Scriptures of the Old and New Testaments. Edinburgh: T. & T. Clark.

Eliade, Mircea
1969   *The Quest. History and Meaning in Religion.* Chicago: University of Chicago Press.

Erlich, V.
1965   *Russian Formalism: History-Doctrine.* Paris: Mouton.

Finkelstein, Louis, ed.
1969   *Sifre on Deuteronomy.* New York: The Jewish Theological Seminary of America.

Fish, S.
    "Literature in the Reader: Affective Stylistics." *New Literary History* 2: 123–162.

Friedman, M.
1880   *Midrash Pesiqta Rabbati Im Tosafot Meir Ayin beshem Magen David.* Vienna: Kaiser.

Funk, R. W.
1975   *Jesus as Precursor.* Semeia Supplements 2. Missoula, Mont.: Scholars Press/Philadelphia: Fortress Press.

Gager, John
1975   *Kingdom and Community.* Englewood Cliffs, New Jersey: Prentice-Hall.

Ginzberg, Louis
1961   *The Legends of the Jews* (7 vols.; eleventh impression). Philadelphia: The Jewish Publication Society of America.

Goldin, Judah
1955   *The Fathers According to Rabbi Nathan.* New Haven: Yale University Press.

Graham, D. C.
1954   *Songs and Stories of the Ch'uan Miao.* Smithsonian Miscellaneous Collections, Vol. 123, No. 1. Washington, D.C.: Smithsonian Institute.

Gray, John
1963   *I and II Kings* (The Old Testament Library). Philadelphia: Westminster Press.

Greimas, A. J.
1966   *Semantique Structurale.* Paris. Larousse.

Gressman, Hugo
1921   *Die älteste Geschichtsschreibung und Prophetie Israels,* 2nd ed. SAT 2/1. Göttingen: Vandenhoeck.

Gros Louis, Kenneth R. R.
1974   *Literary Interpretations of Biblical Narratives.* Nashville, Tenn.: Abingdon Press.

Gry, L.
1948   "La rume du Temple par Titus." No. 2. *Revue Biblique* 55: 215–226.

Gunkel, Hermann
1917   *Das Märchen im Alten Testament.* Religionsgeschichtliche Volksbücher II. Tübingen: Mohr.

Gunkel, H. and Begrich, J.
1933   *Einleitung in die Psalmen. Die Gattungen der religiösen Lyrik Israels.* Hand Kommentar zum Alten Testament. Göttingen: Vandenhoeck and Ruprecht.

Guttgemanns, E.
1971   *Offene Fragen zur Formgeschichte des Evangeliums.* 2nd ed. BEvTH 54. Munich: Kaiser.

1971a   *Studia Linguistica neotestamentica.* BEvTH 60. Munich: Kaiser.

1975   " 'Semeia'—ein Zeichen der Zeit! Zu einer neuen linguistischen Zeitschrift." *Linguistica Biblica* 35: 84–106.

Habel, Norman
1971   *Literary Criticism of the Old Testament*. Philadelphia: Fortress Press.

Harrington, Daniel, et al.
1976   *Pseudo-Philon, Les Antiquités Biblique*. Sources Chrétiennes 119–30. Paris: Cerf.

Harrison, R. K.
1969   *Introduction to the Old Testament*. Grand Rapids, Mich.: Eerdmans.

Hartman, G.
1975   "The Voice of the Shuttle: Language from the Point of View of Literature." Pp. 337–355 in *Beyond Formalism*. New Haven: Yale University Press.

Heinemann, Joseph
1971   "The Proem in Aggadic Midrashim" in *Studies in Aggadah and Folk Literature*, eds. Heinemann & D. Noy. Jerusalem: Magnes Press.

1971a   "Profile of a Midrash: The Art of Composition in Leviticus Rabbah." *Journal of the American Academy of Religion*.

1974   *Aggadot we-Toledotehen: 'iyunim behishtalshelotan shel masorot*. Jerusalem: sifriyat Keter.

1977   *Prayer in the Talmud: Soms & Pattons*. Berlin and New York: de Gruyter.

Heinemann, Yizhaq
1954   *Darkhe Ha-Aggadah*. Jerusalem: Magnes Press, pp. 15–164.

Hempel, Johannes
1930   "Rudolf Kittel." *Zeitschrift der Deutschen Morgen ländischen Gesellschaft* 84: 78–93.

Hirsch, E. D.
1967   *Validity in Interpretation*. New Haven and London: Yale University Press.

Holladay, W.
1964   "The Background of Jeremiah's Self-Understanding: Moses, Samuel, and Psalm 22." *Journal of Biblical Literature* 83: 153–164.

1972   "The Covenant with the Prophets Overtwined: Jeremiah's Intention in 'Terror on Every Side' (Jer. 20:1–6)." *Journal of Biblical Literature* 91: 305–320.

Hoy, David Couzens
1978   "Hermeneutic Circularity, Indeterminacy and Incommensurability." *New Literary History* X: 161–173.

Hyman, Aaron
1964   *Toldoth Tannaim Ve'Amoraim* (in Hebrew, 3 vols.).
              Jerusalem: Boys Town.

Hymes, D.
1960   "Phonological Aspects of Styles: Some English Sonnets"
              in *Style and Language*. Ed. Thomas Sebeok. New York.

Isenberg, Sheldon and Owen, Dennis E.
1977   "Bodies, Natural and Contrived: The Work of Mary
              Douglas." *Religious Studies Review* 3/1: 1–16.

Jakobson, Roman
1956   "The Metaphoric and Metonymic Poles." *Fundamentals
              of Language*. 'S-Gravenhage: Mouton.

1971   *Selected Writings*, I. The Hague and Paris: Mouton.

Jakobson, Roman & Morris, Hale
1956   *Fundamentals of Language*. 'S-Gravenhage: Mouton.

Jaynes, Julian
1976   *The Origin of Consciousness in the Breakdown of the
              Bicameral Mind*. Boston: Houghton Mifflin.

Jepsen, Alfred
1963   "The Scientific Study of the Old Testament." Pp. 246–
              284. *Essays on Old Testament Hermeneutics*. Ed. Claus
              Westermann, trans. J. L. Mays. Richmond, Va.: John
              Knox Press.

Kara, R. Joseph
1881   *Perush Yirmiyahu*. Ed. A. Slossberg. Paris: Libraire A.
              Durlacher.

Kaufmann, Y.
1945   *Toledot Ha-emunah Ha-yisraelit* II/2. Tel Aviv: Dvir.
              Abridged in *The Religion of Israel*, Chicago: University
              of Chicago Press, 1960.

Kitchen, K. A.
1966   *Ancient Orient and Old Testament*. London: Tyndale.

Kittel, Rudolf
1900   *Die Bücher der Könige*. HKAT I 5. Göttingen: Vanden-
              hoeck.

1925   *Geschichte der Volkes Israel*. Vol. 2. 7th ed. Stuttgart:
              Kohlhammer.

Kristeva, Julia
1969   *Sēmeiōtikē*. Recherches pour une semanalyse. Paris: du
              Seuil.

1970   *Le Texte du Roman*. Approche semiologique d'une struc-
              ture discursive transformationelle. The Hague and Paris:
              Mouton.

1971   *Essais Semiotique*. Eds. J. Kristeva, J. Rey-Begove, D. J.
              Umiker. The Hague and Paris: Mouton.

1974   "Comment parler à la littérature." *Tel Quel* 47: 27–49.

1974a   *La Révolution du langage poétique.* L'avantgarde à la fin
                du XIXᵉ Siècle: Lautrémont et Mallarmé. Paris: du
                Seuil.

1975   "D'une identité l'autre." *Tel Quel* 62: 10–27.

Köller, Wilhelm
1975   *Semiotik und Metapher.* Untersuchungen zur grammati-
                schen Struktur und communikativen Funktion von Meta-
                phern. Stuttgart: J. B. Metzler.

Kuhn, Thomas S.
1970   *The Structure of Scientific Revolutions.* 2nd ed. enlarged.
                International Encyclopedia of Unified Science, Vol. 2,
                No. 2. Chicago: The University of Chicago Press.

Lacan, J.
1968   "The Function of Language in Psychoanalysis." Trans.
                with notes and introduction in *The Language of the Self,*
                by A. Wilden. Baltimore, Md.: Johns Hopkins Press.

1970   *Ecrits I.* Paris: du Seuil.

Lang, H.
1973   *Die Sprache und das Unbewusste.* Frankfort am Maine:
                Suhrkamp.

Lauterbach, Jacob
1933–35   *Mekilta de-Rabbi Ishmael.* 3 vols. Philadelphia: Jewish
                Publication Society.

Leach, Edmund
1976   *Culture and Communication.* London: Cambridge Uni-
                versity Press.

LeDeaut, Roger
1963   "Abraham et le sacrifice d'Isaac." Pp. 131–212 in *La
                Nuit Pascale.* Analecta Biblica 22. Rome: Pontificio In-
                stituto Biblico.

Levi, I.
1912   "Le sacrifice d'Isaac et la mort de Jesus." *Revue des
                études juives* 64: 161–184.

Lévi-Strauss, Claude
1975   *The Raw and the Cooked.* Introduction to a *Science of
                Mythology,* Vol. 1. New York: Harper. 1st ed. 1964.

Lieberman, S.
1973   *Tosefta Ki-Fshutah.* New York: Jewish Theological Sem-
                inary.

1973a   *Tosefta: Nashim.* Vol. 4. New York: Jewish Theological
                Seminary.

Luzatto, S. D.
1876   *Erläuterungen über einen Theil der Propheten und*

Hagiographen. Hebrew with parallel German title. Lemberg: Verlag I. Menkes.

Mandelbaum, B.
1962   *Pesikta de Rav Kahana.* 2 vols. New York: Jewish Theological Seminary.

Marmorstein, Arthur
1920   *The Doctrine of Merits of Old Rabbinic Literature.* Reprinted 1968. New York: Ktav.

Marshak, Alexander
1972   *The Roots of Civilization.* New York: McGraw-Hill.

Mauchline, J.
1962   "I and II Kings." in *Peake's Commentary on the Bible,* rev. Ed. M. Black. London: Nelson.

Montgomery, James A.
1951   *A Critical and Exegetical Commentary on the Book of Kings.* Ed. Henry Snyder Gehman. New York: Scribners.

Moore, George Foot
1927   *Judaism.* Cambridge, Ma.: Harvard University Press.

Muffs, Yochanan
1975   "Prophetic Prayer" (in Hebrew), *Molad* 204–210, No. 7. Vols. 245–246.

Noth, Martin
1943   *Überlieferungsgeschichtliche Studien,* reprint. Tübingen: Max Niemeyer, 1957.

1948   *A History of Pentateuchal Traditions.* Englewood Cliffs, New Jersey: Prentice-Hall, 1972; originally published in German.

1956   *Geschichte Israels.* 3rd ed. Göttingen: Vandenhoeck.

Patte, Daniel
1976   *What Is Structural Exegesis?* Philadelphia: Fortress Press.

Perlitt, Lothar
1965   *Vatke und Wellhausen. Geschichtsphilosophische Voraussetzungen und historiographische Motive für die Darstellung der Religion und Geschichte Israels durch Wilhelm Vatke und Julius Wellhausen.* BZAW 94. Berlin: Topelmann.

Perrin, Norman
1974   "Eschatology and Hermeneutics: Reflections on Method in the Interpretation of the New Testament." *Journal of Biblical Literature* 93: 3–14.

1976   *Jesus and the Language of the Kingdom.* Philadelphia. Fortress Press.

Petersen, Norman
1978   *Literary Criticism for New Testament Critics.* Philadelphia: Fortress Press.

Polzin, Robert
1977   *Biblical Structuralism.* Semeia Supplements. Missoula,
            Mont.: Scholars Press/Philadelphia: Fortress Press.

Prijs, L.
1966   *Die Jeremiah—Homilie Pesiqta Rabbati Kapitel 26.*
            Stuttgart: W. Kohlhammer.

Rabbinovicz, Raphael
1960   *Diqduqei Soferim* (in Hebrew; 12 vols.). Repr. New
            York, Jerusalem, Montreal: no publisher indicated.

Reventlow, H. Graff
1963   *Liturgie und prophetisches Ich bei Jeremiah.* Gütersloh:
            Gütersloher Verlagshaus Gerd Mohn.

Robertson, David
1977   *The Old Testament and the Literary Critic.* Philadelphia:
            Fortress Press.

Robinson, James M.
1963   "The Historicality of Biblical Language." Pp. 124–158 in
            The Old Testament and the Christian Faith. Ed. Bern-
            hard W. Anderson. New York: Harper & Row.

Rofé, Alexander
1970   "The Classification of the Prophetical Stories." *JBL* 89:
            427–440.

1974   "Classes in the Prophetical Stories: Didactic Legenda and
            Parable." *VT Suppl.* 26: 143–164.

1976   "The Story of Micaiah ben Imlah and the Question of
            Genres of the Prophetical Stories." Pp. 233–244 in *Re-
            flections on the Bible,* Vol. 2. Tel Aviv: Don Publishing
            House.

Rosolato, Guy
1969   *Essais sur le symbolique.* Paris: Gallimard.

Rudolf, W.
1958   *Jeremia.* Handbuch zum Alten Testament 12. Tübingen:
            Mohr.

Ryle, Hubert E.
1892   *The Canon of the Old Testament.* London: Macmillan.

Safouan, Moustafa
1968   "De la structure en psychanalyse, contribution a une
            theorie de manque." Pp. 139–298 in *Qu-est-ce que le
            structuralisme?* Ed. by O. Ducrot, *et al.* Paris: du Seuil.

Saldarini, A. J.
1975   *The Fathers According to Rabbi Nathan.* Version B.
            Leiden: Brill.

Santayana, G.
1927   *Interpretations of Poetry and Religion.* New York:
            Charles Scribner's Sons.

de Saussure, Ferdinand
1966   *Course in General Linguistics.* Ed. C. Bally and A. Sechehaye with A. Riedlinger. Trans. by W. Baskin. New York: McGraw-Hill.

Schachter, Melech
1959   *The Babylonian and Jerusalem Mishnah Textually Compared* (in Hebrew). Jerusalem: Mosal Harav/Kook.

Schäfer, P.
1975   *Rivalität zwischen Engeln und Menschen.* Berlin: de Gruyter.

Schechter, Solomon
1887   *Aboth de Rabbi Nathan.* Vienna. Reprinted in 1965. New York: Feldheim.

1961   *Aspects of Rabbinac Theology.* New York: Schocken. Orig. ed.: 1909.

Schneidau, Herbert N.
1976   *Sacred Discontent: The Bible and Western Tradition.* Berkeley and Los Angeles: University of California Press.

Schoeps, H. J.
1946   "The Sacrifice of Isaac in Paul's Theology." *Journal of Biblical Literature* 65: 385–392.

Scholem, Gershom G.
1971   "Revelation and Tradition as Religious Categories in Judaism." Pp. 282–303 in *The Messianic Idea in Judaism.* New York: Schocken.

Scholes, Robert
1974   *Structuralism in Literature.* New Haven: Yale University Press.

Schwally, Friedrich
1892   "Zur Quellenkritik der historischen Bücher." *ZAW* 12: 159–161.

Sellin, Ernst
1927   "Hugo Gressman—Gedächtnisrede." *Zeitschrift für die alttestamentliche Wissenschaft* 45: vii–xx.

Shaffer, Elinor S.
1975   *"Kubla Khan" and the Fall of Jerusalem.* Cambridge: University Press.

Shelley, P. B.
1957   "A Defense of Poetry." P. 536 in *The Portable Romantic Reader.* Ed. H. E. Hugo. New York: Viking Press.

Smith, Barbara H.
1968   *Poetic Closure: A Study of How Poems End.* Chicago: University of Chicago Press.

Soter, Istvan
1970   "The Dilemma of Literary Science." *New Literary History* 2: 85–100.

Spiegel, Shalom
1967   *The Last Trial.* Trans. Judah Goldin. New York: Pan-
(1950)   theon. Hebrew original. *"Mē-'aggādôt Hā-'agēdâ."* Pp.
               471–547 in *Alexander Marx Jubilee,* Hebrew Section.
               New York: Jewish Theological Seminary, 1950.

Starobinski, J.
1975   "The Inside and the Outside." *The Hudson Review* 28: 333–351.

Strack, H. L.
1945   *Introduction to the Talmud and Midrash.* Philadelphia.

Streane, A. W.
1896   *The Double Text of Jeremiah.* Cambridge: Deighton Bell & Co.

Sublon, Roland
1975   *Le Temps de la Mort.* Strasbourg: Cerdic.

Tannehill, R. C.
1975   *The Sword of His Mouth.* Semeia Supplements Missoula, Mont.: Scholars Press/Philadelphia: Fortress Press.

Theodor, J. & Ch. Albeck
1912–36   *Bereshit Rabba.* 3 vols. Berlin.

Vermes, Geza
1961   "Redemption and Genesis XXII." Pp. 193–227 in *Scripture and Tradition in Judaism: Haggadic Studies.* Leiden: Brill.

Via, Dan O., Jr.
1975   *Kerygma and Comedy in the New Testament.* Philadelphia: Fortress Press.

Volz, Paul
1910   *Der Geist Gottes.* Tübingen: Mohr.

Von Rad, Gerhard
1964   *Das fünfte Buch Mose: Deuteronium.* ATD 8. Göttingen: Vandenhoeck.

Wellhausen, Julius
1876–77   *Die Composition des Hexateuch,* 4th ed. Berlin: de Gruyter.

1878   *Prolegomena to the History of Ancient Israel.* Eng. trans. 1957. Cleveland and New York: Meridian Books.

Wendel, A.
1932   *Das freie Laiengebet im vorexilischen Israel.* Leipzig: Pfeiffer.

Westermann, C.
1965   *The Praise of God in the Psalms.* Richmond, Va.: John Knox Press.

Wilden, Anthony
1968   *The Language of the Self.* Baltimore: John Hopkins Press.

Wink, Walter
1973   *The Bible in Human Transformation.* Philadelphia: Fortress Press.

Wolff, Hans Walter
1974   *Hosea. A Commentary on the Book of the Prophet Hosea.* Hermeneia. Philadelphia: Fortress Press.

Würthwein, Ernst
1967   "Zur Komposition von I Reg 22 1–38" in *Das ferne und das nahe wort. Festschrift Leonard Rost.* Ed. Fritz Maass. BZAW 105. Berlin: Topelmann.